JEREMY THOMAS AND DR
FOREWORD BY STEPHEN FRY
YOU DON'T HAVE TO BE TONY
FAMOUS HUGHES
TO HAVE MANIC
DEPRESSION
THE INSIDER'S GUIDE TO MENTAL HEALTH

With *invaluable contributions from:*
Dr Liz Miller MB BS, AKC, FRCSE, MRCGP, BA(Psych), Dip Occ Med, MSc
Karen Cowan, BSc(Hons), MSc, Post-MScDip., C.Psychol.
Chris Filmer-Sankey RMN
Sarah Cellan-Jones BSc(Hons) MA

MICHAEL JOSEPH
an imprint of
PENGUIN BOOKS

MICHAEL JOSEPH

Published by the Penguin Group
Penguin Books Ltd, 80 Strand, London WC2R 0RL, England
Penguin Group (USA) Inc., 375 Hudson Street, New York, New York 10014, USA
Penguin Group (Canada), 90 Eglinton Avenue East, Suite 700, Toronto, Ontario, Canada M4P 2Y3
(a division of Pearson Penguin Canada Inc.)
Penguin Ireland, 25 St Stephen's Green, Dublin 2, Ireland (a division of Penguin Books Ltd)
Penguin Group (Australia), 250 Camberwell Road,
Camberwell, Victoria 3124, Australia (a division of Pearson Australia Group Pty Ltd)
Penguin Books India Pvt Ltd, 11 Community Centre,
Panchsheel Park, New Delhi – 110 017, India
Penguin Group (NZ), cnr Airborne and Rosedale Roads, Albany,
Auckland 1310, New Zealand (a division of Pearson New Zealand Ltd)
Penguin Books (South Africa) (Pty) Ltd, 24 Sturdee Avenue,
Rosebank, Johannesburg 2196, South Africa

Penguin Books Ltd, Registered Offices: 80 Strand, London WC2R 0RL, England

www.penguin.com

First published 2006
2

Grateful acknowledgement is made for permission to reproduce the following:
Comments from www.alcoholicsanonymous.org.uk, Carol Titley, psychotherapist.
Extract on pp. 170–71 taken from 'I Never Discuss My Mistresses or My Tailors', Nick Paton Walsh,
14 October 2001, *Observer* website, copyright *Guardian* Newspapers Limited 2001.
Extract from *Waiting for Godot*, Samuel Beckett, Faber & Faber Ltd.
Extract from *Touched with Fire*, Kay Redfield Jamison, copyright © 1993 by Kay Redfield
Jamison. Reprinted with permission of The Free Press, a Division of Simon & Schuster
Adult Publishing Group. All rights reserved.

Set in Galliard
Designed and typeset by seagulls.net
Printed in Great Britain by Clays Ltd, St Ives plc

A CIP catalogue record for this book is available from the British Library

ISBN-13: 978-0-718-14968-0
ISBN-10: 0-718-14968-8

contents

foreword by stephen fry

Whether you are cheerfully anonymous, gloomily famous or unhappily infamous, there are pages in this book that have something for you. There is nothing po-faced, earnest or phoney in what you are about to read. What you will find is honesty, humour, insight and help.

We all know the ineluctable law of gravity as it applies on this earth. Most of us who have experimented with such things know the equally ineluctable law that dominates the life of the drug user, drunk or chocoholic – the law that states 'there is no such thing as a free buzz'. In other words, that every high will be followed by an equal (or greater) low – the downer, the hangover, the blood-sugar crash. It seems that inside the human brain the same relentless, capricious and damnable laws insist on operating. What goes up must always come down.

Many of us who have been diagnosed as bipolar find the manic half of the equation beguiling in the freedom, expansiveness, energy and optimism it brings. We are kings of the world, nothing is beyond us, society is too slow for our racing minds, everything is connected in a web of glorious colour, creativity and meaning. We find too that the inevitable descent matches each characteristic with devastating exactness. What was light is now dark, what was coloured is now grey; the optimism is replaced with pessimism, the self-belief with self-contempt, the energy with sloth, the expansiveness with suffocating constriction. The cruel precision of this reminds one of all the Manichean oppositions in myth and legend, from Zoroastrianism to Darth Vader: 'If you only knew the power of the Dark Side.' Well, we manic depressives do know the power of the Dark Side.

Not only is Manic Depression, Bipolar Affective Disorder, whatever one chooses to call it[1], one of the most common mental health conditions

---

1. Personally I prefer Manic Depression. Bipolar isn't quite right – the condition isn't really just about two poles, there are mixed states in between. Besides, why not give it a title that names the effects?

in the world, it is also one of the most serious. The life of the manic depressive is frequently shorter and less healthy than the life of the rest of the population, and it is not only suicide that shortens it, although heaven knows suicide is a grave enough problem. Often the easiest way to cope with the horrors of perpetual cycling between mood swings is to intervene with our culture's most readily available solutions: alcohol and narcotics. They may be bad, but they can appear to overcome or at least mask the tyranny of mood swings in a more or less controllable way. For the sufferer who has never been diagnosed, self-medication of this kind comes all too easily, as I can attest myself. Of course, the cycles beneath grow wider and more savage and the need to blot them out all the greater, and in this way the problem will remorselessly scale itself up. Those living with a manic depressive are under strain enough, but with addiction and all its behaviours on top, the outcome is predictably disastrous: families and friendships are rent asunder and misery is handed around to all within range.

For people like me, blessed with a good education, loving parents and loyal friends, making my living in an arena of bohemianism, where eccentricity and wild behaviour are regarded as almost the norm, if not outright desirable, things could have been so much worse. The creative 'celebrity' working in music, comedy or the arts has all kinds of advantages when living with manic depression. The mania looks like artistic temperament and can be harnessed to achieve impossible deadlines and fine creative work; the drinking and drug-taking go with the territory and raise no eyebrows. The depression, almost by definition, goes unnoticed – it takes itself off to weep in private for a few weeks until it goes away. Media types don't have to clock into the office, wait on tables, stack the shelves or attend team-leader meetings. They tend to run their own timetables and much oddity and unreliability is forgiven them.

All these advantages can conspire to make manic depression seem almost a trophy, a kind of designer accessory that adds interest and depth to the media personality. In my case, however, a dreadful and upsetting breakdown in 1995, which I am still trying to understand, and a full, final farewell to cocaine some years later convinced me that it was worth speaking out about my condition, even at the risk of sounding like yet another moaning, post-rehab celeb pleading for public attention and admiration. I know that in the case of sexuality, well-known people coming out has helped enormously, despite the irritation it may give to some. The stigma surrounding mental health issues is every bit as great as that surrounding sexuality and perhaps my openness may be of benefit for those who believe their condition to be hopeless and isolating.

For despite everything I have said about the seriousness and morbidity of manic depressive illness, there is a light at the end of the tunnel, and it isn't only, as one might believe when depressed, the light of an oncoming train.

This is a field in which psychiatry, genetics, neurology and endocrinology seem to combine in as yet dimly understood ways. But it is a field still very much in its infancy and one being taken more and more seriously each year. There are strategies for coping, medications, therapies and approaches thst yield real results. There is a whole new generation of psychiatrists, general practitioners, therapists and self-help groups more aware than ever of the nature and gravity of manic depression, and they have at hand a whole new armoury of medications, techniques and resources, an armoury which is growing all the time in reliability, safety and availability.

One such resource is this book. Compiled and written by people who know what they are talking about, as opposed to 'experts', following Jeremy and Tony's trajectory as patient and doctor in the Manic Dialogues is like sitting inside an old-fashioned railway compartment and overhearing a fascinating private conversation that is at once informative, unpretentious and funny. The Insider's Guide is like a *rough guide* to everything you always wanted to know about mental health but were afraid to ask. And in between there are nine wonderfully poignant life stories featuring, amongst others, a rampaging manic depressive farmer, a streaking convent girl and a man hell-bent on trying to steal a train.

That it is available now, and that it has been written to help, and illuminate with insight and laughter an area of our lives that has been shrouded in shame and darkness for far too long, makes this hard old world we have to live in just a little bit better. It will teach you that you are not alone, whether you are reading it because you are manic depressive yourself or because you live with or care for someone who is. It will pull no punches, but it will also encourage you to believe that there is *hope*. Hope is unique in this universe in that it alone is immune to those ineluctable laws: only hope can rise and rise without ever falling to earth.

introduction

However bright eyed or bushy tailed you may or may not be, this book is for anybody interested in mental health and trying to understand how human beings tick; irrelevant of age, income, status, sex or creed. This is *not* the definitive book on mental health, but is intended as an informative and entertaining guide.

Respect and acknowledgement are due to John Cleese and Robin Skynner's *Surviving Families* for providing the inspiration for the format of the Manic Dialogues. The backbone of the dialogues is an intimate discussion between two long-time friends, patient and GP, tracing an *actual* manic depressive's journey and trajectory from ignition and flight to what seemed an irreparable crash landing to eventual reconstruction. The reason for the dialogues being tape recorded was to attempt to capture some uninhibited conversation that was neither contrived nor stuffy but candid and insightful and of some real use to others. The dialogues are down to earth, easy to read, occasionally funny and, hopefully and above all, truthful.

Topics include: the major symptoms and characteristics of manic depression *and* depression; denial, the pitfalls of trying to get help and answers; suicide; relationships; self-esteem; families; pets; the doctor's point of view; creativity and depressives; alcoholism and addiction; sex; and black humour.

The Manic Dialogues aim to provide a comfortable seat at the table for *anyone* interested in learning more about mental health.

The Life Stories have been written and generously submitted by our anonymous contributors and are drawn from a diverse geographical, cultural and age range. Every story is genuine and written in each person's unique style.

Their inclusion and purpose in the book is to show that this illness can affect anyone at any stage of their life. Most importantly the stories may provide identification and hope for others by showing the different ways of coping with and overcoming the illness. The stories are often brutally honest, poignant, courageous and never lacking in a sense of humour.

The Insider's Guide provides a straightforward explanation about most common mental health problems facing the majority of people in their daily lives. Originally designed to be a glossary accompanying the Manic Dialogues, as more questions needed answering, the glossary took on a life of its own and grew into an A–Z guide! Apart from dealing with the main subjects associated with mental health and manic depression, the guide also deals with topics some people may be afraid or embarrassed to discuss with their doctor or anyone else.

Whether your interest lies simply in finding out about coping strategies for depression, skunk, anorexia, addiction to gambling or websites for therapists, the guide will hopefully provide an answer to your enquiry or show you a way of finding out more information. Apart from discussing causes and effects, the guide tries to illuminate what can be done to prevent a particular mental health problem occurring, how to treat it and where to get help.

a note from the authors

Jeremy Thomas: Why did I decide to write this book? To bastardize a current expression, I am certainly *not* the only manic depressive in the village. Nor has my condition or experience been that much worse or more serious when compared to others. However, I wanted to write about my experience of manic depression and other mental health issues because I believed it was way past time to demystify and de-stigmatize mental illness in the UK. I also wanted to read a book that actually explained in plain English what certain illnesses were, what they were not and what you could do about them.

The idea to write the book arose while researching a TV documentary about manic depression which had been inspired by my good friend and GP Tony Hughes. Having been a grateful patient of Tony for over twenty years and fully aware of his complementary knowledge of manic depression, there seemed no better choice of co-author for this book than him. As usual, Tony was his generous self and, after only one application of the thumb screws, graciously accepted my offer. A plan was struck to borrow a friend's flat overlooking the sea in Brighton and to go and record and write the Manic Dialogues and subsequent Insider's Guide. The only argument was who would be sleeping in the real bed and who would sleep on the sofa bed.

To put my own experience into context, I need to turn back the clock. After riding a bumpy rollercoaster of adventure, I was diagnosed as suffering from manic depressive psychosis in January 1981 and hospitalized at the Bethlem Royal Hospital. Eighteen months later, I became friends with an intriguing man in his late twenties, called Tony Hughes. He was a doctor and a painter, had a pretty girlfriend called Fiona and drove a blue Renault 4. Six months later he became my doctor, a role he patiently performs to this day. I soon began taking a mood stabilizer drug every day and have done so ever since. A year went by, and Tony was rechristened

Dracula on account of the amount of blood he extracted from my unsuspecting arm while testing for lithium levels.

On 12 March 1993, after a spectacular career at the bar, I finally gave up drinking and joined a very anonymous organization. Prior to this point, I was allergic to words like group and therapy and felt slightly nauseous at the sight of any self-help books. However, like many other people, I was always secretly hoping to find just the 'right' book to shed light on to my situation. In hindsight, a straightforward and amusing guide to manic depression and good mental health would have been unbelievably useful in those intervening twelve years.

We all want to be seen by others as Mr or Ms or Mrs Sane, Groovy and Wonderful, certainly nothing too different from the rest of the pack. Also, unless you are a poet, comedian, novelist or rock star, having manic depression is not the coat of colours most people would choose to wear. Mental illness isn't considered to be terribly manly unless, perhaps, you happen to mask it with a bottle of vodka or tequila and endless talk about football or bullfights.

I have always belonged to the category of people who need to burn their hands on a hot stove at least seventeen times before finally believing it might not be a good idea to continue touching it! Unlike some less fortunate friends, though, I have survived the last twenty-five years of ups and downs and, thanks to various people too numerous to mention, have a wonderful life today. Pass the sick bowl time, I know. That doesn't mean that there have not been dark clouds or moments of total doubt, gloom or elation, but more that I have learnt ways in which to manage my own mental well-being.

It's 2006 and stigmas and suffering are no longer compulsory. Yet everyone at some point in their life is going to be directly or indirectly affected by some form of mental illness; so it's probably better to be more informed than less. If you don't want to become mentally ill, try your best to be mentally healthy. Should any of my references appear inappropriate or flippant, please accept my apologies – I do not take the subject of mental illness lightly, but rather believe it is *sometimes* better to deal with the subject in a lighter vein.

Dr Tony Hughes: ... So why did I write this book? Having researched for three years, meeting many of the leading lights in the field and reading widely around the subject, we had to largely hand over development and filming of a documentary on manic depression which we had been making with Stephen Fry, apart from any other reasons due to our own professional commitments. It thus seemed a great opportunity to co-write a book when Jeremy, my dear friend and partner in the original TV documentary project, suggested it.

It has meant a return to one of the main reasons I began studying medicine – my interest in psychology – and arose directly from my ventures into the world of the arts.

I felt the chance to mix some humour with such a serious subject might give it broader appeal. In this way I hoped our book might be able to make a worthwhile contribution to the understanding of this illness that is so close, and yet so far from everyone's experience of joy and despair.

the manic dialogues

prologue

Jeremy: Driving down from London to record these tapes, I recalled an amusing and quite apocryphal story. It was shortly after when we had first met in 1983. Having spent six successful years in the music industry, I was just coming to the end of a two-year rollercoaster of manic depression. Your girlfriend had been working for me in a first-floor garret in a wharf by the side of the Thames in Battersea. You probably don't recall but about a month later she left just as the financial rug was being pulled from beneath my feet. I had five bank accounts that were all overdrawn and most of my assets were the clothes I was wearing and they were a little tatty. I was suddenly in a very serious situation. House gone, investors gone, girlfriend too. And now the remains of the business – in fact everything, except Ned.

Tony: The cat.

Jeremy: Of course the cat. Well, Ned and I were living in my little first-floor office, which I was days away from losing too. And there were just writs everywhere, from everyone. And one of them was from a mini-cab firm.

Tony: A mini-cab firm?

Jeremy: Whenever I was about to go even vaguely bonkers, you could always tell because a mini-cab account would appear, and then receive a serious hammering. But this was the grandmother of all mini-cab accounts – I'd racked up a bill the size of a small planet, which hadn't been paid. And like everything else, it was meant to be paid but couldn't be paid.

And that morning one of the guys who owned the office below mine came running up pretty scared and said, 'Listen, there's a Mr O'Nasty and His Very Large Friend downstairs from some mini-cab firm. They say they're here to collect.'

I knew something terrifyingly bad was going to happen – kneecaps at the very least, with a bit of defenestration and broken legs thrown in as well. Anyway, Mr O'Nasty and the Very Large Friend walked into the office. 'We want paying Mr Thomas – now,' the less huge one hissed through his teeth. I gulped and suggested I made them a cup of tea. Mr O'Nasty snarled in the affirmative and I left them to look at all the writs lying on my desk. Fully expecting to be maimed at any moment, I came back and told the guy the truth – I had tried to raise some money, thought I had raised the money but I'd failed, and now had absolutely no money at all. I simply couldn't pay him.

He'd been really angry before. But he looked at me, sighed deeply and said, 'Don't look so worried, we're owned by a public company, and they make allowances for this sort of thing.'

Then, buttoning up his coat, he continued, 'Listen, it may all seem like an irretrievable mess to you now but you'll sort it. You're the type who'll bounce back one day. People can. People do. So will you. One day you'll rise up from the ashes.'

And with that they both got to their feet, nodded and left.

Tony: Did you believe him?

Jeremy: No.

a short walk
around manic depression

Jeremy: Well, boyo, here we are then, gazing out to sea through an open fifth-floor window with only two squawking seagulls to distract us. But where do we start? Beginning, middle, end? I did consider breaking the ice with a joke about Manic Depression being a town in Mexico or something to do with the weather, but perhaps the best thing would be to try and explain exactly what it is.

Tony: Well, there's a common assumption that manic depression is very bad depression. It's actually a condition in which there is a disorder of mood, but mood swings between high (manic or the lesser extent called hypomanic) and low, though there can be complex mixes in between those two.

In a hypomanic state someone feels speedy, confident, needs less sleep, thinks fast, and often has a sense of life being fantastic. If full-blown mania develops this can get completely out of control with speech and thoughts scrambling at a terrifying rate.

The depressive state is where you're low. So it's the one that people normally understand because most people have felt low. When it is bad it is really bad, and can get as bad as someone feeling suicidal.

Now depression is one side of an axis from well to being low. Manic depression, on the other hand, is a swinging between high and low, which is less common.

Jeremy: And how common is it?

Tony: It is thought that one per cent of the population has manic depression classed as the most severe level of 'bipolar 1'. A larger percentage, perhaps five per cent, has a milder form of the condition called 'bipolar 2'. Many people in their lives have episodes of severe depression, maybe up to as much as ten per cent, and at least according to the figures it would seem that women have a far higher prevalence of depression.

Jeremy: Is that correct?

Tony: Well, the studies show that, but I think it is partly because women are more open about their feelings and thus the figures are skewed.[2] I think a lot of men get depressed and don't even admit it to themselves. However, manic depression is entirely even-handed in its sexual preference.

Jeremy: Why has this new expression 'bipolar' suddenly come into being?

Tony: I think bipolar is an American concept, probably brought about because mania had all the historical connotations of people being locked up and behaving in a very bizarre and frightening manner. Bipolar is a softer concept which describes the two poles of the high and the low. It can include people with mixed states – in other words, there is a certain amount of excitability mixed in with depressive illness too. So a person

2. This is a complex subject and has to be seen in the context of history, politics and religion.

may be desperately depressed and suicidal, yet be having thoughts spinning round at high speed in their head which come from the manic pole of illness.

Jeremy: I know it's only a name but I'm still a 'manic depression' fan.

Tony: I rang the Dual Diagnosis[3] headquarters in California the other day and the phone was answered by Clancy, the man who actually runs the unit there. He is a sufferer himself and he corrected me when I talked about manic depression. He said, 'Over here we call it Bipolar.' He was quite definite.

Jeremy: At least he could make a decision! One of the strange and annoying things about being depressed is an inability to be definite or make any decision. It's a terrible feeling when you can't decide whether to get up off the sofa to make a coffee or tea, or make a phone call, and then when you have finally dragged yourself up and made your drink or your call, you just sit back on the sofa again. It's a small aspect of that sort of terrible depression, but it's quite a paralysing one and can quickly compound internally. You start saying to yourself that you really are a dreadful person because you can't even decide whether you're going to make a cup of tea or a cup of coffee.

Tony: Of course your self-image in depression is exactly the opposite from mania, isn't it?

Jeremy: Yeah, it's low self-esteem personified, accentuated and magnified. And with every hour of sleeplessness it starts gaining in power. Sleep is a very good indicator of what the hell's going on with your mental condition. If I find myself leaping out of bed at a quarter to five in the morning, having a shower and then a bath, then watching the Open University or breakfast television and summoning mini cabs at six in the morning, an upward swing can be accurately forecast!

---

3. Dual Diagnosis: Term from the USA used to describe the co-existence of an alcohol or drug problem with an emotional or psychiatric problem – often alcoholism and manic depression. See page 199 of the Insider's Guide.

Tony: But we also know that one of the symptoms of depression is waking up early, having had an unsatisfactory sleep.

Jeremy: In a depressed state, I normally can't get to sleep until 1 or 2 am. Then I wake up around 4 to 4.30 and toss and turn, while my head churns like a cement mixer with the blackest of thoughts. The more this happens, the more the depression gathers strength.

Tony: And everything seems increasingly negative.

Jeremy: In a depressed state, you tend to believe that the glass is permanently empty, and that even the 'half full' concept is a thing of the past. Sometimes, my actual reality was pretty terrible, and sometimes it wasn't at all, but I still saw it as terrible.

That last perspective was largely caused by an immensely persuasive voice saying, *What you've done before has all been luck.* The small voice of reality may put in a word and say, *Well, it can't be, you've been very successful, you've had lovely girlfriends.* But the negative voice cuts back in with, *Look mate, that was all luck, you know you conned all those people into liking you.*

This is such a powerful self-destructive voice that it can disable your perception into believing that these dark thoughts are in fact reality.

Tony: You have no insight into your condition.

Jeremy: Absolutely right. The other thing that happens in a really depressed state is terrible moments of paranoia. This is a state where you are constantly asking people what they said and then processing their reply in your mind for any signs of treachery, mockery or conspiracy.

A lot of this paranoia is internalized and as it builds and builds, you can believe people are against you and that the world is conspiring to trip you up. In a way it sounds quite funny, but it's not so funny when you're going through it. Anyone who has ever had a bad experience smoking marijuana will be able to identify with this state.

Tony: It's part of the low self-esteem, isn't it? You feel so wretched and that it must be visible, and you imagine that people are watching you.

Perhaps during this phase you imagine people can see how pathetic you really are? You can no longer hide this 'weakness'?

Jeremy: I don't like the word weakness in this context but yes, it's all ultimately part of low self-esteem, and the paranoia is like a wave that comes in and out. It can get out of control – unless you treat it.

portrait of the artist as a young gloom

Tony: Do you still get depressive episodes?

Jeremy: I do get gloomed periodically, but I'm lucky because they are never too acute. Lithium tends to act as a safety net for these things.

Tony: How was it when they first started?

Jeremy: I experienced two bad depressions when I was a teenager and then again in my early twenties. But I didn't tell anyone that sort of information. It was sort of la-di-dah, you know, grin and bear it. Perhaps they were dress rehearsals for the full monty that came later.

I do remember various times – messing up exams and breaking up with a girlfriend or something like that. But I usually masked the gloom with alcohol and work.

Tony: A temporary release?

Jeremy: I have always known I was veering towards any sort of depression if I found myself going into sweet shops and buying bars of chocolate.

Tony: Because chocolate helps depression, doesn't it?

Jeremy: When I start buying eight Mars bars in one go I know I'm in trouble.

Tony: Yes, I have on occasions been known to buy a triple Bounty.

Jeremy: Tony, all this time I had you down as a Marathon man!

Tony: The point is, it's also a craving for sugar, isn't it – and simple gratification? Why doesn't one always eat sweets? Because they aren't good for you!

Jeremy: Yes, but doesn't chocolate have some connection to the endorphins that produce this mild pleasure?

Tony: That's one of the reasons depressives like it so much.

Jeremy: Yes – you're going to try anything that will make you feel slightly better. Depression at its worst is physically painful, where your solar plexus is knotted and all you want to do is …

Tony: Pull the covers over your head and never really look out again.

Jeremy: It's tricky, especially when you have people going, 'Cheer up, buck up, it could be worse, a penny for them,' and all that crap. But once you recognize your own signs, and have a few techniques up your sleeve, the best thing to do is to head for a safe place and try your hardest to activate what you've learnt.

Tony: Perhaps we can discuss your ways of spotting the trouble signs and specific coping techniques later?

Jeremy: It's going to cost you a box of Mars bars, at least!

asking for help

Jeremy: There are a lot of people out there who have this illness but don't have a diagnosis and remain untreated. Quite a few of them end up in prison. This is serious stuff.

Tony: Oh yes, very serious. The issue here, I suppose, is coming to enough of an acknowledgement that you get diagnosed – and then treated. But that's a hard journey in itself. Your own story makes that clear.

Jeremy: When I first had this illness full blown, back in 1980, the major problem was being ashamed or embarrassed about the situation and not being able to talk about it to anybody. I come from a groovy, ok family, with no real history of mental problems, except possibly my dad's black moods. We all knew …

Tony: But the family never went near the words 'mental illness'?

Jeremy: No.

Tony: So what chain of events triggered your manic depression?

Jeremy: Well, in many ways I had brought on the situation myself. My mother had recently died, and I had changed from being employed in a big company to joining forces with a friend of mine in a much smaller company.

It all felt very cold all of a sudden, even though everyone believed the new venture was going to work out. I'd had quite a lot of success, but suddenly there was a voice saying, *Hey, none of that was because of you.*

From being a positive person, I became someone gnawed by doubts that I just didn't dare share with anyone. It was weird – a self-belief melt-down.

Of course I tried to push it away. I didn't want to let the side down. So despite the mounting depression, I just carried on. Besides, I didn't know what to say to anybody. I went to the doctor once, which I didn't really want to do. And he said, 'Well, we'd better give you some anti-depressants.'

Tony: Time has moved on and nowadays, doctors would usually not give anti-depressants without finding out first about family history and whether there are any signs of bipolar mood disorder. Because actually they could send someone into a hypomanic state. Anyway, did you get on with them?

Jeremy: No, I didn't like them *at all!* They seemed to make no difference whatsoever. Perhaps I was too impatient. Also at the time, the external world was lousy, business was bad, and there was a recession. I tried to pretend that's what it was, but in fact I felt it was all me – all completely my fault. It was bad enough for my business partner, but just hell for my girlfriend. I actually dumped her, thinking in some mad, superstitious way that she was the problem.

Tony: Alcohol was featuring quite largely at this time?

Jeremy: It was. But there was no pleasure in drinking. It was like a really bad anaesthetic. And when it wore off, I felt worse than before.

The critical thing to understand about young men, and maybe these days young women, is that they don't want to look weak in front of their friends, or peers – or anybody. ESP – Embarrassment, Shame and Pride – those are things that particularly screw young men up, because they prevent them from admitting there's a problem and seeking help.

Tony: So what organizations have you come across that are a back-up for situations of despair?

Jeremy: Nowadays there's Mind, the Depression Alliance, the MDF,[4] and smaller more personal organizations such as the Charlie Waller Memorial

---

4. See **Manic Depression Fellowship**, page 234 of the Insider's Guide.

Trust who have a great site for students.[5] Not forgetting the Samaritans who are a tip-top organization in any crisis.

There's so much help out there, that's the thing. Twenty plus years ago when I came out of hospital the only information available was through a bi-monthly magazine you could subscribe to called *Lithium News*. I did discover a book in the USA called *Mood Swing*, a year after that.

Tony: You mentioned the Samaritans. Can you talk about the time that you felt suicidal?

Jeremy: I can remember it so clearly. It was a few weeks after I'd been released from hospital, and with no girlfriend I was on my own in this bleak flat, trying to front it out. And I remember going to bed around midnight, and I'd been given these sleeping pills. I swallowed three of them. They were really powerful and the psychiatrist had said only ever take one and all the usual and I thought, *If I take another four that should do the trick.*

Tony: Do the trick of putting you to sleep so you never wake up?

Jeremy: That's what I was thinking. But I was also very frightened. One moment, *Do it!* The next, *Don't!* That sounds a stupid thing to say, but bearing in mind all the other drugs I was taking from the hospital like chlorpromazine, I was feeling weird enough anyway.

Tony: And now you were effectively playing Russian Roulette.

Jeremy: Except I was lucky. I had a marvellous psychiatrist who I trusted. He had told me that in moments of real worry, whatever time of night it was, to ring him, and I rang around half past twelve that night, and his wife answered the phone and she went, 'Oh yes, hang on.' And I heard her sigh and say, 'Darling, it's for you.'

Tony: A line she had perfected.

Jeremy: He was great. I think he just said, 'Yes, it is an awful feeling but it will go, believe me.' I said, 'How do you know it will go? How can you

---

5. See page 295 of the Insider's Guide.

be so sure?' He replied, 'Well, having been a psychiatrist for twenty years, I've seen a lot of people like you go through hell and come out the other side okay.'

Tony: And how long did your conversation in the middle of the night go on?

Jeremy: Not long.

Tony: It reminds me of that Birmingham radio problem page phone-in show about twenty years ago. Somebody rang in two seconds before the end of the show, and said, 'I've got this terrible problem. Nobody's prepared to listen to me,' and the guy on the radio said, 'I'm so sorry but now we've come to the end of the programme'!

Jeremy: Oh no!

Tony: But seriously, it's very difficult to be a doctor and be phoned at 3 o'clock in the morning when you've got a full workload the next day. Theoretically, you might end up having a conversation that could go on for two hours. That's why the Samaritans are so good because they are there for you any time of the day or night.

Jeremy: They are, and they know what they're doing. That's their business and they are a great organization.

Tony: But it does count for a hell of a lot that you could have such faith in your psychiatrist and that he was so willing to go that extra mile for you as a patient.

Jeremy: That was a big deal because in the end, when you get that far down and you are actually thinking I'll just piss off, you really do need to believe and trust in somebody. I was very lucky because he knew the situation was potentially dodgy and that's why he did what he did. I was also very lucky to have a great family around me anyway, though I would never have phoned them.

Tony: Why not? Is it because you thought you'd already used up their goodwill?

Jeremy: No, that came later. It's odd because sometimes, in those crisis points, you don't want to speak to your nearest and dearest. Maybe if I was thinking of topping myself now I would speak to them. I am sure they would be immensely flattered!

Tony: Why did you end up losing their goodwill?

Jeremy: It's exasperating and exhausting to be around someone who is manic. More so when there are repeated episodes. Although a manic person can be the real embodiment of affection and enthusiasm, charm and fun, they can also behave like a nasty drunk and say terrible things to members of their family, knowing exactly which buttons to press.

Tony: Well, that doesn't sound too bad!

Jeremy: Yes, but when it's coming from someone with a loud Napoleonic confidence, it can be extremely unpleasant. Imagine this same hyperactive, bumptious, highly critical, verbose person, borrowing money, getting into fights, repeatedly running up debts and trying to coerce as many friends and family as possible to join in with the latest ill-thought-through scheme. Needing to be bailed out of trouble, borrowing things that they shouldn't, making inappropriate suggestions to close friends' daughters. Perhaps behaving in exactly the same way to how they had when they were ill before. Then when his or her family try to suggest their sibling might be in need of help, that same manic person is hugely offended at such 'insults' and tells everyone to stop conspiring and interfering and eff off.

Tony: So that's when families often withdraw goodwill and say enough is enough?

Jeremy: Family members are not saints. There's a limit to how many times people will or can put up with someone repeating the same mayhem.

Tony: In the end, you and your family came to understand the condition and things levelled out?

Jeremy: Yes, but I certainly put them and my close friends through the wringer a few times. Fortunately, they are a great bunch, very resilient and switched on. Mind you, a lot has happened in twenty-five years.

Tony: Meaning?

Jeremy: You grow up, you make more mistakes, and you learn. Anyway, I think that in those days life was very different. It was way before Princess Diana went on TV and was talking about her 'issues', and at least fifteen years before Morrissey and The Smiths went on *Top of the Pops* singing 'Heaven Knows I'm Miserable Now'. There was still this ridiculous embarrassment about being mentally ill. Did you ever know my school chum, Will?

Tony: I think that I met him once.

Jeremy: Well you know that story.

Tony: Took a shotgun to himself, didn't he?

Jeremy: No, no, he didn't. Will was somebody I went to school with. He was 6'2", went to Oxford, good-looking, bright, thoroughly nauseating because he was also a nice guy. He became a TV commercials director, and was about to get into directing feature films. I used to bump into him on the King's Road, always with his arm around a gorgeous girl, and it was like, *You've got everything, you bastard!* And there's me struggling with my Safeway's bags trying to attract the attention of some passing pink Mohican punkette.

I always used to think that Will had it all in the palm of his hand. But then, a few months later after his thirtieth birthday, he was found at 3 o'clock in the morning, naked, hysterical, running down the street. The police and ambulance grabbed him and sectioned him into Charing Cross hospital. The next night he got out onto the roof and threw himself off.

Tony: Had he never said anything, or talked about it to anyone?

Jeremy: I don't know what the problems were. But that's the point – no one did. Apparently, he was someone who didn't or couldn't talk about what was really going on. And there are lots of people like that. People who say, 'I'm not a touchy feely person, I'm not a pills person, and I'm not a talk person, either. So *please* leave me alone.'

Tony: So somebody with your 'ESP', as you call it?

Jeremy: Sure. You must have met loads of patients like that.

Tony: Oh, yes. Still the British stiff upper lip, and, 'There's no such thing as a problem. One can only achieve by doing practical things. You can ignore the mental side, because that's just the machinery that does the work.'

It's a bit like when patients come to me for advice about psychotherapy. I say firstly, I'm not in favour of the New York five times a week on a couch talking about the poodle, but neither am I in favour of the British stiff upper lip.

Jeremy: There is a balance to be found somewhere.

Tony: What about farmers during these terrible epidemics, living on their own, miles from anywhere, who don't want to feel a sense of weakness at all? Some of them end up taking their own lives. How bloody awful it must be, living through that, on your own, miles from anywhere. We've all got breaking points, all got vulnerability. Conversely, I have patients of mine who say, 'I can't complain about this, it's not as if I am starving in Ethiopia.' The fact is we don't live in Ethiopia and we all have our own set of challenges. It's just so important to talk!

Jeremy: We're making amazing progress with the physical side of medicine which is fantastic, but we haven't done enough to promote good mental health. You are not a bad or a weak person if you get depressed, or if you're a manic depressive. But of course neither does it make you worthy of canonization!

obstacles to acceptance
– lack of self-worth

Tony: What do you think are the fundamental obstacles to manic depressives accepting their condition?

Jeremy: Manic depressives – along with addicts/alcoholics – have a strong tendency to low self-esteem, low self-worth, in the same way they do to self-importance and grandiosity. They are also often highly intelligent and high achievers. I think the low self-esteem is not just part of a depression but more part of the overall package.

To mix my metaphors, manic depression isn't a holiday destination that you go to for a few days and then come back from.

Tony: So are you saying you feel vulnerable because the illness taints you and makes you feel that you're weak and less important than other people? Or do you feel that's simply the personality of somebody who is manic depressive? In other words, is it that chicken or the egg thing again?

Jeremy: There's no doubt that in some cases the stigma surrounding mental illness can make someone feel innately bad about themselves or worse. It's a nasty paradox that people who are feeling bad can believe that by admitting it they are only going to feel worse. But manic depressives often turn things in on themselves and bash themselves up.

Tony: Because their expectations of themselves are too high?

Jeremy: Yes, often in a manic phase the expectations become even more unrealistic, but it doesn't matter because you believe you can do just about anything anyway.

But in a low-level depressive phase the person concerned can quickly slip from, *I should be doing much better than I am, I'm intelligent, I'm this, I'm that*, to, *I was never going to succeed at this anyway.*

Tony: So how did you find your own way through this shifting landscape?

Jeremy: The only way I learnt to deal with it was to accept that the answer lies in the simple common sense stuff of taking some action and setting realistic goals. A common danger for manic depressives is taking on too much. You have to learn to position the high jump at four feet as opposed to thirteen. But it's much easier said than done.

Tony: I agree. But I also want to fly the flag for psychotherapy which I believe is fundamentally important in helping. Psychotherapy sounds like a very grand, or maybe even irritating, word. But it's really just a way for people to come to terms with their condition. There's lots more about this in the Therapists pages in the Insider's Guide.

Jeremy: Let's just put it at a very basic level: I accept that I am a manic depressive. I accept that I have to take lithium, that's the way it is. I'm not angry about it, I accept it.

Tony: And acceptance of course means appreciating that it is a long-term illness and one that is, generally speaking, a condition for life. Therapy doesn't necessarily work first time round for everyone. Some people need to experience the school of hard knocks to achieve the same thing. One such lady had her life turned upside down by a horrendous house fire. She sought answers in Buddhism, which teaches that life is full of such suffering. She finally realized she couldn't have the perfect life she had been hankering after, and came to accept her illness, and found some real inner peace.

Jeremy: It is vital to have somebody to talk to. I don't just mean in a corny, folksy way, but anyone having any mental health illness needs to talk to somebody who is a sympathetic listener more than anything else. We mentioned my school friend, Will – was he too stiff upper lip, or just frightened of baring his soul?

Tony: And Will was an individual with so much to offer.

Jeremy: Yes.

Tony: Who couldn't see it himself?

Jeremy: But in a way, this is the point of what we're doing here. Perspective … and that there is life after …

Tony: … a diagnosis.

Jeremy: Whether you go into one of the old-fashioned Bleak House-type mental hospitals or one of the trendy clinics that have a press office and jacuzzis, even now some people worry about being tainted with stigma. Am I really a weirdo? Will this get worse? Will I ever be a normal human being again?

Tony: Although the diagnosis can be perceived as being a long-term 'life sentence', important breakthroughs in treatment are coming from scientific research. There really is hope here. But put that aside – progress really can be made by what people do for themselves.

Jeremy: And surely, there are lots of other medical 'life sentences', aren't there? You must have lots of patients who are diabetic?

Tony: Exactly. In this regard it's no different to a diabetic needing to take his insulin. It's really the same as any of these other long-term medical problems, one needs to take responsibility and accept that one has a problem.

Jeremy: Most of us have got something wrong with us. It's all about having the right attitude. Your condition doesn't need to be the centre of conversation at a party, but neither does the whole room have to fall silent when the words 'manic depressive' are mentioned. Back in the 1960s lobotomies were still being performed. And even more recently unwanted relatives were ending up being incarcerated in 'mental hospitals' long term.

Tony: All sorts of awful things used to happen, and still do in some parts of the world.

Jeremy: R.D. Laing was right when he said if you treat somebody in a weird way, they will probably behave in a weird way.[6]

Tony: It certainly came through to me loud and clear when I was a medical student in Birmingham seeing the Victorian asylums which were the psychiatric hospitals. And then I went off to work in a brand-new beautiful unit in Perth, Australia, and noticed the difference in the feeling of the whole place. The patients had exactly the same medical problems, but in a clean and cheerful environment the relationship between patients and doctors was just so much better.

The most important thing is the staff. If you have caring, interested staff, the whole thing works. But, of course, if staff work in poor surroundings … it goes round and round.

Jeremy: The whole thing is about attitude, isn't it? I read the Sainsbury Mental Health Foundation's vision for 2015 report in which they predict that in less than ten years' time every GP's surgery will have a mental health care person attached who you will go and see, for routine check ups. There would also be somebody at every school, qualified to deal with emotions, psychological disturbance and teenage mental issues.

I suspect it will probably all happen one day, because in the end everybody will cotton on that maintaining good mental health is as important as looking after yourself physically.

---

6. *Sanity, Madness and the Family*, R. D. Laing and A. Esterson.

hair of the black dog – alcoholism, addiction and depression

Tony: Let's talk about alcoholism, addiction and depression. What's the difference? And can they all be successfully treated with one programme, or 'method'?

Jeremy: There is a lot of common ground between manic depressives and alcoholics, let alone depressives. There are many fellowships dealing with a multitude of addictive behaviours that one day soon could all be handled by one twelve-step fellowship like Addictions Anonymous.

But be warned – alcoholics and manic depressives tend to want to have their own clubs and can be prickly, territorial creatures!

Tony: What would you recommend?

Jeremy: Well, rather than start something new, it might be better and quicker to build on what already exists. I will probably be shot for saying this, but there are many things that everyone can learn from each other. For example, the MDF runs a fantastic course on self-management, but it doesn't have the AA-style talks or 'chairs', where a member comes and talks for fifteen minutes about their experience.

Tony: Does the speaker in an AA meeting have to be somebody who is successful? Because perhaps the only way it can be helpful is to hear about a success.

Jeremy: I think hearing someone talk about unadulterated success might be faintly nauseating. In my experience, good old honesty about the good *and* bad times is what people like hearing. Just as in reading a novel or watching a film, it's great news when we can identify with one of the characters.

Tony: For example?

Jeremy: For instance, if Terry the Taxidermist is attending a meeting but is really hacked off, what is important is that he tells it how it really is. 'This is what is happening to me, and I'm fed up with this and I hate my doctor and I hate my psychiatrist and if only I could get a better job and have the guts to ask Tracy the Zookeeper to go out with me ... moan, moan, moan.' Somebody who has been listening from around the table might say, 'Well thanks, Terry the Taxidermist, I went through similar stuff like that, but I've been around long enough now to know it will get better.'

Tony: Do you feel from the MDF meetings you've been to that there is the same feeling of well-being that you get from AA?

Jeremy: I think what's really important is that these are both organizations that work through respect and anonymity. They must be safe places for their members, because people need to trust that confidentiality will be kept by everyone. So I don't want to say too much here.

However, I think the MDF is more a process of practical help, with an emphasis on people being able to unload their frustrations about coping with the illness.

Tony: My interest is in seeing whether the so-called Dual Diagnosis meetings that exist in America could help people here who have got addictive problems and manic depression. If you didn't by chance have an MDF meeting nearby, would the structure of an AA meeting help? I'm of the opinion it probably would.

THE MANIC DIALOGUES

Jeremy: You seem very interested in finding out about AA and the like. Shouldn't we be focusing on manic depression?

Tony: I know. But I suspect, Jeremy, that there is a connection between them all, and I would be grateful for your patience!

Jeremy: I'll try and answer your questions, Inspector Morse, but I was nowhere near the scene of the crime at the time.

Tony: I get the impression that AA meetings are a sort of 'hypnosis', but where you discharge your angst. And by the time you come out you feel different – a bit, well, uplifted?!

Jeremy: Well, in the meetings I've attended people may nod off, but I've yet to see someone in a trance. All I can tell you is that there is a certain power. Perhaps it's because of the number of people in the room. Or perhaps it's something completely different. Whatever it is, it works.

Tony: I would suspect that it is a little bit like going into a church. I'm not a believer or a non-believer.

Jeremy: I'm like the old Monkees song, 'I'm a Believer', myself – with a bit of doubt thrown in.

Tony: I am an agnostic, but when I come out of a church, I do feel a sense of calm. I mean, I have only been to one AA meeting, but it wouldn't surprise me if it was the same.

Jeremy: Yeah, but Tony, let's just turn this round. What about you? Do you have any peculiar bats flying around in your belfry – so to speak?

Tony: I suppose I have got my own set of 'addictions', or minor obsessions as one might call them. It might be true to say that everyone is an 'addict' in his own way. To my mind, we could all benefit from something like AA, if we could persuade ourselves to do it.

Jeremy: How do they affect you?

Tony: They can lead to a cloud that just won't clear.

Jeremy: People never stop to think that their own doctors might suffer from gloom and anxiety at times. Doctors have a huge suicide rate, don't they?

Tony: It is one of the highest; strangely, the highest being dentists.

Jeremy: How weird. But what about your anxiety and gloom? How does it affect you, and in brief, how do you deal with it? Physician heal thyself?

Tony: I think I do feel a sense of distress during the winter, for example, when I don't see the sun for a while. I like to see the horizons and, like my grandfather who was unhappy in the Lake District, I am not exactly in the right place for that in London in the winter, though I love it for other reasons.

Jeremy: Thanks for sharing that.

Tony: Well, I don't normally say those sorts of things to my patients.

Jeremy: Maybe you should?

Tony: It reminds me of the patient who went to their GP and the doctor said, 'You think you've got problems, take a listen to mine!' It's great to open up from time to time but I am there to help patients and not the other way round.

'But I don't want to go among mad people,' Alice remarked. 'Oh, you can't help that,' said the Cat. 'We're all mad here. I'm mad. You're mad.' 'How do you know I'm mad?' said Alice. 'You must be,' said the Cat, 'or you wouldn't have come here.'

Lewis Carroll – *Through The Looking Glass*

THE MANIC DIALOGUES

madness and genius – creativity and depression

Jeremy: I'm thinking back to Will and the time when he looked set to make some interesting films. There seem to be a lot of suicidal depressives and manic depressives in literature and the arts. What was that book – *Touched with Fire?*

Tony: Yes. The author, Kay Jamison, came up with a whole list of writers, poets, painters and musicians who have had affective disorders – in other words, disorders of emotion.

She hasn't separated the great and the good into manic depression and depression per se. However, there has always been this question, 'Do you have to be mad to be a genius?' And there are plenty of answers on both sides of the equation on that. Could Einstein have been a genius, if he hadn't been such an isolated individual? Had Einstein had three kids and a car in the garage, would he have been the same boffin as he was?

Jeremy: I never met him, but why couldn't Einstein have had three kids and a car in the garage and still be a genius?

Tony: Well, cars weren't so good in those days, and he'd have been late for work.

Jeremy: I guess it's all relative.

Tony: It's always the chicken and the egg problem, isn't it? There are plenty of creative people who are very emotionally stable and very bright. With manic depression the side people normally associate with creativity is the manic pole. In other words, the intense activity, the lack of sleep, the sense of over-confidence, the fast thinking, which of course spills over into a situation where, however creative the ideas originally were, they're no longer of any value. The ideas scatter so much from one to the next, and the person has no ability to keep them in any order, till they're lost in confusion.

Jeremy: Very interesting, doctor.

Tony: There is a psychiatrist in America who apparently is trying to capture some of these fantastic ideas and to make a fortune with them.

Jeremy: Cheeky so and so! He'd better not come over here and pinch any of ours.

Tony: He's a psychiatrist in California who looks after chief executives with manic depression. His aim is to harness the brilliant ideas they have before they go into a state of mania when they can no longer use them. Sounds a pretty good idea to me – in fact, strangely enough, one we had as well!

There have been many studies looking at the connection between madness and creativity and realistically speaking there's no definitive answer. On the other hand it is true that many of these wonderful creators, composers and artists have been tortured by mental disorder over the years.

Jeremy: Well, let's look at some of those – Tchaikovsky, Schumann, Schubert, in terms of composers. Some people have even said Beethoven as well. Then of course Kurt Cobain from Nirvana, Ian Curtis of Joy Division, and Screaming Lord Sutch to name just a few.

Tony: And so many writers too – Virginia Woolf, who they said 'enhanced parties like champagne', till she died in despair by suicide.

Jeremy: And Ernest Hemingway – a 'man's man' who everyone thought of as a tough guy. Till he shot himself.

Tony: And he was an alcohol abuser as well.

Jeremy: Big time. Strange, isn't it? People have this idea of manic depressives as being sort of wimpish, which is just so wrong.

Tony: Kay Jamison has written another book called *Exuberance* in which she describes the healthy expression of enthusiasm for life in creative people and how they have used it.

She illustrates this with examples of extraordinary people and their incredible zest for life. One such is Richard Feynman, the brilliant American mathematician, whose enthusiasm knew no bounds. His lectures were so exciting that students loved them, and when asked how many hours in the day he worked, he said he had no idea because the line between work and play just didn't exist. But he was described as being a very poor tutor in fact, because he wasn't able to calm down and explain to a student on a one-to-one basis how to correct his mathematical errors. There's little doubt that this sort of energy blends into hypomania, when it spills out of control. There is no definitive *line* between mental health and illness.

In Katherine Graham's autobiography *Personal History* she speaks of her husband, Philip, who used to run the *Washington Post* that she owned. He was a manic depressive who unfortunately …

Jeremy: Committed suicide.

Tony: Yes, he did. She describes hearing him speaking on the telephone to President Kennedy while in one of his grandiose hypomanic phases, saying aggressively, 'Do you know who you're talking to?' Apparently, Kennedy replied, 'Yes, I do know that I'm not talking to the Phil Graham that I have the greatest respect for.'

President Kennedy said there was a fine line in Philip between his madness and his genius. In reality, though, of course it is so fine that there is hardly any line at all.

Jeremy: But going back to the creative side…

Tony: Well, you say that, but all these things are creative. You don't have to be in the arts world. Inventors are creative, mathematicians, physicists, scientists, too. All science means is a thirst for knowledge. Creative people don't have to be artists in the art field at all.

Jeremy: I think when people say creativity they are talking about the written, visual or performing arts.

Tony: I think it's the ability to think outside of the box that makes these inventors, scientists and mathematicians so great. Their thinking is so fantastic because it's not in a rigid line. They're using the connections in their brain to think in other ways.

Jeremy: Yes, I think that's valid. But what's the connection to the artistic process of creation? I would venture to suggest that most manic depressives have an extra layer of perception and sensitivity.

Tony: In *Touched with Fire* Kay Jamison describes writers and poets as having a higher incidence of manic depression, but in the studies she's done the link's not so clear-cut in other forms of art like painting.

There were other studies by Nancy Andreasen, Professor of Psychiatry at the University of Iowa in America, and Felix Post, an English psychiatrist who really came to much the same conclusion.

Jeremy: So it's the writers and poets who get the brunt of this illness?

Tony: Those were the two that came out most clearly associated. But you're a writer. What about you? What difference has it made?

Jeremy: It has taken me to a lot of different places, physically and metaphorically, so my experience might be broader than quite a lot of people's. That extra sensitivity thing is an ability to feel certain things more deeply and in turn be doubly intuitive about what people think and what they are feeling. Likewise, if your mind has already visited the weirdest places while being high or low, it gives you the freedom to step back into places 'normal' people wouldn't dream of going. Certain mental territorial fears have been taken away. Sounds awfully poncy, I know.

Tony: No, I'm interested in your view that your disposition has given you an extra sensitivity. I think that's something worth exploring.

Jeremy: Perhaps it's the internal version of a writer who externally has licence to behave in a certain way. You can be going home when everyone else is going to work. You can be a little moody, don't have to wear the suit to work. You can express yourself in a flamboyant or dramatic way.

Tony: But you've got your deadlines as a writer; though they're not the same sort of deadlines a journalist faces working on a newspaper.

Jeremy: Manic depressive writers are not Martians. They can meet deadlines. They can even own media empires! Maybe it's a good time to also remind ourselves about lithium and creativity. There are often moans that taking lithium deadens your soul and flattens out any creative spark in you. For me, it's the thing that has helped me to be able to write. You can't write properly if you're marooned at one end of an upended seesaw.

Tony: I remember reading the Carrie Fisher book *The Best Awful* where she describes wanting to stop being on mood stabilizers because 'all the magic had gone'. It's sad that most of her 'magic' seems to be based on a fragility of mood. But it's a great book.

Jeremy: My suggestion would be to keep checking that you are on the right dosage of medication by having regular blood tests.

Tony: You live life very close to the edge, don't you? You enjoy that and that's why you benefit from the lithium. If you led a quiet life, with a nine-to-five job and a car in the garage, you might possibly be able to afford to get away with not taking lithium. However, your constant travelling, exposure to financial stress and writing deadlines suggest you like to live in that manner, which of course is exciting in itself.

If life has no magic for someone unless they're hypomanic or high on drugs, it seems pretty sad.

Jeremy: I do understand Carrie Fisher's point, but I don't agree with it. What are we doing here today? Drinking fresh coffee, looking through the window at a beautiful sea and writing this book. Isn't there a certain magic in that?

Tony: Sure, definitely. And we are lucky to be able to appreciate it.

tears of a clown – comedy and depression

Jeremy: And of course, there are comedians.

Tony: Yes, comedians. People whose intensity of mental energy is extraordinary. I often wonder if the price of huge emotion and intellectual energy is depression. And the price you see being paid for these extraordinary, high-powered performances – you don't get anything for nothing – is that you must be utterly drained when the performance is finished. If it accumulates enough, being drained leads to depression.

Jeremy: Yeah, that's a great point. Going back to comedians, Tony Hancock was certainly an alcoholic depressive.

Tony: So was Frankie Howerd.

Jeremy: I didn't know that.

Tony: A desperately unhappy man.

Jeremy: Poor old Frankie Howerd, he was funny. But Kenneth Williams was also a depressive. And Peter Cook was a depressive alcoholic. The Gloom List can go on and on.

Tony: Do you remember that lecture we attended about Spike Milligan where we spoke to his television director, Joe McGrath? He said what a particularly selfish and difficult man Spike was – though what a joy as well!

Jeremy: That was a real surprise.

Tony: I'd like to go into that idea of the selfishness though, because it's something that I feel I can ask you and you've said historically that you feel there's some truth in it. Are you born selfish, or do you have selfishness thrust upon you?

Jeremy: I can recall particular depressive friends who can only think and speak about themselves – endlessly! You hop round to their place to announce you've had your leg amputated, and they say, 'Yeah, well, but my vacuum cleaner has run out of dust bags ...'

I don't think 'selfish' is really the correct word. It's more about being self-obsessed, or self-absorbed.

Tony: The Now Back To Me syndrome.

Jeremy: Which can be quite funny. But I think that people in this state are caught up in the headlights of their illness.

Tony: So it forces people in on themselves – it becomes internalized, doesn't it? But a sudden depression can of course happen to Mr Extrovert Man with Three Kids and the Car in the Garage. He is absolutely knocked for six because he has no concept of how to deal with this situation at all. He doesn't have any coping mechanisms, and regards it as a huge failing.

Jeremy: You're obsessed with those three children and the garage!

the 'gift' of manic depression

Jeremy: Some people with manic depression see it as a 'gift' that enriches their lives and marks them out as special.

Tony: Well, it's true there have been studies suggesting that manic depressives often have a higher than average IQ at school. Studies were done in Iceland in the eighties by Professor of Psychiatry at the University of Iceland John Karlsson, looking at groups of patients that were psychotic in hospital, including people with schizophrenia. He looked at hospital groups with psychotic patients and came to the conclusion that these families had slightly higher success rates in life.

There has been another study by Nancy Andreasen, again suggesting a slightly higher IQ. I suppose it is nice to feel one is in a special group with some pretty cool dudes in it, even if, like most of us, you are not a mini Einstein.

Jeremy: Most people who have had manic depression will have probably suffered some serious loss in their life. Consequently, by way of compensation, it is tempting for them to believe that they belong to some unique club. After all, if you look at the roll call of manic depressives in the Insider's Guide, it's a pretty impressive list.

Tony: But you don't need to be famous – you just need to have the condition.

Didn't Kay Jamison have an interesting point at the end of her book *An Unquiet Mind*? She'd been asked whether she would rather have had manic depression than not. She said that she would rather have had it – the 'Gift'.

Jeremy: As I mentioned previously, it does give you a heightened sensitivity in which you can sometimes see things more quickly and perhaps in a lateral way that other people can't manage. It's not something where you have a choice, where you can say I wish to surrender my gift, please, or I'd like to return this manic depression, thank you. It's like having a radio inside your head set to a separate digital long-wave frequency. You've either got it or you haven't and the only question is what you do with it.

Tony: There are plenty of successful people out there who lead fulfilling lives with this condition.

Jeremy: Absolutely.

Tony: One doesn't have to be a major achiever in a huge corporation to have a degree of success.

Jeremy: Quite right. Although there are some extremely successful manic depressives running huge corporations, particularly in America. The difficulty in this country is that we live in an age where success or contribution is measured by what you earn and what you possess. My idea of success is a person with or without this condition, who happily lives in a railway carriage, perhaps on a disused railway siding, but where through some ingenious device there is basic electricity, drainage and running water. Otherwise, they make do with whatever they have, surviving without any income, but with two dogs and three cats, ten chickens, a vegetable patch, a solar-powered shower and CD player, five bicycles and the use of a nearby brilliant library. And maybe he or she has got a wife or husband, three kids *and* a garage for the bicycles. So perhaps, on second thoughts, it's a large railway carriage, left over from the Royal Train or Orient Express.

Tony: Well, I'm afraid I think I'm going to answer in a less romantic manner! Success is the ability to make the most of one's abilities and to accept one's limitations, and in my view it is the degree of balance between those two things which makes a successful individual.

Jeremy: Quite so, milord.

love, relationships and manic depression

Jeremy: You wanted to talk about sex.

Tony: Sex – and mania. And dis-inhibition.

Jeremy: Dis-inhibition. Now, I thought that was the French word for getting undressed. It sounds so sexy to me but of course really means the opposite of being inhibited. And most of us are quite inhibited in the way

we conduct ourselves. We don't take off our clothes at the drop of a hat nor do we go and talk to absolute strangers and within five minutes invite them home for dinner.

Tony: But in a state of mania, you do.

Jeremy: Yes. Let me give you a very mild example. Early one Sunday morning, seven o'clock, I bicycled from Battersea to Ten Downing Street. I walked up to the policeman outside the front door and started talking to him about the importance of bodyguards and unarmed combat. We had a very lucid conversation. Now, I don't normally go out bicycling at seven in the morning to Ten Downing Street to talk to the policemen outside.

Tony: Not about unarmed combat!

Jeremy: Another example. I used to loathe going up to girls and saying, 'Hello, do you want to come and have a drink with me?' or whatever. Hated that, and was always quite shy. But in a hypomanic state, I would go up to *any* female and say, 'I think you're absolutely gorgeous and you should come and have lunch with me immediately!' While staying at a hotel, I once borrowed a room service waiter's uniform, so I could deliver breakfast in bed to a girl I was anxious to become better friends with.

Tony: Simply no reservations at all!

Jeremy: Five hundred per cent confidence.

Tony: Either she's interested or she slaps your face and tells you to buzz off. Carrie Fisher's autobiography *The Best Awful* reminds us that kind of full-on behaviour is very much more socially acceptable in Hollywood!

Jeremy: Perhaps. But although it's like having incredible social confidence, it can easily get you into trouble.

Tony: And of course that would lead on to sexual dis-inhibition I guess, the normal sexual mores that we have and the way we guard our sexuality become somewhat loosened in a state of hypomania, don't they?

Jeremy: Your sex drive goes into a fifth gear and you feel hugely confident and as if you're on permanent heat. Which some people might feel they are on anyway. Suffice to say, you are on full flirt alert, full on all the time and you're wanting and having as much sex as possible.

Tony: You? Even more than normally!

Jeremy: Much more, yes, I mean it's interesting that the desire for sex is much greater.

Tony: And tell me about your performance.

Jeremy: I beg your pardon, doctor, I thought this was a family show!

Tony: We discussed this the other night, didn't we? And we were saying that basically you will be more adventurous in your display of sexual interest, which in a partner who's open to receiving such things could be very exciting.

Jeremy: I am not *so* sure.

Tony: Or are you just careless and selfish?

Jeremy: Rampant would be a better word. However, looking at both sides of the coin, if your manic depressive partner has been in a depressive phase for the last four months, you very well might welcome a phase of slight mania!

Tony: A certain friend of mine, who hadn't been in a relationship for a while, recently began seeing a woman who became hypomanic for the first time. I suspect he was delighted, until they both realized she was unwell.

Jeremy: And exhausted. I think it's funny, because you also start acting out certain fantasies. I don't mean this to read like the back page of a men's magazine, but that male fantasy of having a girl in every port, and wouldn't it be marvellous to have a mistress or two, can easily start to happen. You can easily slip into that *demi-monde* and you're very good at it because, no pun intended, you can keep it up, in all sorts of ways. But the sex thing can actually get out of hand and when I say get out of hand, that means people can get themselves into some very unsuitable liaisons.

Tony: Dangerous liaisons?

Jeremy: I'm sure Count Dracula's surgery has treated patients exhibiting the unfortunate results of unsuitable behaviour. And manic depression doesn't discriminate between the sexes. This behaviour is equally distributed between men and women – as are the consequences. And then when your boyfriend or girlfriend or husband or wife discovers, they might go ballistic, and might not be …

Tony: Terribly impressed. So let's talk about how relationships can be affected by this condition.

Jeremy: This is really important. And it's not just the sexual liaisons and indiscretions that can be so damaging. If you're married or partnered up, and you've got children, the really serious problems can occur through putting your family at serious risk financially. I can recall two or three ex-girlfriends in particular, who were extremely supportive and put up with an awful lot. But in the end they just couldn't hack it any more and left. It was always too much of an emotional rollercoaster, feast or famine, too much insecurity and too much having to look after someone, and not enough of being looked after.

Tony: Perhaps your partners didn't actually know when you were hypomanic, because in those phases you were so charming and effusive in your demonstrations of love. I remember reading in your book of an episode where you took over the top deck of a bus to charm one of your girlfriends.

Jeremy: Taking Leave is a work of fiction!

Tony: All right, I'll believe you! Okay, so can you give an illustration from real life which demonstrated your affection and undying love to your partner? In a hypomanic phase, when you were gathering momentum?

the tale of a champagne breakfast, and a very understanding girlfriend …

Jeremy: Here is a classic example. I was in New York exactly a year after my first manic episode. I had returned there after my big fall from grace, full of great intentions to prove that I could pull off certain business deals without going nuts. I wanted to show everyone that I was okay, particularly my new girlfriend, X. To show willing, I even agreed to leave my one remaining credit card with my brother.

Tony: When exactly did this take place?

Jeremy: December '82. However, my good intentions did not extend to running up a massive bar bill and being kicked out of the first hotel I had been staying in.

At the next hotel, I ended up falling out with the rather tired and emotional manager. The result was that he impounded my passport until after the last flight to London had left. It was Christmas Eve and I found myself completely stuck without any money in New York. Standing in the phone booth of a smart hotel lobby, I reversed the charges to X, the new girlfriend. I said I was stuck and she told me she'd ring me back in five minutes. When she did, she said, 'Right, I've checked you into the hotel with my credit card and am arriving tomorrow morning at JFK. I'll have $500 in cash and you'd better come and meet me at the airport!' She'd changed her whole Christmas plans for me.

Tony: She was a nice girlfriend.

Jeremy: She was amazing.

Tony: That's a girlfriend we would all look for!

Jeremy: So, I thought to myself, *Well, I've got to go and meet her at the airport and I can't just pick her up in an ordinary taxi, that wouldn't be much of a greeting. After all, it's Christmas Day.* So I booked a stretch limousine and on the way to the airport bought a bunch of flowers that were so big, I actually fell over trying to carry them.

Tony: How did you pay for them?

Jeremy: I'll get to that. Well, you know how everyone used to say I looked like a dead ringer for Dudley Moore? I went straight up to the very nice head of BA Customer Services and told her that I was Dudley Moore's twin brother, and that the lady who was arriving shortly was incredibly important and could they do something special?

The lady from BA was fantastic and arranged for X to have special clearance through security straight to a champagne breakfast in the First Class BA lounge, which they kindly let us have to ourselves. X was a little taken aback to see a stretch limousine waiting outside, but was then distracted by the flowers.

And so we went to stay in the lovely hotel, and it was only three days later that X found she couldn't use her credit card anywhere as her entire limit had been blown.

The point is that it was all so well intentioned – the romantic gestures were sincere and heartfelt. I'd just also happened to use her credit card number to pay for the limousine and flowers …

Tony: You were very romantic, and not a little chivalrous, but you were also not well at the time.

Jeremy: I think it's a really tricky thing because more than anything manic depressives need to be involved in a good relationship. And if they can't be in a relationship with a human being, then they should have a good one with a dog or a cat or whatever.

We don't use the word 'mad' here – we prefer 'crazy'...

Pearsall.

Tony: One of the other advantages of being in a relationship is your partner can watch out for stages when you're becoming unwell. Because, as you say, you are not aware of being unwell and a partner can press it upon you that things are not quite as well as you think. And if they catch it early enough they can perhaps persuade you to take appropriate measures to correct that. The wonderful book by Judy Eron, *What Goes Up,* describes how her manic depressive husband was unwell for a whole year with hypomania, having stopped taking his lithium. And eventually came down with a massive depression that ended in his tragic suicide.

Jeremy: Yes, it was well told and frighteningly real.

Tony: But the point she makes throughout the book is that you must get in early, to try and impress upon or force your partner to take medication or see the doctor or friends.

Another thing she emphasizes is that you, the non-suffering partner, have this desire to be loyal and trusted by your loved one, and can feel bad talking behind your partner's back, when perhaps that's exactly what you need to be doing. You absolutely should be talking about it to friends and partners and doctors, to tell them what a bad situation you're both in and that he or she is unwell.

Jeremy: None of us *wants* to be disloyal or seen to be going behind some-one's back, or undermining someone. When I was even vaguely hypo-manic I used to get furious with people if I thought they were conspiring behind my back.

Tony: The person in a state of hypomania wants to stay there, because it's such a nice state to be in. So much so that they will be manipulative and maybe aggressively resist the overtures of the partner.

Jeremy: Yes. But as we've said, the person who is hypomanic doesn't necessarily think there's anything wrong with them – except for being surrounded by bloody annoying people misunderstanding them. When Judy Eron's husband announced, 'I'm trying an experiment in not taking lithium anymore,' *that* was the point where she lost her grip of him. When someone's given up their medication which has proven to work, it's a fairly big danger sign.

Tony: So often people are secretive. And then they just suddenly say ...

Jeremy: 'I have stopped taking it.'

Tony: And, 'Why do I need this medication when my other friends don't? What's so wrong with me? I am okay now, so why can't I be like every-body else?'

Jeremy: Likewise, what's wrong with just accepting that you have to take two pills a day? Yes, they might make you slightly overweight, but if that's just going to keep the whole thing together, accept it – and work out if you want to. I think a lot of people think they're being made to take part in a remake of *One Flew Over the Cuckoo's Nest*, where there is some awful nursing sister standing behind the drug hatch with a pharmaceutical axe in her hand.

Tony: Yes, it's the idea that the doctors or the medical team are the enemy. But it's not your life in their hands – it's your life in *yours*. And thank God lithium and the other products are around, because life was very different before these medications.

thinking big – the unaffordable side of manic depression

FINANCE MANAGER

Jeremy: As we were talking about before, something that's very common to manic depressives is grandiosity and delusions of grandeur.

Many manic depressives in the extremes of mania have historical, religious delusions, very often thinking they are Buddha, Marilyn Monroe, Napoleon or Jesus Christ – or that they are married to one or the other. Most believe they are on a mission. In my first bout of mania in America, I elevated myself to the status of a British Peer, a position which nobody doubted, including myself, by the end!

Tony: This was when you became Lord Thomas?

Jeremy: I am still searching for the ten thousand acre estate that goes with the title.

When someone is really manic, it is not as if they're frothing at the mouth with their eyeballs rotating in opposite directions. It is often someone who looks normal, behaves in a totally plausible manner and looks the part, save that they might appear restless and speedy; otherwise they are 1000 per cent convincing. I think that's the funny and the frightening side of it.

Tony: Another frightening side to it is the manic depressive's attitude to money. Sort of, *I deserve these things and I want them, not some time in the future but literally now. It doesn't matter what it takes, I'm going to have them.*

Jeremy: When you're manic three of your many middle names are 'Mega Confident', 'Multiple Schemes' and 'Impetuous'. You want three red Alpha Romeos for yourself, your wife and your secret girlfriend – and a new house to go with each of them. You quickly dream up an idea to set up a network of two hundred 'Alpha' car wash service garages across the country. Meanwhile, there's a tiny little voice squeaking, *You haven't got the money.* But a much bigger voice is going, *Well, of course you've got the money, because this and that deal will be coming off soon, then there's that other one in America and maybe Germany, and anyway any bank with any imagination will be begging to finance the whole operation and at worst you can always sell back the cars and hey it's okay.*

Tony: And litigation? Manic depressives are fairly keen?

Jeremy: My wonderful old psychiatrist explained to me many years ago the difference between a normal person and a manic depressive in a manic phase. A normal person has a terrible car crash, where perhaps they break their leg and are quite aware of how painful it is, probably feel a bit sorry for themselves but are thankful it's not worse. In a manic state, a manic depressive is totally delighted that they've broken their leg because it means they can not only sue the driver of the other car for a giant sum of money, but also the car manufacturer for the inexcusably flaccid airbags and probably the ambulance driver for not arriving at the scene of the accident quickly enough!

Suing people and being involved in all manner of litigation becomes an enticing and compulsive challenge: 'I don't take any crap from *anyone*, I don't put up with this or that. *You* may, but I don't – and by the way, that is largely because I am descended from Napoleon.'

welcome to the rollercoaster

Tony: How did your main or 'first' episode take off? Can you unpack some of the baggage surrounding the story?

Jeremy: After my mother died, I decided to put a few things to the test. It was time to leave the safe and successful world of employment and go out into private practice with my good friend to start a new record label. However, after only a few weeks it became apparent that something was wrong, but I couldn't identify what it was.

I felt very sort of blue inside and was worried, it was like, *Jesus Christ, what's going on, I can't afford to have anything go wrong here, keep going, keep going!* So I kept on, trying to get the business going, but I found it very difficult.

After a few more weeks, I was having difficulty sleeping, finding it difficult to concentrate, being terribly forgetful, and thinking, *Oh my God, this is all going completely wrong.*

My thinking became very muddled and all sorts of superstitious things ran through my head. I looked for any external reason to blame and any external action to repair matters – almost like not walking on the cracks in the pavement.

For some reason I thought it must be my girlfriend. It's her, I really shouldn't be with her, I've obviously got to leave. This is after her trying to help me in those months. So I left her in a terrible situation. But things just got worse, they just got worse and worse.

Tony: You also didn't like where you were working, did you? Compared to the bright lights of the West End?

Jeremy: The location was pretty awful but that wasn't relevant. What was relevant was that in my mind it had become clear my luck had run out. It was just the real me now, coming to the surface – this hopeless person.

I knew the company would fail, that every record I was making was a complete waste of time. My mind would magnify and project everything in the future as a total disaster. I would half pretend to be positive because I simply didn't know what else to do and what was really going on. It had been bloody awful for my girlfriend. Now it was bloody awful for my friend and business partner. He was very supportive. I was talking to all sorts of people but didn't tell anybody the same story. So it was excruciatingly difficult for my friends to know what to do.

Tony: But were you *really* talking to anyone?

Jeremy: Not really. People would say, 'Oh, you're really down.' And I was like, 'Yeah, we've got no money in the business.' And then they would say, 'Ah, well, it's the lack of money that's causing it.'

Tony: So you would talk about superficial things?

Jeremy: A girlfriend of mine, who had lived in America and was quite therapy minded, said, 'Look, you're going through a real crisis.' I told her, 'Oh, you're being American on me.' And she said, 'Look, I lived with you, and I can tell you're cracking up.' And I just said, *'Don't say I'm cracking up!'*

As the weeks went by, as the months went by, it got worse and worse. And in the end I turned round to my partner and said, 'Look, I'm going to leave the music business, it's obvious that I can't hack it anymore.'

It got to the point where I thought, *I think I will actually end it all.* But I had amazing friends, and a particularly supportive brother. And in the end I didn't do it, but it came very close.

Tony: How long had you been feeling like ending it prior to this? Because you did actually even try to kill yourself.

Jeremy: The drama of it! Yeah, I even rang the *Times* births and deaths column to place an entry about my death that day.

Shortly after that 'rock bottom' moment something extraordinary happened. My old boss called me up. I went to see him and he said, 'Listen, I can't stand seeing you in this state, I want to offer you a job and we'll pay you so many thousand pounds a year.' It was good money at the time. His words suddenly switched something on in my head – *Would you really give me that job?*

I went back and I saw my partner and I wouldn't have left him in the lurch anyway because I felt bad enough about what had happened. Within a couple of weeks I went hell for leather for work, and I soon got the girl-friend back and it all fell back into place. In the ensuing few months I used so much whisky as my rocket fuel I should have been sponsored by Bells.

To cut a very long story short it ended in me coming up with the scheme of all schemes that was going to make more money than was passing through the Bank of England, let alone Las Vegas. It really was a very good idea, but like many ideas born of manic episodes, simply not thought through enough.

It eventually involved two trips to New York, and on the final trip I did actually go completely off my rocker and elevated myself to the House of Lords and installed myself in the most expensive hotel suite in New York with twenty-four-hour bodyguard protection, two stretch limousines and many *wonderful* new friends. Apart from music interests, my new empire took in aeroplane leasing, chartering trains and redeveloping residential property in Harlem. And that didn't include the wondrous schemes I was setting up in London. I had total faith that, given a little time I could make every single project successful and be a multi-millionaire by the tender age of twenty-seven.

Ah, goodness me! I was utterly convinced I was going to take over the music business and most of New York State into the bargain! If it hadn't been for two great friends who were also coincidentally in New York on holiday I think it would have ended with the bodyguards getting really quite upset and all sorts of other terrible things happening.

My two friends realized something was seriously wrong, acted accordingly and called the hypodermic cavalry. I was flown home, heavily sedated, straight into the Bethlem Royal Hospital, West Wycombe, Kent, no interview required.

Tony: For two months.

Jeremy: Yes, indeed.

Tony: So what about after you left the Bethlem?

Jeremy: I'm fairly clear in saying that this period was one of the worst times of my life. I was still trying to get my business idea off the ground. The problem was that my confidence had reduced from 500 per cent to about fifteen per cent, and because I owed such a lot of money, and the scheme was already so ambitious, the pressure became too much, and I dropped down into a bad gloom.

It was a serious depression that lasted about three or four months. It ended up with me selling the house to pay off most of the debts. To get a place and then to lose it four years later was a bad blow. Far worse was that all the confidence, power and ability I had felt before had just vanished, and was being replaced by the same feelings of hopelessness and failure I had experienced a year before when I changed jobs.

Tony: A bad case of *déjà-vu.*

Jeremy: Yes, that's right. I think I went adrift then for some time, and it was really unfortunate, I didn't have any work or ability to work. I'm lucky to have had great friends and family but even they found it difficult to cope with. I was being treated as an outpatient at the Maudsley but really just hating it, and hating everything actually.

Tony: What medication were you taking at this time?

Jeremy: I was taking lithium, but I almost didn't see the point, because I just felt so bad. I was living on my own, well, I had the cat but it was extremely tricky. To say that reality was kicking in was something of an understatement.

Eventually, several months later, after selling up and camping out at different friends' places for weeks, I began looking for work. I had been drifting badly towards the edge but somehow managed to reverse the direction. Then out of the blue, exactly the same thing happened: another chum from the music business rang me up and said you shouldn't be doing nothing, can't stand to see you like this, come and be in my company. The next thing anyone knew, I'd got this together and that together and off I went. I was convinced I was getting better but the illness swung back again.

Tony: In hindsight, how did that happen?

Jeremy: I had sent a tape of a song to a big record producer in New York and most unusually, he loved it and was considering recording it with a big-selling artist (Leo Sayer). I became convinced that my presence in New York was essential and that my redemption and readmission to the centre court of the music business were only a few weeks away. Joining the dots, this then took me on my trip to New York without a credit card which ended up in meeting X with the flowers and stretch limousine at JFK airport.

Tony: Those opportunities, though, come from you being a sociable, outgoing, warm and humorous kind of a guy, don't they? Do you think that fits in any way with your emotional character? What made you attractive enough for people to ring you up and say, 'Come on, you can't be this down, come and have a job!' I think you had better bottle that as well! Do you think that's the same thing that made you very vulnerable?

Jeremy: I've no idea but take me to the bottling plant.

Tony: I mean, because you were jolly, outgoing, and a bit superficial – maybe? – you were not very grounded and therefore possibly a bit vulnerable?

Jeremy: I was probably all of those things but I was also quite good in the music business, quite good at finding groups and marketing and selling and all that crap. So if you have a certain personality, it's much easier if you're groovy, outgoing, then yes, people want you around, that's true.

Tony: And then you've got that innate sort of enthusiasm, which you would then fuel with alcohol?

Jeremy: I am enthusiastic in normal circumstances. But in a slightly manic mood, I could be cooking on gas *and* electricity ...

Tony: So you're kind of motoring?

Jeremy: You're motoring and most of the time you're also Mr Good Vibes where everyone around is going, 'He's such a good laugh, he's so great.'

You always over-accentuate the positive, so it becomes very tricky for others to know what's really happening. Nobody wants to be the wet blanket.

Tony: Weren't you suspicious that your new situation was being fuelled by alcohol?

Jeremy: No, because in those early days it was wonderful to feel good again or normal or what I thought was normal, or even vaguely up. I didn't care what it was that was getting me there.

Tony: And then we met six months later.

Jeremy: My shenanigans in New York, Paris and Hamburg were all winding down, just coming to a close then.

Tony: My girlfriend of the time was working for you.

Jeremy: The lovely Fiona!

Tony: We got on well and I recall offering to be your doctor on the principle that I would not charge you, for the time being, till your status in the industry was restored!

Jeremy: Still no bill and it's only twenty-two years later!

Tony: I'm still waiting for a large bonus and in five years' time, perhaps a Cadillac?

Jeremy: I was thinking of giving you a small Lear jet.

Tony: Those first couple of years that I was with you, we were obviously catching up with the background, but to some extent as you say, you weren't too bad. But then it wasn't long till you had that terrible car accident; what was that about?

Jeremy: I fell asleep while driving the car on the way back from a weekend binge and hit a remarkably solid lamppost. I didn't have a seatbelt on, and went through the windscreen.

Tony: Broke your mandible and glass pierced your eye.

Jeremy: That was an interesting experience. I broke my jaw in two places and a piece of glass went through my left eye.

Tony: Has your vision been damaged for ever?

Jeremy: Yes, unfortunately.

Tony: You've had a couple of other incidents with the police where I believe you've lost your licence?

Jeremy: Yes, I'd lost my licence in '79 the first time, and again two years later and then again in '87.

Tony: They were all related to the alcohol?

Jeremy: They were indeed, milord.

Tony: And then the following year, I see a note that we referred you to have a psychiatric review, including the time when your depression had increased, but also you were sleepwalking. Now do tell us, dear fellow, a bit about your *somnambulism*!

Jeremy: It sounds as if we are in an episode of *Just a Minute*! I think that a combination of taking lithium, Dalmane sleeping pills, and a fair quantity of alcohol caused me to sleepwalk. But this wasn't just sleepwalking round the bedroom. This was out of the bedroom, and out of the front door, down a flight of stairs, and out of the building.

Tony: And, of course you were ... naked!

Jeremy: I used to wake up and find myself standing like a new-born baby in the strangest of places. It was quite odd but perhaps a trifle more odd for the passing milkman.

Tony: So the psychiatrist said cut back or stop drinking altogether; what was your reaction to that advice?

Jeremy: I didn't want to. It was an attitude of *I know I should but I won't.* I used to experiment with moderating my drinking instead.

Tony: A few hours without alcohol!

Jeremy: Well, only drinking white wine with soda, or only drinking a half or two of Guinness a day or something.

Tony: We were keeping an eye on your lithium level periodically throughout the years. I wasn't getting the impression that you were ever hypomanic, and it seemed your depressions were more a reaction to circumstances – a bad time at work or busting up with your girlfriend or things of that nature. But do you think those lows had been induced by alcohol?

Jeremy: They were certainly helped by it.

Tony: During the years of '80, '81 and '82, you were suicidal and having manic episodes, when you were wildly out of control.

Jeremy: Oh yes, and the year after as well. I think the point really about this period is that if you drink excessively and take lithium, it's rather a stupid idea.

Tony: Plus the fact you probably were not taking the lithium regularly.

Jeremy: No. In the end – by '84 – I was taking it correctly. Presumably, if you see a patient every week, you're going to find out a lot more about what's going on with them. In my case, I was only going to come and see you as little as possible. There were probably a lot of things that happened which perhaps you didn't know about.

Tony: Perhaps you didn't want to tell me about them.

Jeremy: It's possible.

Tony: And you were probably secretly aware that a part of the reason was that you didn't want to face up to it.

Jeremy: When you've had bad manic depressive episodes, you want to be back on the straight and narrow, but you also want to have a good time. Getting pissed was the easy option and, if you're pissed most of the time, it's great. That was what I largely did in the early eighties up until the point where I decided to get my life back on track.

the angle-poise light moment

Jeremy: Back in the dark ages of late 1987, when men were men, women wore shoulder pads and a Mars bar cost 12 pence, I had been bankrupt for three years. My solicitor informed me that if I could obtain a clean bill of health, an MOT certificate from the hospital in which I had been incarcerated, there might be a possibility of getting an earlier discharge from bankruptcy.

Tony: What happened?

Jeremy: I went down to the Bethlem hospital and saw this lady psychiatrist I'd not seen before. However, she insisted she'd helped look after me when I was ill in hospital six year earlier, and knew all about me. I said, 'Fair enough. So let me make this easy for you. All you've got to do is sign the piece of paper and I'm out of here.'

Tony: And then you'd be discharged from the bankruptcy?

Jeremy: Hopefully. Anyway I thought it would be a piece of cake to get the paper signed, but soon discovered otherwise. So she says, 'Well, I'm not quite sure I'm going to sign that yet, because we need to discuss one or two things first. On my file here it says you were drinking rather a lot, and if anything we also thought you were an alcoholic.'

I then had this amazing cat and mouse game with her where I was perhaps economical with the truth by suggesting that I only drank half a bottle of wine every other day with a friend. She was going, 'Yes, of course you do, you liar,' and in the end it got very heavy, really eyeball to eyeball. Christ Almighty! I had only gone there to pick up an MOT certificate, not get the Spanish Inquisition! She finally said, 'Look, I'm just not going to sign the piece of paper unless you start telling me the truth ...'

Tony: Did she use water torture?

Jeremy: Far worse. The main trick she played on me was when she picked up the telephone and said, 'I've got your file here with some telephone numbers of old girlfriends. Would it be okay if I rang a couple of them now to ask if alcohol caused any problems in your relationships?'

I reached for the telephone and said, 'I wouldn't do that, if I were you.' And she said, 'Really? So you must think that I'm right.' She was skilful.

Actually I'm very grateful to her, even though it took a long time to follow her advice. Her point – and maybe I am labouring it – was that I could not drink in the way that I did, *especially* with this condition. After much huffing and puffing and smoking for England, Ireland and Wales, I said, 'I'll tell you what I'll do, I'll give up for a year and if I do that, it means I'm not an alcoholic – okay?'

Tony: Did she withdraw the whip?

Jeremy: She said, 'Why *won't* you stop drinking, permanently? You must, you've got to understand that you've got to stop. In fact, you do understand, but why won't you?'

It felt as if I had two angle-poise lights shining into my eyes and matchsticks being shoved under every fingernail. In the end, I said to her, 'Listen, if I stop drinking, I won't be funny, and if I'm not funny then no one will like me.'

Tony: That must have been really hard to say.

Jeremy: It was. I said to her, as if I'd just imparted some state secret, 'If you ever tell anybody what I just told you, I'll be back to sort you out!' She said, 'Well, you know I think you'll be fine and you'll be all right, you're a funny guy.' I was thinking, *No, I won't be all right.*

Tony: What actually happened? You went through November and December with your usual conviviality and then what happened?

Jeremy: I always used to go to the same gang of friends every New Year's Eve. That evening I got absolutely off my face – so off my face that at the end of the dinner, when everyone was going home, they said we'd better give you a lift, and I refused point blank and insisted on walking. The walk would probably be about four or five miles and it was also freezing cold.

The next thing, I woke up the following morning, fully clothed, with my hand twice the normal size it should be, and my forehead covered in blood. And I thought, *That's interesting, I wonder how that happened?*

I had no memory of what had occurred at all, but I did think then that, maybe, just maybe, I should actually stop drinking for a year.

Tony: So you did.

Jeremy: Apart from one or two Irish coffees … yes.

it's up to you

Tony: We've got to around 1988 in your story.

Jeremy: Yes, '88 into '89.

Tony: At this time you were still running your own record label?

Jeremy: I was working for somebody, running an alternative and punk label up until '89. Then a French company wanted to set up a record company in England, so I agreed to run that. At that point I had quite a clear head, having not drunk for nearly six months, so I decided I was also going to set up a company to tap the new opportunities for record sales in Eastern Europe.

Tony: During that dry spell did it not occur to you that you were functioning far better than when you were drinking heavily?

Jeremy: I don't know whether it's because I knew I could eventually go back on the sauce but it wasn't too bad. It also meant that I had a lot more energy and could work really hard. I was very pleased about that.

Tony: So were you able to successfully combine running the French company and doing your Eastern European thing?

Jeremy: It was difficult but I managed for a while. Then, despite selling 200,000 copies of Technotronic's 'Pump Up the Jam' in the former USSR, the coup that dislodged President Gorbachev sadly dislodged Blue Baltic Records as well.

Tony: Did you try and get paid in vodka? Okay, and then?

Jeremy: In 1992, I then met a very nice Australian girl and followed her out to Australia to see her. When she came back we had a big problem with the immigration authorities, which involved her being sent home and coming back three months later on a fiancée visa.

Anyway, we ended up getting married, and though this coincided with a period when I'd been trying to stop drinking, and although things looked very good on the outside, it wasn't quite so hot on the inside.

I wasn't sure if I wanted to be married, and didn't know what to do. I didn't know who to talk to, either. I didn't think that I would talk to you, because you're a chum and you know it sounds crap, but sometimes the squabbling in one's own head is too weird to impart. I became convinced that I must see someone. So I went to see this psychiatrist that you arranged.

It was actually very funny because after he said to me most politely, 'Now, Jeremy, what seems to be the trouble?' I just rambled on for about half an hour non-stop. When I finished speaking, he looked at me with such horror as if to say, *Did I REALLY need to hear all that garbage?* He told me I needed to join a group, and I went, 'I am not a group person.'

Weirdly, the next thing that happened was that I ended up joining jolly old AA. It happened by accident, in the sense that a friend of mine tricked me into going, 'Just for the craic you understand,' he said. Well, you don't really go to AA just for the craic, do you?

Tony: When you say your friend tricked you, what was the –

Jeremy: Oh, he just said, 'You should go, have a laugh, because it's terribly funny, just go.'

Tony: Was it a useful experience for you?

Jeremy: Yes, it certainly was, though part of me did worry that I was joining the Moonies.

Tony: I have certain patients who should go to AA but won't because they have not reached desperation point. Is there any way to help them go?

Jeremy: You can tell them about it, give them phone numbers of people willing to help. The rest is up to them. You can lead a horse to water … You have to decide to go there for yourself. I guess that many people are put off being in a group, because they fear that a spotlight might be shone on them, or they may be asked a question, neither of which ever happens in AA anyway.

Tony: But it does work, which is wonderful, isn't it?

Jeremy: It does work and in the first year of being a member, I met more manic depressives than I had ever met in the preceding ten years. And I heard more things that made more sense *to me* than anywhere else I'd ever been.

This is not meant to be an advertisement for AA. The important thing in all of this is *deciding to do something about the problem and talking to someone*. That is the first port of call, whatever road you choose.

getting the
information you need

Tony: We were talking about some patients often having an 'us and them' attitude to the medical profession. You illustrated it quite nicely, by saying that when you were in hospital some of the patients regarded themselves as prisoners in a ward, and the doctors and the nurses as prison guards.

Jeremy: Perhaps most people who are manic see the medical team around them like that.

Tony: We've had lots of people talking to us about their views on it. Only yesterday I had a resentful email saying, 'When *they* got my medication right, eventually …' People need to realize that even with all our advances in medical science, we don't have all the answers. People can feel very resentful about this and that's why we need better communication from doctors and psychiatric nurses.

Jeremy: I suppose that there are some doctors who are less good at communicating with people and others who simply have too many patients to deal with.

Tony: I think also the doctor can be arrogant because he doesn't know the answers and is afraid of admitting that. 'We' don't, is always a good way of saying it, because it's not the doctor as an individual. Nowadays, particularly when the whole idea of the paternalistic, know-it-all doctor is somewhat passé, it's very important for a caring communicative doctor to get that across.

Jeremy: Hopefully, this book might spread the word a bit in a reasonably palatable manner that doctors are actually human!

Tony: Really?! But back to being a patient. Being given a diagnosis of manic depression is a frightening thing. Having to take on board something you never realized you had is quite something to follow for the first time. All of those questions that come up in your head have to be answered slowly, bit by bit, over a period of time.

Jeremy: Maybe in this country we should review the way that information is delivered. I think the danger is, if you're a manic depressive or depressive, and you have a stay in a hospital where somebody gives you a diagnosis, when you come out, you might panic and think, *Oh my God, what does all this mean, am I a total weirdo? How do I find out?*

Well, most people these days find out everything by going on to the internet, and typing words into Google. Now, providing you have access to a computer, that can give you a certain amount of information, but I think it would be so much better if we had more psychiatric nurses in the community who come round and actually sit down and have a cup of coffee and say look, this is the story.

Tony: Sometimes, I find patients come into my room with more knowledge than I have about an area of medicine. But I actually still have to translate what they've read into a context and framework, because reading something on the internet can give incomplete information which can be very harmful.

Jeremy: Your point being?

Tony: The important thing is to communicate with people who know about their subject, face to face, so don't only read and don't only look at the internet, talk to someone.

Jeremy: This is where something like meetings of the Manic Depression Fellowship come into their own. You're going to meet other people who are in the same boat.

When I first came out of hospital, after a pretty serious time, I had the opportunity of trying to put my business back together again. I went hell for leather, but I just couldn't do it. I was furious and upset, shaking my fist and thinking, *God, I've failed!* A great friend of mine came to see me and said, 'Listen, you're not seeing things how they really are. Don't you see that you've been really ill? If this was a physical illness, you'd be going to the seaside to have a six-week rest.'

Tony: Or at least have time off to recuperate.

Jeremy: Yeah, and he said, 'You've got to heal.' I think if you smashed your head in physically, you would be taking serious time out to heal it. What's the difference between the internal and external head?

Tony: I think that's a very good point.

pet therapy

Pearsall.

Tony: I remember you mentioned a man with a stammer at an MDF meeting who said his life had changed the day he got a dog. You said that it was a very good illustration of being taken out of one's self, by taking on responsibility for something else.

Jeremy: When you wake up, you have to feed that dog, and then you have to take it out for a walk. That dog never gives you a hard time, but it really loves you – unconditional, slobbering love is hugely important and gives people a reason for going on.

Tony: Pets really are good for our well-being as we can give them unconditional love, and they are so dependent on us. They are company when we are alone and need our care, often just when we don't feel like giving it; which is usually the most important time for us to have to give it.

Do you recall coming to the surgery when Laggan, my Labrador, was there?

Jeremy: Of course.

Tony: I had a mad love affair with her, and unconditional love is the phrase – except after that favourite Labrador affectation, the roll in the dead fox. But all that talk about me and Laggan was just tittle-tattle.

Jeremy: Come on, Doctor Hughes, be serious.

Tony: Laggan used to get me out walking. I still walk, but when she was alive Laggan and I were a pair.

Jeremy: It was very good to come to a doctor's surgery that had a dog snoozing in the kitchen.

Tony: Though these days, when everything is so fastidious, you wouldn't be able to do that.

Jeremy: When did you get her?

Tony: 1990.

Jeremy: Thirteen years!

Tony: I remember the grief when I had to have her put down because she had cancer. It was so bad she was having fits, but of course on the morning she was due to be put down she was on remarkably good form. I remember standing over the vet as he injected into her leg and then she was no more. It was absolutely gutting – like killing your best friend. But then, of course, there's always the cat, Tuscany.

Jeremy: Can you describe Tuscany?

Tony: Tuscany is a cute cat, and one of my PA receptionists called Kim adores cats. I am able to tease her considerably because I tell her stories of filling Tuscany full of oil paint from the top end and then squeezing her like a toothpaste tube and using her tail to paint with, which of course sends Kim running round the house screaming at the very thought.

Jeremy: We all know that deep down, you really love Tuscany.

Tony: Yeah, Tuscany is okay, Tuscany's okay. And your relationship with Ned was for seventeen years?

Jeremy: I acquired Ned in 1978. What's funny about Ned is he stayed with me through thick and thin, through all of my ups and my downs. I moved something like twelve times and he moved too.

Tony: Because cats aren't naturally peripatetic creatures.

Jeremy: No, they like their routine basically.
   Speaking of which, you remember me telling you about X, the lady with the credit card in New York? After that we lived together for three years. She put up with a lot of crap and big up and down mood swings and boozing. I am not proud of it but I am of her. Anyway, in the end we had one row too many, and I said to X, 'I'm sick of this, I'm sick of this relationship, and sick of you and sick of this flat.' And she went, 'Well, that's fine, because actually you're living in *my* flat.'

Tony: So what happened?

Jeremy: She said, 'I'm not going anywhere, but when I come back tomor-row, you're not going to be here anymore, bye …' As she walked out of the room, Ned walked into the room and looked at me, as if to say, 'What the hell have you gone and done now?'

Tony: You were homeless?

Jeremy: By sheer luck I found an absolutely perfect basement garden flat the next day.

Tony: This was chosen primarily for Ned, you mean?

Jeremy: He had told me this time he had to have a garden, you see. The place was owned by an old Scottish lady who lived in the rest of the house. It was a perfect flat in a brilliant location. I used every inch of charm to persuade her I was suitable. Finally she said, 'Well, I think you'll do –

when do you want to move in?' I said, 'Marvellous. Is there any chance I could move in now?' And she said, 'Yes, I suppose so.' Then, just as I was leaving to get my stuff, she called out, 'You don't have any wee pets, do you?' 'No,' I said, 'only a wee cat.' She shook her head. 'Oh dear, no, I'm so sorry, because I've got a wee dog and he doesn't like cats at all.'

I had to give up this amazing flat for that bloody cat!

Tony: The price of love, eh?

Jeremy: Mind you, when it came to that time in 1995 when I had to have Ned put to sleep it was a tricky moment to say the least. I was surprised at how bad I felt, especially during those first few weeks of going home each night when you're so used to hearing a large cat trundling towards you.

Tony: I know what you mean. I can't decide whether to get another dog.

Jeremy: No, you must do! Having a dog or cat, or even a hamster or a goldfish, gives you something to look after that'll also look after you.

Tony: Well, maybe not the goldfish.

shrinks, loss and the doc on the couch

Jeremy: I thought you made a very good point when we were talking about the difference between blues and depression. You said you *should* feel sad when a human being, or your cat or dog has died, and that there's no point trying to stop that feeling or mask it.

Tony: The key is to acknowledge it, but also to move on. These two things have to move in parallel or the grief will never change. Even though the grief will one day subside, the love for that individual will never change.

Jeremy: And triggers for manic depression and depression are so often bereavement and loss.

Tony: Not only for depression, but loss of a loved one can also lead to hypomania, which is an interesting counter-intuitive reaction. It may happen as a result of insomnia and the gathering storm in the mind from exhaustion.

Jeremy: Well, I can imagine, if you had lost somebody but couldn't deal with it and had a tendency to be a workaholic, you could work yourself so hard that you end up being like a spinning top.

Tony: I think the advantage of the nine-to-five work pattern is that the routine protects people in some ways. A potential problem for an artist, for example, is that he can work till five in the morning, and then he's so excited by his project he will create an artificial insomnia just from simple enthusiasm which will tip vulnerable people into hypomania. Their trigger would literally be over-exuberance or – as you might say – a workaholic attitude.

Jeremy: And without any sleep, going on and with alcohol and drugs, you can flick into that manic swing. Taking drugs and alcohol is putting petrol on the fire.

Looking back before I was diagnosed and before we met, my mother died and I just decided that I would go on to a form of autopilot. I did the funeral, then thought, *Now I'm really going to go for it.* And four, five months later I changed my job, and tripled the stakes as it were.

Tony: Was that too soon? Because they always say with a major drama in one's life one should never do other dramas at the same time, if you have the choice.

Jeremy: Dead right.

Tony: If you lose a parent, don't break up with the girlfriend at the same time?

Jeremy: Definitely not. And with the benefit of what I and we know now, absolutely. But then I was somebody who didn't talk to people about the sort of stuff we're talking about now. I just sort of felt desperate to keep going, which is just what I did do. Then about another three months after that, I really sank way down into Gloom City International. When I was diagnosed a year later, it allowed people to put it all into an irritatingly neat ball: 'Ah, yes! It was the death of your mother which you obviously didn't get over, and so this has happened.'

Tony: Do you still pray, being a Catholic? The reason I ask is because I do, even though I'm agnostic. I do in a way because it exists, prayer, although it's a bit of an existential concept. I don't think there's anyone out there listening, but it can act as a strengthening tool. I am fairly spiritual in my view on life, though, I have to confess, it usually happens during the biggest dramas of my life. But I am certain that I benefit from it.

Jeremy: I think that's great, I really do.

Tony: I remember that year I lost my mother, Laggan died and then a serious relationship ended painfully. I put it euphemistically but it was traumatic in the extreme and exhausting, and emotionally a huge burden, and I remember a considerable amount of praying that month.

Jeremy: And would that take the form of being on your own at home?

Tony: Well, I was giving thanks for Laggan and my mother, but I was also praying for the well-being of this girlfriend, hoping that she would be okay because she had a lot of things to deal with in her life. I had a ritual. I would sit in the dark, cross-legged in my living room, facing Strasbourg, and I would recite this mantra with my eyes closed, in a lotus position, hoping that somehow if there was any force out there it would strengthen her.

Jeremy: How do you cope as a doctor – or psychiatrist for that matter – with these very difficult periods when you also have to sit through patients droning on about themselves? You've mentioned prayer, but how do you manage?

Tony: I suppose if you're going through a bad patch like that, it helps in a way not to think about your own situation for some hours. However, the experience of loss and pain in one's own life can do nothing but strengthen a doctor.

Jeremy: So do you feel as a doctor that the process of dealing with other people's problems on a daily basis is a way of getting out of yourself?

Tony: I think it can be. At the end of the day you would return to your own pain, but for some hours it's been masked by occupation with other people's issues. But that's the same for everyone.

Jeremy: Please carry on.

Tony: We've talked about a particular colleague who can sometimes perform on stage in a very amusing way whilst underneath experiencing great anguish. If only he could express this sometimes, he says. There is this something within you, but as a professional – a comedian, doctor, whoever – you have to rise above that to perform. I'm sure you do the same in your field. If you've got your own personal issues going on at a given time, you still have to sit at your desk and work.

Jeremy: The truth of it is that the general public still tend to either idolize doctors and psychiatrists, or the opposite, but few of them ever wonder how they actually cope.

Tony: Well, going through my divorce and other difficult times, I've spoken to colleagues. Having colleagues made the initial leap to ask for help a little easier. The big advantage of speaking to professionals rather than friends is that they are independent, so aren't involved in the problems. For example, I had a relationship problem some years ago and my partner at the practice, who fortunately was very familiar with this area of medicine, recommended I do a course of psychotherapy to look into the causes.

Jeremy: Really?

Tony: I thought it would be helpful, and I might learn some interesting things about myself. However, after a year of staring at the ceiling and talking about my dreams I wasn't quite so convinced, but it was this particular individual's method. It was certainly useful, though, reflecting on the origins of my behaviour and I would highly recommend it to anyone, but perhaps not in that manner.

Jeremy: Did you ever do anything else?

Tony: Yes, I've also attended Insight courses as a way of learning more. Insight is an American creation otherwise termed 'EST without the angst'! A group of people – maybe 100 or so – cooped up together for a few days, baring their souls to each other.

Jeremy: I've always thought that EST was a dangerous kind of organization.

Tony: I found it difficult to accept initially. Exposing one's soul to individuals that you had never met before was okay because there was no previous relationship! It seems very strange and rather an odd idea, but was actually richly rewarding and gave a good feeling – no doubt from the

Having an imaginary friend is very common, Mr. Penrose...

Pearsall.

close contact, openness and, for a while a reduction in the 'ego' we all have. But it can be dangerous for people who have serious psychological vulnerabilities, so it is worth discussing with one's own doctor before doing it, if in doubt.

Jeremy: It's not for me, but maybe works for people who really know what they're doing. But not for anyone in their early days, or who are stumbling along just out of hospital.

Tony: I totally agree with that.

Jeremy: The most important thing for anyone is to be able to trust whoever they are talking to, and feel completely safe in doing so.

I remember, when I asked the first psychiatrist I ever had how on earth he was able to put up with listening to all of his patients' stuff all day, he said, 'At 5.35 every evening I walk onto a squash court and knock hell out of the ball for forty minutes. I play every evening and by the end of a good session on the court it's all gone and I'm okay again.' What a great way to deal with it.

Tony: But I think it is particularly difficult for psychiatrists. The problems they are dealing with are not superficial. The problems are not ones you can fix with a hammer and chisel. They require a sensitivity – a human relationship forming, and in a relatively deep manner.

Jeremy: Up until the age of about twenty-six, my understanding of psychiatrists was gained through watching them portrayed on TV and in films. A psychiatrist was somebody with a notepad who you'd tell your secret weird thoughts to, lying on a couch while they wrote it all down.

Tony: I think it's a big problem for people who have no experience, and why should they know? Going to see a psychiatrist might sound like the end of the world, when in fact it's just going to see a chap who knows more than most about the mind's problems and moods. Most of them are extremely kind, gentle, intelligent folk who can be very supportive.

Jeremy: Absolutely. But it is also interesting that a lot of people don't know the difference between a counsellor and a psychotherapist, a psychoanalyst and a psychiatrist. Even if you don't have much money, or you're shy or frightened, arrogant or rude or whatever, it's important to know who can help you.

Tony: It's not easy, even for doctors, to know that therapists are good, because it's not like saying, well, this doctor saved 99 per cent of appendices! But you should still be better off going to your doc for advice about who to see than looking in the back of the local rag, even if you do not need a medically qualified psychiatrist.

Jeremy: But it can be very difficult for some people to ask for help.

Tony: They often say that seeking help is at least half of the cure – half way towards being better and being well again. Walking through the doctor's, counsellor's or psychotherapist's door is half the battle.

keeping it up,
keep going

Tony: Carrying on through your notes, on the physical side of things, back in '95 your libido was very low, wasn't it?

Jeremy: Yes, the libido was trailing along the floor.

Tony: We were questioning whether that was psychological in origin, or whether there might have been a physical cause.

Jeremy: Yes.

Tony: So we offered you the choice of either having a digital rectal examination or a trans-rectal ultrasound scan.

Jeremy: Oh my God, don't remind me!

Tony: And because you thought it would be less personal I packed you off to the hospital and you ...

Jeremy: I didn't fancy your middle finger plan, perfectly formed though it might be! It was quite funny because I thought by going to this very snazzy hospital it would just be a scan where they would guide this electronic scanner over my nether regions and that would be it. What I didn't realize was that something resembling a small electronic elephant's tusk would be mounted up my arse.

Tony: I think *rectum* is the more appropriate word, Jeremy.

Jeremy: That was bad, yes! I'm just remembering actually, it must have been around this time, that I went into a funny sort of mood, worrying, *God, I've done my first three or four years of AA and I feel really glum, running on low voltage – I'm fed up.*

I went and saw DK at the Priory Hospital in Roehampton again and said I needed a 100,000 mile service and some Prozac. He asked me why I wanted the Prozac. I told him I'd discovered one or two of my more cheerful friends had been taking it for some time and thought to myself, *Well, no wonder they were so bloody cheerful!* DK said to me, 'Look, you cannot take anything like Prozac, because it might make you manic.'

Tony: His advice was spot on! What did he recommend you do?

Jeremy: He said, 'You've got to keep going.' He suggested reading two books that he knew were very helpful for people with a dual diagnosis of manic depression and alcoholism and all that stuff. I got the books[7] and thought, *Oh my God, I'm turning into a self-help twat.*

But actually they were very helpful. Like a lot of people, I thought I knew what all the jargon meant, right down to the tired old joke about denial being a river in Egypt. It made a difference being recommended to read these books by a professional whom I respected.

Tony: And your mood lifted?

Jeremy: Eventually it did. But it had been easy to get into a fug where I thought, *I've given up doing this, stopped doing that, my marriage hasn't succeeded and work is not taking off as I had hoped. Is this really as good as it gets?*

Tony: Did you think the marriage and the work had not succeeded in taking off because of your mood? What kind of interaction did you feel was going on?

---

7. Earnie Larsen & Carol Hegarty, *Believing in Myself*; Earnie Larsen, *Stage II Recovery: Life Beyond Addiction.*

Jeremy: There was nothing wrong with my wife, she was lovely. The work had been okay, a little up and down. Overall, I was blocked and still hadn't worked out a lot of stuff or whatever you want to call it.

Tony: And what happened to that baggage?

Jeremy: It's tempting to say I left it going round a carousel at Luton airport. But it was largely dealt with by going through the twelve-step recovery process, living on a Greek island for a few years and by writing *and* finishing my book. It all came out in the wash, even though that wash took a hell of a long time.

Tony: Perhaps you needed to change your profession.

Jeremy: Yes, I was extremely fortunate to be able to give up the music business and become a full-time writer.

Tony: But that's a very hard thing, being a writer, because you don't have any structure there, and by definition you have to be very introverted at the time to dream up things to make a living. That's potentially a huge stress emotionally, but by the same token very rewarding?

Jeremy: Count Dracula, you can't make an omelette without breaking eggs.

using the tiller and maintaining a steady course

Tony: You made a decision to live in a manner that is not easy emotionally but, aided by not drinking any more, you've made a real success of it for the last twelve years.

Jeremy: Thank you. People have said to me, 'You've got your property back, you are re-married, you are writing another book, a film script, everything's going so well, you've been sober for years, what do you need to take that lithium for?'

Tony: And what do you say in response?

Jeremy: Listen, I don't want to take pills, but after questioning various psychiatrists around the world as well as your good self, it seems it's far better to take it.

There are also a lot of people around me who in the past have had to pick up the pieces, so why should I put them at risk? Most importantly, I am now very happily remarried and all is well, and I have no intention of jeopardizing that or anything else because I couldn't be arsed to take a couple of pills a day. If someone said to you, 'Excuse me, you've got a heart murmur and if you don't take your tablets you'll have a heart attack,' I suspect you would take the tablets.

Tony: We're very lucky to have it. Fifty years ago there was no such thing and it's just like insulin for diabetics, where people actually died. No, you take it and you're grateful and you live a life.

Jeremy: It all comes down to balance and using your common sense and having somebody you can really trust to talk to.

Tony: The advantage we've had in our professional relationship is that we are chums and in many respects we've been able to share a lot of our life outside the medical aspects. I've known your situation very well, being close.

Jeremy: Yes, it's been great, and I think there's a lot of benefit in having a long friendship and doctor–patient relationship, in which you can refer back and see this and that.

Tony: We were talking about the time restrictions facing a GP. You were suggesting, very usefully, that anyone visiting a doctor should bring a written list of problems with them.

A lot of patients who come to see me come back and say, 'Oh, I forgot to ask you this.' Or when they've been to a specialist, they've come back frustrated because they forgot to ask them such and such. It's very important to tell your doctor what he or she needs to know and what your problem is. And providing he is a good doctor, he will go through it carefully.

Jeremy: Particularly with people who have got mental health problems. For men it's very important, because if you are feeling a bit depressed you might go to see the doc but what happens when you get inside is that the doc says, 'Oh hello, Fred, good to see you, how's everything?' And you say, 'Oh, fine, it's absolutely fine, there's no problem at all, actually I've just got this spot on my nose and yes, my little toe is playing up ...'

Tony: That often seems to be the pattern of conversation when patients come and see a doctor. They wait until the last thirty seconds of the consultation before they say, 'Oh, by the way, I'm getting divorced tomorrow and I can't cope ...' Which is the real reason they came in the first place!

Jeremy: I have a great Greek friend, who says, 'You British are all round the twist, you've got all these psychiatrists and therapists. We don't need psychiatrists in Greece, we *talk* to one another. If we've got a problem we go and talk about it, it might take all day or all week but we sort it out.'

Tony: There's this great British tradition that problems don't really exist and if they do, you can brush them away, and they'll never reoccur, and that *strong* people don't have problems.

Jeremy: The danger is that if you keep it inside you, internalize it, it's just going to get worse and worse. It's a psychological cliché to say that depression comes from suppressed anger but clichés are often remarkably true. The problem with anger is that it's often something stuffed down inside over a long period of time, that one day explodes everywhere, so to speak.

Tony: The toughest people have vulnerabilities; we can be Jean Claude Van Damme or Mr Schwarzenegger and be physically hugely strong but still have vulnerability. It's not an admission of human failings, it's simply being human.

The advantage of coming to terms with these things is that it can open up a whole new part of your life. Instead of saying, 'I'm all right Jack,' you can admit certain fallibilities, which makes you more empathetic to the rest of mankind.

Jeremy: Doing something about it is the hardest thing but also the most important. And we're not all the same. When my hunting-shooting brother gets fed up – and he is not renowned for talking about his inner soul – he will go off and climb a hill, go for a ten-mile walk, cycle around the park all day. I think he expels a lot of his stuff in that way. Maybe my brother's Golden Retriever is his secret therapist?

Tony: Exercise is wonderful. But while it may get rid of the results, it doesn't actually get to the root of the problem.

Jeremy: We've come a long way in these discussions, and we've come a long way together in the last twenty-three years.

riding the waves and using the coping tool kit

Tony: Okay, I agree but let's not forget that it is *possible* to improve one's mood through effort. It's better to do something than nothing. So what techniques have you found helpful?

Jeremy: Well, my rules are: Try to get at least six or seven hours' sleep per night and have a siesta if appropriate. Make sure you eat and have plenty of water. If you want to have positive self-esteem, do esteemable things. Take the dog, cat, hamster or hair dryer for a good daily walk. Make a list of four things that need your attention including two things you don't want to do, and do them to make yourself feel better. Do not take life or yourself too seriously. Listen to some music and make contact with a good friend. Actually the MDF runs a course where you can learn a lot of tricks on how to manage your illness.

Tony: We could probably all benefit from going on these sorts of courses at some stage in our lives. It's just that people with this particular illness and associated illnesses are not brilliant at looking after themselves.

Jeremy: It's very important to have a daily routine of fixed things to do, like getting up in the morning, and writing a list of the day's objectives.

Tony: I remember a man at an MDF meeting talking about how he wouldn't have any food in his flat, in order to get out of the house. His rule was to be out of bed when his alarm went off but to have no tea, no coffee, no newspaper, no bread in the house – so he would be obliged to get out, because he knew the despair of being in the flat on his own would make things worse. He felt that if he could only get out of the door to his local café to have his coffee and a sandwich then his mood would start lifting.

Jeremy: A slightly unusual approach but whatever floats your boat.

Tony: Everyone has their own way of doing things and I think the key is to learn one's own methods. The point is, if you have this routine, come high or low water you can still follow it.

Jeremy: It's much easier when you've got into that habit. Then you can always do it, every day. It's like having a mental handrail.

Tony: So basically you're saying the techniques you learn in the good times, you can take into the bad times with you?

Jeremy: Hopefully, there won't always be bad times. Yet, undiagnosed and untreated, manic depression is a very serious illness and should not be underestimated. Although we both joke about it, it is extremely serious; one in five manic depressives end up committing suicide.[8]

Tony: So what's changed in your approach to staying sane compared to around ten and twenty years ago?

Jeremy: Twenty years ago there was hardly any information on manic depression or related topics. Ten years ago I had loads of information but only used it in a fire-fighting capacity. Today, I try and use the information on the basis of prevention being better than cure.

---

8. In their book *Manic Depressive Illness*, Goodwin and Jamison concluded that an average of nineteen per cent of manic depressives take their own life.

Tony: Meaning that you take your medication regularly and don't drink.

Jeremy: Yes, but much more than that because when you stop drinking, a jack-in-the-box addict can keep popping up with other things to deal with.

Tony: You mean all the smoking, drugs, food, work, relationships, gambling, etc?

Jeremy: Yes, so I try to live in the real world these days without having too many distractions or any anaesthetics. I avoid putting myself in situations that are likely to be dangerous, however much I might want to do them. So, for example, if someone was to invite me to Las Vegas for the weekend, to gamble in casinos and so forth, I would decline. Twenty-five years ago, I would have gone and probably tried to co-pilot the plane and break the bank. Ten years ago, I would have still gone but hoped I could have got away with it. Now I hope I can make the right choice.

Tony: Some folks might say you were just being a lot more sensible!

Jeremy: Conversely, if I find I am suddenly buying fifty items a day from e-Bay because of the compulsive buzz of buying, I have to take that as a sign too. Well, it's all about understanding your limits and what makes your tick-tock tick, isn't it? Boring, I know, but it's better to be boring sometimes.

Tony: What about you and money?

Jeremy: I always loved the idea of having oodles of money and would only think in terms of being the Big Cheese of Big Cheese Global Industries, earning trillions and taking over all the mousetraps and cheese boards in the world. Alternatively, in the opposite mood, I was often a creepy version of Uriah Heep wondering if I was quite good enough to get a job sweeping up the cheese crumbs from the factory floor. Those times have long gone and hopefully I now steer a midway course. Although I can catch myself composing the odd Oscar acceptance speech for a script I have only written five lines of.

Tony: I am sure Ned was behind those mousetraps. Go on with the changes.

Jeremy: With apologies to T.S. Eliot: I have measured out my life with parking tickets. When I first came out of hospital in 1981, my orange VW beetle had so many parking tickets on it and *inside* it and up its exhaust, I couldn't find it for three weeks. Two months after giving up the hooch in 1993, a bailiff came to the door with a bill for £1400 in unpaid parking tickets. That took me two years to pay off. These days, if I get one parking ticket, I need to attend a meeting of Parkaholics Anonymous and have a lie-down.

Tony: Parking who?

Jeremy: Only joking. But I do take it seriously and if I was to suddenly get loads of them and toss them into the back seat, my wife, you and the man on the Clapham omnibus would be entitled to think there was something bad brewing up.

Tony: So what other coping tools do you have these days?

Jeremy: They probably all sound daft to anyone else. But not rushing and trying to be still, once or twice a day are paramount. Not frying two eggs while speaking to the travel agent on the phone, vacuuming the carpet and changing the murky water in the goldfish tank at the same time. Making sure that I have enough sleep and don't overdo the caffeine.

Remembering to try and appreciate what I already have in my life.

Writing is very important, as is doing things to take myself out of my own head. Helping other people, maybe helping the elderly neighbour in the garden. Listening to music and playing squash. Living within my means but ensuring I have a laugh and not taking myself too seriously are vital. Finally, going to regular meetings, whether they are AA or MDF.

Tony: Is that your equivalent of going to church, do you think?

Jeremy: Maybe it is. So many people are terrified of using the words God, church or religion these days but I don't mind. These meetings work for me and for loads of other people. But so can yoga, Buddhism, Jungian-based psychotherapy, being a Quaker or a Roman Catholic, or many other things. Having some sort of a spiritual life that is rooted in common sense is the key. No pun intended but all roads lead to Rome, so just find your road.

desert island risks …

Tony: I first began visiting the wonderful island of St John's Revelation in 1984. You came out and stayed with me in 1995 and also fell in love with it, and started visiting the island to write.

Jeremy: Yes, I started writing a couple of film scripts there and really liked the place. So much so that on St Patrick's Day 1998, I went to live there with the specific goal of writing *Taking Leave*.

Tony: It must be pretty tough living on a small Greek island, particularly when you've forsaken alcoholic beverages.

Jeremy: Correct.

Tony: I imagine being on your own and writing about stuff inspired by your own life in a small community was difficult. Or was it the best thing?

Jeremy: It was difficult, but when I look back now, I laugh because I thought it was going to be so terribly easy! *Oh marvellous, life on a Greek island, sunshine, gorgeous girls, swimming, writing – easy!*

But to go somewhere where, at first, it was raining all the time, freezing cold, no telephone, no girlfriend, not even a friendly goat, and to write an actual book, a novel? It was very lucky for me that I didn't go completely barking. The only reason why I didn't was that I had a good friend there and started a routine straight away.

I got on with the writing, and there's a school of thought that says all writing is therapy. And the combination of having a routine that included daily walking, which turned into squash, which turned into swimming, and having human contact, helped keep me on the straight and narrow.

Tony: It must have been very difficult to remain sober in the evenings when the whole island's custom was to drink vast quantities of ouzo. Was that difficult or not? What happened without your AA support group?

Jeremy: No, most of the time it wasn't too bad, only when what I call a 'Fuck It Moment' arrived.

In the bar they had a wood-burning stove, which each night I used to park my arse on. Then you'd have Stavros saying every night, 'Why you no aver drink, why don't you aver proper drink? Was wrong with you? Why you only drink Fanta?' That used to drive me mad. Small things are often the worst!

Writing the book was the biggest thing I've ever done and the actual process of being on an island like that in a tiny community, having never lived away from home before, was like a growing-up stage I didn't know I had to do. I learnt a lot from it.

Tony: Yes, that must have been a kind of self-assessment, self-healing, opening and re-exposing all those wounds, thinking about letting them air a bit. Did you find it to be too introspective or was it in another sense a kind of release?

Jeremy: I think that the difficulty was that the book was drawing on a large part of my manic depressive experience, particularly when I was gloomed or when I was off my rocker in New York.

Tony: I think it was also an acknowledgement of your value, in a funny way, when you were writing about some of your own experiences. You'd been through a very difficult phase, which perhaps you felt had been a failure, and when you turn that about it's an acknowledgement of its significance to you and perhaps to other people.

Jeremy: Yeah, but funnily enough therein lies the rub. What was tricky was that I wanted to utilize that experience but wanted to write a novel and not an autobiography.

I wrote it in the third person originally, but then had to rewrite it all in the first person three years later. I'm very proud of what I did but it was tough because I guess it was like having the therapy that I'd never had before.

The fact that the book was written, and no humans or animals were killed or injured in its making, should be taken as a testament to the determination and staying power of all other manic depressives and recovering alcoholics.

Everyone has a capability to do something like this. My only warning would be that wherever you go in the world, remember that you always end up taking yourself along as well.

Tony: Some people think that by travelling one can escape from oneself, from the inner *me*, and of course you can't.

Jeremy: No, unfortunately you cannot. But I was very lucky because during the time I wrote *Taking Leave* fantastic people came into my life who were very kind to me, and put up with my peculiar *creative* ways.

Anyway, moving on a few years, I moved to America where the final thing that happened that amazed you, and me, was that I managed to stop buying two packets of Marlboro Red each day and gave up smoking.

Tony: You said that was more difficult than alcohol?

Jeremy: It was, there's no doubt about it. I had smoked since the age of twelve and heavily since the age of fifteen. I smoked so much I should have had a neon sign on the side of my head saying I was sponsored by Marlboro. Those Marlboro Red cigarettes have got some interestingly bad chemicals in them and when I finally gave up, yes, I thought I was going out of my mind. It was like giving up drinking and going into the Bethlem for the first time, even with two new huge Nicorette patches glued to my backside every twelve hours. It was a *very* interesting experience. And why is that? He asks a doctor.

Tony: There can often be terrible depressive repercussions.

Jeremy: For people who stop smoking?

Tony: Sure. You had the physical addiction, which probably didn't last so long after stopping, but you then had to deal with all the psychological issues.

Of course, there were the years of habit, but what do you think they were in your case? Was it that you thought it was quite cool to smoke? Do you think it was the idea of the nipple substitute, that it was a security thing, putting something into one's mouth, between one's lips?

Jeremy: It's definitely to do with nerves – something that gives you something to do with your hands and probably something to put in your mouth. Also if you're angry, it's a sharp inhale, exhale, and then you stub it out. What I realized is that it's not just nicotine but the chemicals they put in cigarettes that fuck you up. I had no idea of how bad it would make me feel when I tried to stop. It was unbelievable.

Tony: And what happened?

Jeremy: My memory went completely. I lost three sets of keys, mobile phone, couldn't remember where my bloody car was … It was awful, and I came very, very close to drinking at that point. I was living with this nice Californian girl who was really keen that I should give up as she knew a lot about giving up stuff herself, so she was quite a good taskmaster.

Tony: She got out zee whip!

Jeremy: Yes! But why do I seem to attract so many women with whips?

Tony: Which you dealt with in the appropriate Catholic flagellation manner.

Jeremy: I did indeed, Father!

Tony: And did you put on weight?

Jeremy: A tyre around the mid-torso, yes.

Tony: Of course, women complain about this, perhaps more than men do.

Jeremy: I was more bothered about how it affected me mentally. Even though it all lifted after six weeks, it was pretty awful.

Tony: Do you think it was tied in some way with manic depression? Well certainly it's a mental illness, isn't it, addiction?

Jeremy: Where do you draw the line? Certainly, we know physically and medically it's a really dumb idea to smoke. But for some people smoking is the only pleasure they have. They might not drink, eat sugar, drink coffee, eat meat. What else are they going to do? Eat daffodils?

I'm not telling anyone to stop smoking, but what I know now is that many people use nicotine and cigarettes to control other feelings bubbling underneath. The nicotine and nasty chemicals that are in cigarettes are far more harmful than most of us realize. What a sanctimonious old git I sound!

Tony: Far be it for me to say … It must be the Benedictine coming out in you – again!

Jeremy: So, Dracula, why not tell the panel what's happened to *you* in the last three or four years?

Tony: Well, okay. Following on my return to acting in some fringe theatre, I felt I would like to make a short film. I went to do a film-making course and by chance the documentary we were studying was *The Man who Mistook His Wife for a Hat* by Oliver Sacks, the English neurologist, who lives in New York. It was made some years ago but I hadn't seen it and it turned out to be something quite Pentecostal.

THE MANIC DIALOGUES

I decided to try and make a documentary on a neurological/psychiatric subject myself. I set about the project by talking to several of my colleagues including the eminent neurologist Dr Frank Clifford Rose. He was the founder of the World Federation of Neurology and had put on some symposiums on art and neurology. He suggested one or two things. But it was only a few weeks later, when you, Jeremy Thomas came into the consulting room, that I suddenly realized – in a blinding flash – that the project should be about manic depression which is intimately entwined in your exotic persona.

Jeremy: I am going to have to take that as an enormous compliment.

Tony: No, seriously, it's because it's such a compelling medical problem. It's those hypomanic episodes which mirror so many extraordinary things in life, a mixture of comedy and tragedy, that fascinate me. This is really where my interest was born with its potential links with creativity and lateral thinking.

Jeremy: During the last three years your idea for the documentary has come together and is going out this year, and that's a major achievement. You have a wonderful French girlfriend and you still have Tuscany the cat. I got married and that's a fantastic achievement, mainly one of incredible daring and endurance on the part of my wife!

Tony: You can say that again!

Jeremy: Seriously, I'm very chirpy. My novel is about to be published, the second one's nearly ready *and* we're doing this book. And that's a really extraordinarily positive outcome since our first meeting twenty-three years ago. Wouldn't you say?

famous last words
(for now) ...

Jeremy: The challenge in being a manic depressive is not to over-inflate that into some great excuse but to keep everything in balance. Whenever I get all bent out of shape, I can recall another fantastic documentary called *Brian's Story*, about a Cambridge-educated lawyer who became an advertising copywriter, and who was alcoholic and manic depressive. The documentary followed him over a period of a year and it became more and more tragic, as his self-destructive nature and inability to deal with life unfolded.

Tony: He killed himself in the end, didn't he?

Jeremy: Sadly, yes. I know it sounds very depressing to talk about, but this illness, if left untreated, is a very serious thing. But you can manage it and you can get on with your life too. In the end, I bounced back. Things could have easily turned out very differently for me and I am aware of how lucky I have been in my life. There but for the grace of God, go I.

I know this woman who had once been a nurse and she was married to a very rich guy, a partner in a big accountancy firm. And she once said to me, 'I'm sick of having these dinner parties where all my husband's friends do is complain that they've only been skiing three times that year.'

She said that if she was Prime Minister, she would make everybody work in a hospital for one day a month, starting with her husband's skiing friends. She said that that would make the world a better place. I agreed.

Tony: 'You have to give to others in order to grow yourself'; a good adage.

Jeremy: We're all shy of saying this stuff and it's a shame we don't have a Swedish-type Prime Minister, who could implement the idea. So, Tony, we've sort of come to the end in a way – for the moment. And I don't know whether we can try and sum up our life tips: all our tips for manic depressives' depressive lives – everybody's lives. *Remember to keep your sense of humour* is the most vital thing, I would say.

Tony: And I was actually going to end the book in my version with one line on the back page: *Go and see a Jerry Sadowitz show!*

Jeremy: Yes!

Tony: He is a great stand-up comedian, with a savage wit that brings a big smile to your face. As you say, it is of course true – laughter is the very best medicine.

Jeremy: You can be a millionaire living in a mansion or you can be somebody living in slightly more humble circumstances, in the middle of a tower block, somewhere in England, or …

Tony: Or even in Wales.

Jeremy: Or even in beautiful Wales. Indeed. But both the problems and the principles are the same. It doesn't matter about the money; it matters about the attitude and whether you can put that into effect. I'm sure there are loads of people who want to scream at me that money makes the world go round, but I still say attitude and action are everything.

Tony: Well done, boyo!

Jeremy: Well done, boyo you! I think that's it, isn't it?

Tony: For the time being …

life
stories

convent girl turns streaker

I got through O levels in a mood of gloom and anxiety. I survived the rest of my convent school through fantasies of suicide, stealing altar wine, regularly cutting my wrists and generally self-harming. Once I threatened to jump out of the third-floor window but was reprimanded for being stupid. From sixteen I spent every opportunity drinking to make myself feel better – this first medication really helped and since diagnosis was another seventeen years away I became reliant on its effect.

I went to agricultural college which was a two-year riot, and I was able to do exactly what I wanted. I excelled academically and socially but it all took its toll. During the first year, looking back, I became non-functioning with only drink to help. I went to a college GP who put me on Ativan, not telling me this was a psychiatric drug that could knock out horses! I popped these and fell asleep in lectures and was more depressed. Again I just survived on boozing and being very ignorant that I had a diagnosable illness.

I went around the world when I was twenty-one. It was a year of boozing, wildness, near scrapes, almost being run over, streaking at night – once I was driving naked with a friend in Darwin, Australia, and we stopped and ran around, but he jumped in the car and left me for a laugh, running around the town stark naked.

A year later I came back to England and got a job as an Assistant House Mistress at a girls' boarding school. During my first night, I was raped at knifepoint. The man had broken into the boarding house whilst I was watching TV in my room, slammed through the door and pinned me down.

From that violent rape at twenty-two I battled with undiagnosed post-traumatic stress disorder and bipolar. Overnight I went into alcohol and prescription drug abuse. I felt that I had something to hang my mood on and was given Temazepam to sleep and the odd bit of Diazepam.

Somehow the thought of suicide was my 'Get out of Jail Free' card, and ironically, this fantasy kept me going!

Life was not all down, just a huge struggle. I would always be the one to be dared – a red rag to a bull. I used to love being dared but now I hate it as I know I will end up doing it.

I even excelled at jobs, always being asked to stay longer or accept a long-term contract.

In my early twenties I did settle in a job for three years and for a joke I entered Secretary of the Year and found myself sitting next to my boss at a presentation dinner at the Ritz.

Without a doubt the bipolar has given me a boost to being success-ful. I can cope with my lows and am able to function without too many clients noticing. Occasionally, I am suffering such anxiety and depression that I rearrange meetings. However, with bipolar I have always been a brilliant employee as I am able to work two or three times faster than an average person. When I have a low episode I end up working at a steady pace which is more in line with a 'normal' person.

A cycle of up and down, alcohol abuse and getting into trouble led to a mini impulsive decision to walk out of my life at the age of thirty. I impul-sively spent the proceeds of the sale of my studio flat by buying antiques abroad to ship back to the UK – one of my disastrous business ventures. I disappeared for a year in the Pacific and worked in New Zealand. By this time I was two years away from admitting myself into the Priory.

I was unable to pace myself and during depressed episodes my body would almost shut down and I would be in bed for a few days which I called 'charging my batteries'. Then I would become very excitable and flash my tits even at the arrivals section of Auckland airport!

A year later, I came back to England extremely depressed and was only capable of doing temping jobs and lodging with a friend. I then worked for a lady who is now my business guru and between us we came up with the idea of Personal Time Saver (www.personaltimesaver.co.uk).

I started the business during mixed episodes of depression and hypo-manic states, still undiagnosed. Needless to say, my life fell apart at thirty-two and I admitted myself into the Priory.

Bipolar Type II was not diagnosed for another year as I was treated first for post-traumatic stress disorder and alcoholism. Since bipolar can be difficult to fully diagnose I struggled along and it wasn't until I streaked across the Priory lawn at night that it was diagnosed!

Since being diagnosed and stopping drinking, the treated bipolar has stabilized quite well. My particular condition when the bipolar is manageable and running quite well comprises three to four stable weeks, then two weeks of hypomania, then four to five days of depression, and then back to three to four stable weeks.

I have established a business which I have devised to fit in with the behavioural and mental health aspects which are so unsuitable for a nine to five job.

The frequent hypomania is a fantastic asset to any business as I can work into the night and work extremely fast, achieving what a normal person may achieve in two or more days. Being my own boss allows me to work as much as I like and also to take time off whenever I like.

If I need a rest I will take a siesta or power nap. I have tailor-made my business to my bipolar.

Starting from a mere laptop and pushbike, I have managed to establish a successful business which led to a BBC TV documentary about my business. I was also awarded the Start Ups Women in Business Award which was an outstanding achievement and an honour.

Would I want it any other way? When the depression hits, of course I wish I didn't have it. But when I am excelling and receiving enormous positive feedback from clients and doing wild and fun activities, I really wouldn't swap my life with anyone else's. My motto is, 'Just do it, in an impulsive bipolar way!'

As for the future? I fear that my bipolar might develop into Bipolar I and that my hypomania might get out of hand, causing me to become noticeably insane and, ultimately, sectioned.

On the positive side, I see my condition as a gift which helps me to get so much out of life and be a go-getter. Perhaps the pros cancel out the cons. I can't imagine being normal and I think I would only want to be normal for a week – otherwise life would be very dull.

I hope that one day I will find a kind, supportive, fun chap who I can share my life with – as for having children, that is another matter. 'Thy will not mine' is all I can say and trust.

coming to terms with manic depression

They say: 'Life begins at forty,' and I always felt that this would be true for me. It wasn't that I hadn't enjoyed life, but having married just short of my seventeenth birthday with two sons arriving by the time I was nineteen, life had not been easy. I felt that 'middle age' would be my time of life.

Now, when people say: 'Life begins …,' I tell them not to believe it because all that happened to me was that I went mad! Well, I did. Shortly after my fortieth birthday I had my first psychotic episode, nervous break-down, manic episode or whatever terminology we choose to describe the indescribable. I'm not going into detail here because I have a success story to tell, not a book to write, and time and space are limited. Suffice it to say that, whilst on holiday in Majorca, I lost my mind. I became deluded, obsessive and convinced that my husband, Jim, was Jesus. I didn't tell him this at the time because I thought I had a mission: to return him safely to England, where he could be joyfully received as the Messiah!

I knew something was wrong and we called the doctor the day before we were due to fly home. He prescribed some form of medication, I don't know what it was, advised me to stay out of the sun and drink plenty of water. We followed the advice and put my 'odd' behaviour down to sunstroke. Jim, of course, didn't know just how oddly I was behaving inside my head.

Well, we arrived home but things rapidly escalated with my behaviour becoming more and more bizarre and uncontrolled. I ended up on a psychiatric ward, sectioned under the Mental Health Act, and diagnosed as suffering from manic depression or bipolar affective disorder, its modern title. I spent a month in the hospital, being allowed home in the third and fourth weeks for a day and then weekend leave.

I was devastated. My family were devastated. I cannot express here the absolute horror of that first major episode and the subsequent labelling for life. Manic depressive – me, Helen, a manic depressive. The horror and bewilderment expressed in the faces of those who loved me so dearly; and all the time knowing that we had seen it all before. That we had lived through the horror of it all before.

Why had we lived through it before? My father, still alive at the time of my first episode, had been institutionalized for the best part of fifty years. He too was a manic depressive. Here I was, stupefied by the same medication (Largactil) prescribed for my father. What did the future hold for me? Would the nightmare and stigma of mental illness haunt my family for another generation and perhaps beyond?

Four years on, I cannot say that it has been easy. Almost inevitably, severe depression followed the manic episode. Months of not feeling anything like myself; of not being able to do the things I had always done. Obviously I couldn't go to work but I was determined, perhaps too determined, to get back to work. At the time, returning to work was my overriding goal, symbolic of my return to normality. I returned to work after three months but it was another three before I was anything like my 'old self'.

In those four years I have learnt an awful lot about the illness. Through this research I hope I am beginning to learn more about myself and how to control and modify my moods and their effects on others. I have learnt that I am not, nor do I wish to be, alone; that there is an awful lot that can be done; that things have changed since the days when my father became ill. Tragically it is too late for him but it is not too late for me.

I have joined the Manic Depression Fellowship (MDF) and attend a self-help group where we share our experiences, fears, hopes and objectives for the future. There is still, very much so, a stigma attached to mental illness, but there is a lot of positive progress being made. Care in the Community has received a lot of criticism, sometimes rightly so, but it is the way forward for the majority of people suffering from mental illness.

The MDF promotes a programme of self-management for those suffering from the illness. The basis of this programme is the same as many recommend for the promotion of a healthy lifestyle: diet, exercise, relaxation, reduction of stress and enjoyment of life. This approach, together with appropriate use of medication, is working for many, many people with manic depression.

I myself am enjoying life. I have a happy home life surrounded by the love of Jim, my family and friends (I'm going to be a grandma for the first time in July!). I'm fortunate in that I love swimming and can regularly be seen cycling around the neighbourhood and beyond.

I did have a further psychotic episode at Christmas two years ago, perhaps in part due to my dogged determination to beat the illness and fight it myself. Fortunately, I now have an excellent support team: Jim, my family, friends and an understanding GP. It is not always easy to listen to advice or to swallow the medication but I am cautiously optimistic for the future. Perhaps life begins at forty-four!

ian, still cycling after all these years

I loved my childhood because my mother would let me go anywhere I liked. My father, on the other hand, was a control freak. On one occasion he threatened me with the dreaded 'boarding school' as he pinned me against the living room door! He had a habit of leaving my mother in order to shag anything wearing perfume. Many years later, after my mum's funeral, I eventually learned from her sister that my dad was seeing a redhead whilst my Mum worked in Troon post office, and he made wooden toys for sale in the local toy shop. That was a milestone. After passing my eleven plus and going to the local all-boys grammar school, my father walked out, to sleep above his newly created shop with his teenage sweetheart, a woman he was later to marry.

I suspect my mum was manic depressive but in those days no GP had read Kay Jamison. My mum would complain of her 'nerves', but despite this, I loved her to bits and would do anything for her.

Each vacation I would return home from university and do stuff for her and we would enjoy each other's company; she seemed happy but hated him. He tried, unsuccessfully, to get my mother out of her house and even to take her furniture!

Anyway, she had tenacity and stuck to her abode which she never left, eventually dying of a massive heart attack at eighty-something, in front of the telly.

Where am I now?

Well, after having had four 'successful' children – three boys, one girl – and a career I am now at a point in my life where I face the final curtain, as Frank would say.

I am angry at times.

A left-winger most of my life, I cannot help believing that we have finally succumbed to mediocrity. My daughter carries this forward in her lectures to sociology students in her classes. I am curiously proud that she holds a torch for the poverty and ignorance in our age.

My boys play the drums, are totally literate with computers, etc. and my eldest son is a BT engineer – he knows about wires! My thirty-odd-year relationship with my spouse is always in a state of flux, especially when she realizes that I am getting 'high'. This happens every year and for the last two years has ended in a period in hospital.

I quite like hospitalization as everybody (almost) treats you with the utmost respect and it's not a bad place to be. Apart from the last time in which I escaped the psychiatrist and disappeared from the hospital, later to be arrested by the police and escorted back to a locked ward where I had the pleasure of meeting a self-confessed axe murderer and a gentleman who would make me a welcome cup of tea. The next morning I was, of course, transferred to my old ward with a few 'how ya doings?'

In hospital I could mix with my own kind, have a good laugh and get lots of visits and free meals! I also enjoyed relating to other patients: what an amazing mix! I often wondered, during these times, if I was somehow acting as a multifarious member of the human race, sharing and getting wisdom and insight not only into my own condition but others, all of which are distinctly classified as abnormal or dissident or some other label.

As for fellow MD sufferers, well, you have to find your own path through this condition, it's not easy. People may eulogize, sympathize or just medicate (i.e. doctors) BUT they will not understand. During my hospitalizations I met only one psychiatrist. He was Spanish, and told me once in a hospital corridor, 'Do you know, Ian, if you carry on like this [i.e. stop taking your lithium!] you will die!'

I know, now, what he meant by this.

Am I an aerobic exerciser? Yes, I love and loved my bikes. Bring back the bike! Whilst lecturing at the local FE college I often cycled the twenty-five-mile round trip and faced the homeward journey with the wind in my face! I often did marathons and was proud to once be 813th out of 1235 in the Edinburgh marathon, a time of four hours something, what a buzz!!! Great! Endorphins are good things, I know this as, in a previous lifetime, I was a biochemist.

Well, I lost my job as a lecturer and then had to work hard at trying to recoup my life but things turned bad. I fell out with my partner who later sued me. I always fall out with people, especially when I get hyper. My lovely wife is very intelligent and has many interesting friends. I was so glad to be given this opportunity to relay my life. My wife twice put me in hospital during a manic build-up because I was getting so high and was and am intolerable to live with. I spent six weeks the first time and three days the second time, after being arrested by the police when I did a runner from the hospital.

So I've had my ups and downs and now take my lithium as a ritual. However, last autumn I succumbed to the video nasties playing inside my head. I didn't know that even with the lithium I could go so low. In desperation, I went to my GP. He telephoned my psychiatrist immediately and I was put on Citalopram, which is an SSRI, and Sulpiride. Since taking 10mg a day I am a new being! Or to tell you the absolute truth I survive on the minimum dose! My psychiatrist often comments on my under-standing in this respect, and once said, 'Ian, Sulpiride has an extraordinary effect on you; you take a lower effective dose than most patients.'

Thank god for chemistry!

I drink vast volumes of tea and hate alcohol but usually succumb to its charms. I am a self-medicator, often sleepless. I love life but also like being high. I have avoided the downs as a result of the cognitive therapy that I eventually received courtesy of the NHS. I take as much aerobic exercise as I can and love dogs!!!!

married to a manic depressive

I didn't know it at the time, but Rod was in the early upward spiral of a manic episode when I first met him in the summer of 1996. He was talkative, generous, had a self-deprecating sense of humour, enjoyed the local pubs and was very good company. But it didn't seem quite right. He played music, always very loud; he liked taking baths at unusual times of the day and night; he was very much into the 'significance' of numbers; he drove fast and spent hours offloading various confessions (some trivial, others not so) into the early hours of the morning when all I craved was sleep.

There wasn't much we didn't talk about – his twenty-three years in the navy, including two and a half years serving on board HMY *Britannia*, retiring early with the rank of Commander, and his subsequent travels to Antarctica and the Middle East. There was nothing obvious to rouse my suspicions, and even though he mentioned his mother's attempts to continue controlling his life – they were obviously very close even though she apparently still had the ability to irritate him over small things – I just thought that's what some mothers do. I was fascinated by this person who had achieved so much but who had no whiff of pomposity or self-importance.

Not long after, Rod had to leave for a week in the United States.

The day before he was due to fly out, Rod casually told me he was a manic depressive. That day I also learned from Rod that the severe injuries to his legs, with chunks of missing muscle reminiscent of a shark attack, were actually the result of a close encounter with a lorry several years earlier. I didn't like to ask too many questions in case it was still a very sensitive subject and seemed ghoulish. It never occurred to me that the accident might have been deliberately engineered; only months later did

I realize it had been an attempt to put an end to the excruciating mental torture that had developed during one of the most severe episodes.

Rod then told me that he had written a book which he would like me to read while he was away. The book, called *Walking with Angels*, introduced his ambitious mother, whose own potential had never been fulfilled and who then sought to succeed through her son. It was also a roller-coaster account of his time in the navy, burning the candle at both ends yet still being able to perform highly specialized roles in naval intelligence. Then came the exact moment when he first realized he was suffering from depression, triggered whilst working for an uncompromising Dutch admiral down a nuclear bunker nicknamed 'the hole' at NATO HQ at Northwood, Middlesex. Several more bouts of severe depression followed before Rod then became psychotically manic. The bizarre recollections of these episodes, especially those in France, swung me to and fro, from deep sadness to hilarity and back again. The book was impossible to linger over slowly. Written with such speed and momentum, it demanded to be read at a break-neck pace. This was the way Rod did almost everything, fast and furious, and I had to read it numerous times for everything to make sense and fall into sequence. On his return, Rod came to stay for a few days. Rod's mood was definitely elated, and even though I had read his book, I wasn't fully aware what this might be leading to. He was still taking his daily lithium, prescribed to stabilize his mood, but by now Rod's drinking had leaped to epic proportions; all part, he said, of his programme of self-medication. His in-depth knowledge of the illness, obtained by talking to numerous consultants, reading and analysing Kay Redfield Jamison's books and listening to others, was enough to convince me he knew what he was talking about, but I didn't like what was happening. I now know that Rod was becoming psychotic and occasionally paranoid, suggesting friends, strangers and even I might be evil. It all seemed very much at odds coming from someone whose mood had just been lively and exuberant a few weeks before. With little sleep for the both of us for nights on end while Rod talked, played music and became increasingly 'revved up', I was beginning to feel stretched to the edge of my limits; I felt powerless to intervene and could not suggest an alternative, yet strangely, I never felt threatened or at risk at any time.

It had got to the point where I asked him to leave home, but then there was a call from his mother, informing me that Rod had been sectioned in Glenbourne, Plymouth's psychiatric unit, and was asking to see me. I did as I thought any good friend would do and called in to see what had happened and what I could do, if anything, to help. There followed almost a month of severe depression. Rod's animated 'life and soul' mood with the occasional flashes of psychosis had flattened out to become one of total tiredness and dejection. Various types of medication had been tried in the past and this time with a cocktail of different tablets, each one causing various unwanted side effects, Rod managed to come through, spurred on by the burning desire to fulfil another promise and help a friend get aid to Tibetan refugees in the Nepalese camps. Kathmandu must be one of the most inaccessible destinations for a man with very limited mobility, yet Rod, true to form, managed to struggle along and came back exhausted but successful a fortnight later. I realized that Rod could not ignore injustice and inequality in any shape or form.

We married on my birthday in 1999 with close family and friends present. Initially, Rod's episodes were every one or two years, seemingly triggered more often in spring but occasionally in autumn as the days lengthened or shortened, and as the clocks went forwards or back, disrupting his sleep patterns and making him much more vulnerable to emotional highs or lows. At their peak, they could be terrifying and he would fly into rages, drive off with tyres squealing, dissolve into heart-shattering sobs. Occasionally he would self-harm and continue to suspect friends as well as total strangers of being 'black angels'.

These particularly harrowing times were, I believe, made worse by the alcohol which was still part of his self-medication. He would seriously believe he was either the Archangel Gabriel, or a god from Norse, Roman or Greek mythology. He was particularly attracted to Mars and Thor, though even he didn't know why. Brewers *Dictionary of Phrase and Fable* never left his side as he looked for reasons, connections, coincidences and number patterns that would send him into even more bizarre thought processes.

Rod would look forward to hospital: many of his friends would be there and instead of me nagging him into behaving at home, he had full rein to act out and play up to all his weird ideas. I had realized very early, especially after visiting Rod in hospital and seeing other patients who regularly came and went and were readmitted again soon after, that manic depression is never cured, it can only be treated with various degrees of success that depend on the sufferer accepting that there is a problem. Few will seek help in the rising stages of mania when they are all-powerful, all-knowing and hugely entertaining so, unfortunately, professionals will usually only see patients when they present on the deep downward slide into depression, making a true diagnosis that much more difficult. Once carers can be brought in to help recall previous patterns of behaviour, manic depression that may have gone untreated for years can be correctly identified and help offered. Before that point, it may be confused with substance abuse or diagnosed as just straightforward depression.

When Rod is well, which is now ninety-five per cent of the time, he will spend an inordinate amount of time trying to improve inpatients' conditions, having been co-opted on to the Friends' Committee of the local hospital and working as an inpatient visitor to the acute and intensive wards of the psychiatric unit. His own experiences and role as an impartial go-between have helped identify a whole range of different needs. One of his greatest interests is being included on interview panels for mental health service staff, imagining their surprise when someone they last saw as an inpatient is now well enough to be helping to decide their future.

In the last few years, while Rod's episodes may have become a little more frequent, on the positive side, they are less severe. Although Rod still feels he is entitled to them, he has started to take control and tries to stop them before the mood swings take him into full-scale mania. He will talk about 'parallel worlds' and what I believe to be utter rubbish because I can't understand it.

So in the last few months I feel at last that things may be changing for the better. After years of dreading Rod's pattern of mania and depression, I may eventually be able to relax. It will be a huge relief to know that Rod has not only accepted the condition but has gone that much further. When things were at their worst, I would become a thoroughly unpleasant person, partly because I desperately needed sleep when it was the last thing on Rod's mind. It surely wasn't Rod that I detested but the illness that overtook him; the poor chap just happened to be in the firing line for my increasing irritability. Perhaps it was subconscious: by being sympathetic at the height of mania would I have been condoning his drinking which often caused total memory black-outs and a tendency to over-adjust his medication, in turn causing hallucinations. Could it have been a barrier to protect me from some of the unintentional hurt and worry I knew I'd be facing in the following few weeks? Did I know I would need to save all my resources of sympathy and understanding when the depression took hold, as it inevitably did? I cannot really explain, but after Rod's most recent episode which he himself recognized very early on, I hope that this unkind side of me will never re-emerge.

We have both been particularly fortunate in that our local GP surgery and with it the team of community psychiatric nurses and consultants have always been tremendously supportive of Rod through all his stages of illness and well-being. Decisions on Rod's care have been made by all those concerned, including myself, and everyone is kept fully in the picture so that when there is a problem looming, we're all prepared.

I am immensely proud of Rod and his achievements, for the way he has overcome such severe physical and mental pain and damage after his accident, for his understanding of his condition and for his overwhelming desire to help others similarly afflicted. He has rebuilt his relationship with his son and daughter and has mounted a crusade to help de-stigmatize a condition that many people, both famous and unknown, seem to have to some degree or another, but are scared to admit to. He has given so much time to help carers and consultants, medical students and the media to realize that sufferers are real, functioning people who can be assisted in coming to terms with their illness, given a little more time and knowledge of manic depression. As Rod would say himself, there is no stigma attached to having a chemical imbalance in the digestive system, leading to diabetes. Why should a chemical imbalance in the mind, resulting in manic depression, be any different?

not quite the
great train robber

I went to boarding school at the age of ten because my father was a Major in the Royal Artillery and kept getting new postings. As my education would have inevitably suffered, it was decided to pack me off and give me stability. After learning to cope with homesickness, I settled into a new life and began to enjoy lessons and sport. Doing quite well on both fronts, I was approached at sixteen by a large public school and assessed for a full-fees scholarship. This I was awarded and moved from my Dorset private school, in 1990, to a grand establishment in Worcestershire.

I was a good lad, polite and enthusiastic. I had a few bad habits, enjoying the occasional cigarette and beverage. I was pursuing an army career but upon completing my A-levels I became naively seduced by the chimera of Bohemia and I went up to Newcastle University, intrigued by what an unfettered undergraduate life would entail. I had a traditional upbringing, deferential to custom and parental authority but university opened my eyes to challenging ideas and practices. In hindsight, I failed to adjust to the responsibilities of self-sufficiency and coped poorly with the new-found freedom. My path through those undergraduate years was strewn with mistakes and reckless behaviour. By the middle of the third year, I had developed a penchant for excessive partying and avoidance of academic work. I even gave up football to concentrate on wild dance-parties. This is the story of how I ended up in a psychiatric hospital, having gone missing six weeks before finals ...

By the start of my second year, I began to seriously lose concentra-tion. I attempted a project for an American Government module, testing the thesis that 'The CIA is the greatest threat to US democracy'. I had neglected to attend any seminars and lost insight into formal academic expectation. My tutor sneered at the shoddy waffle I presented and consigned the thirty per cent effort to a filing cabinet.

Not only disenchanted with studying, I also proved unable to manage my grants and loans. By March 1994 I desperately needed money, so I responded to a newspaper advert to become an outdoor activity instructor. I was trained on the Isle of Wight and, having returned to Tyneside to resolve personal matters, moved to North Wales. I left the university six weeks before the end of term without having passed any second-year coursework, depressingly in debt. Instructing quad-bikes, command-tasks and ball-sports, I spent four months in the sun and grew fit and happy. I was away from the academic grind as I perceived it and was thrilled to be putting smiles onto faces.

Summers end, as did that one. Little did I know that by the October of the following year I would have been admitted into *psychiatric hospital three times*, diagnosed with manic-depressive psychosis, been through some of the horrors of side-effects and reduced to a functionless zombie-like state, tormented by skewed 'Why did I do that?' memories of passing months that saw me change from a relatively carefree student on lager, with some academic expectations, to a fully-fledged mental patient on lithium.

May 1995 saw me taken into custody by the police in Doncaster, having been reported as a missing person. I was returned to the care of my family and shortly admitted into hospital. The police were involved that day because I had given British Rail personnel cause to throw me off a number of trains that I'd jumped in order to get back to Newcastle. I'd spent two days wandering disconsolately around the capital, swinging from vast heights to unplumbed depths. I had vacated my lodgings up north, friends and tutors having witnessed dramatic changes in my moods and behaviours, on a mission to prove myself as a miracle-worker to entirely fictitious powers resident in London. I did not realize at the time that I was unwell, that sleeping rough on the streets of London is not normal and that roaming up and down the Embankment, considering suicide, is a sign of mental illness.

A most startling manifestation of my unbalanced mind came two hours before the police found me. So intent was I on returning to Tyneside, I reacted huffily upon being discharged from an Intercity train in Peterborough. Dressed in outlandish garb and with no money with which to pay my fare, the conductor had no choice. Blind fool – he couldn't see my destiny. Determined to ascend from whence I'd come, I noticed an empty, two-carriage Sprinter standing idle on a far-flung platform, facing roughly in the right direction and shimmering slightly. Crossing the foot-bridge and entering the empty driver's compartment was easy. Inside, upon the dashboard, perched an instruction manual. I quickly flicked through its pages and began to pull all the levers and press the buttons. I thought that if I could get it started, I would be able to personally steer it to my chosen destination. Unfortunately, the ten minutes I spent as a wannabe engine driver proved fruitless. Although I tried with all my might to steal that train, it proved beyond my untutored skill to achieve such a technical feat and, having located the horn and pressed it a few times, I realized my inspired scheme wasn't going to happen. What is staggering to consider is that during all that time, absolutely no one noticed and my dangerous intentions went unchecked. Imagine the news that night if I had succeeded in starting the train and got it moving! Anyway, frustrated, I retreated from the cab and sat down in the passenger carriage. Within half an hour passengers took their seats and I eventually endured a short return journey up the line, to Spalding. Upon arriving back at Peterborough and being unceremoniously dumped, I jumped the train that took me to Doncaster and into the arms of the law. I was admitted into hospital the next day because my family could not account for my continuing bizarre behaviour and they understandably supported the GP's referral.

In the weeks following admission I performed a number of further acts which form much of the detail of my experiences of being manically psychotic: I disappeared off the ward only to be captured by police forty miles away; I inappropriately propositioned inappropriate females; I set off fire-alarms in the middle of the night, forcing geriatric patients to attend headcounts outside. I threw an empty wine glass the length of a long corridor, at the wall, evaded questions whilst being interviewed by senior medical staff, and often took all my clothes off and ate daisies.

There are many similar anecdotes lying around the insides of my head. Once, I disappeared from the ward, only to be found 400 metres away at a mini-roundabout on a nearby main road. I was lying in the middle of it, on my side, with my head resting in my left hand. I knew that the juggernauts couldn't kill me. Massive artic lorries veered around me as I lay there, invincibly. A nurse arrived and beckoned me to join her and walk 'home'.

I sat my university finals in a psychiatric acute unit. Failing, in such a total sense, was a painful experience in itself for someone who'd always been middle of the road, sporty and successful. Mania was followed by numbing depressions, as I struggled to come to terms with my actions, the on-going symptoms of illness, my failed student career and my new identity as a manic depressive. It didn't feel like I could get better and I spent many months as an agonized and lost soul. Learning to understand and control the condition requires medical care and tutelage; thankfully, these services are available and are improving all the time. Learning to function in the real world, without being held hostage to symptoms or the side effects of medication, is taking a long time. Sometimes I take backward steps but, in more recent years, maturity and experience have enabled me to work effectively towards mood stability and I've accepted the need for medication, within the context of meaningful self-management. Living the life of a full-on manic depressive has been a trial but a few years ago I managed to graduate in politics and philosophy. How I will cope in years to come remains to be seen, but for the first time since being diagnosed, I am correct in believing that I'm finally on the right track.

once a caterer,
not always a caterer

Coming from a secure family background, I suppose you'd call it middle class, there was nothing in my childhood to indicate I would become mentally ill. I had two loving parents and two brothers and one sister.

Life was turned upside down when my father died tragically young whilst I was sixteen and preparing for my O levels. My youngest brother, at the age of thirteen, took this very badly, which resulted in him refusing point blank to go to school. After being badly let down by the system, he eventually took his own life at the tender age of twenty-one. This was to leave a deep scar on all of us and it was two years later that I had my first bout of psychosis.

I lived in North Wales where it is very difficult to find work for anyone, but particularly as a non-Welsh speaker. As a result I always had to travel some distance to find work. I chose catering as I had worked as a waiter during summer holidays and because it allowed me to travel.

After commencing a course in hotel management I was offered a job as a waiter in Switzerland in a four-star hotel; I realized I was learning more there, and decided to stay on after the summer season finished. Typical of me, always doing things the hard way! After two years in Switzerland I came home to start as an assistant manager in a small country town hotel. At first, I enjoyed the job and put everything into it. However, as time passed, I became increasingly stressed to the point of not being able to sleep. My thoughts became rapid and I started to link things that had no connection. I became highly emotional and very nervy; and began to lose my temper which is most unusual for me. Gradually I began to believe there was a conspiracy against me involving the media and that the radio and TV were having a laugh at my expense. Even though I was physically exhausted, my mind was racing so much that I was only able to get a couple of hours sleep per night. I also became very unpopular, something I was not used to being, as I am a gentle and caring soul, but looking back I can understand how others must have perceived me. Eventually, I believed that the SAS were following me and that I was being bugged by someone.

Depressed, broke and jobless, friends I had made in Switzerland offered me a job as head waiter in a 140-seat restaurant 6700 feet up in the Swiss Alps, and I thank them for helping me to put the pieces back together. During my stay there I got my head sorted and applied for a job as a French speaker with a British management company as an industrial catering manager based in Algeria. One week I was at the top of a Swiss mountain and the next in Algeria. The work was hard and the hours long but looking back I enjoyed my time there and learnt a lot.

Having bought a house at home in North Wales, as the contract finished I secured a job as an accommodation manager on a 550-bed oil support barge based in Shetland. Operating amongst people who worked long stints on oil rigs was unlike anything I had experienced before. Eight weeks later, it started happening again. I could not sleep and was highly emotional. The media were having a laugh at my expense, my temper re-emerged and once again, I linked things that were not connected in my mind. I had a sense of *déjà vu* and one day lost my temper with my boss and hey presto was sacked and returned to North Wales.

I was unable to continue the mortgage payments and had to sell the house I had worked so hard for. This time at least I had made a profit so for once I wasn't broke. I avoided hospital but it was nonetheless a painful and humiliating experience. Once again it was a friend who offered me a job and I set off for South Wales.

With the profit from the house I set up as a portrait and wedding photographer, continuing an interest I had had since childhood. After three years I secured a job in Dubai as a photographer. Dubai was hot, 40° every day, and I was happy to have landed a job which I enjoyed and was good at. I now understand that good things happening to a bipolar can be as dangerous as bad things. Within a month and displaying all the normal signs, I went psychotic again. But this time I came to believe that I was the next Messiah. I was terrified and eventually had a row with my employers which resulted in my being sacked once again and handed an air ticket home. I would like to take this opportunity to apologize for my behaviour. Quite simply, I was mad.

Returning home completely out of control, it was not long before I was sectioned and this time diagnosed with manic depressive psychosis/bipolar 1. After a month in hospital, I returned home. The diagnosis was a double-edged sword. On the one hand it explained in part what had happened to me but on the other it would be written in indelible ink on my medical history. Were I to apply for a job which required a medical questionnaire I would have to disclose it. Once again I was home in North Wales, alone, broke, devastated and this time with a life of benefits ahead of me. I was thirty-four.

One helpful thing, apart from an accurate diagnosis and medication that my psychiatrist gave me, was a pamphlet published by the MDF. My involvement with MDF was to play an important part in my recovery as I was to meet many men and women with the diagnosis and to learn of coping strategies.

I joined the management committee of MDF Wales in Newport in 1998 and became a trustee of the Fellowship in 1999. This I found challenging, worthwhile, interesting, and ultimately being a part of the organization replaced the void that was created by being out of work.

During the three years I served as a trustee of the Fellowship, the MDF received lottery funding for their self-management training programme. This is a two-day intensive experience whereby two trained facilitators, both with the diagnosis, lead twelve people with bipolar through every aspect of the condition. This I would describe as the most helpful two days I had spent since diagnosis.

Bipolar for me is two conditions – depression and mania – and I treat both differently. Mania for me generally is seasonal and can start in springtime. Over the years I have agreed with my psychiatrist that I can tweak the antipsychotics within minimum and maximum levels. My insight tells me when I am going a bit high. This can happen very quickly if there are sufficient triggers, usually for me good luck, a new girlfriend or something positive in my life, which raises my mood, risking hypomania. It is at this point I increase my medication to pre-arranged levels and generally get more sleep for a couple of days.

As there are frequently outside unpredictable factors that are triggers for mania, I do not find that a constant fixed dose of medication is the way for me. I would add that I have good insight into my condition and this is tried and tested, and anyone thinking of changing medication should first agree it in advance with their psychiatrist.

Lows, on the other hand, I have to deal with without antidepressants as previously these have tended to send me high very quickly. Depression generally starts around October/November time as the nights draw in. I have learnt that, whilst in a depressive state, I hang onto the notion that it will lift and liken it to a long dose of flu. When very low I tend to withdraw from all but my close friends and family and wait for it to lift.

Whilst in a state absent of either depression or mania I liken my life to that of a skimming stone on calm water. Whilst on the move between mental health meetings, visiting friends, shopping and going for walks, if I were to stop and be alone, my mood would sink like a stone.

Volunteering in mental health may not be everyone's cup of tea, but finding an interest to fill time that will benefit others is a great way to work a little on self-esteem. Doing nothing on one's own on a low income is enough to make anyone depressed regardless of a natural pre-disposition.

I have also long since let go of any desire for material possessions beyond the necessary and this has given me a degree of freedom. Some will talk of retail therapy, but for me it's about being content with what I've got, and not comparing myself to others. This, however, has taken me a few years to develop and I still would like to win the lottery!

steve – the horseman

My name is Steve. I was born the youngest of five on a farm in South Tipperary in 1953. From a young age I tended to be moody and withdrawn at times. I remember one day as I sat under a tree, my dad asked me, 'Why are you moping about on your own?' I was unable to answer his question.

As the years passed, and I grew into my late teens, I became very restless. I came over to England at the age of seventeen to work. Over the following seven or eight years, I moved from place to place, and job to job, until I ended up in North Devon. There I met and married my first wife, and I settled for the first time in years. I went to work in a local factory as a welder, and later as a cell facilitator. We had two lovely daughters in the six years our marriage lasted.

Shortly after we separated I became very unwell; at the time I was suffering with a prolonged back problem which caused me to have many sleepless nights. What with the lack of sleep, the stress of looking after two young children, etc., I was admitted as a voluntary patient to the psychiatric wing of the North Devon District Hospital. It would take pages to explain the delusory thoughts that were swirling about in my mind at this time.

I spent two weeks in hospital heavily sedated; the diagnosis was a breakdown due to stress. I was released and given a concoction of sedatives, but as soon as I got home I flushed them down the toilet. I have always had a fear of taking addictive medication. It might be because I saw the effect they had on my mother when I was growing up; she had a severe breakdown after the birth of one of my sisters, and took medication for many years.

I returned to work three months later, I was in a new relationship, which led to my second marriage, and life looked rosier!

Over the following sixteen years I lived with bouts of depression and mania, but went undiagnosed. I used various herbal remedies including St

John's Wort to help me through. Sometimes I would be at work and I would feel so panicky I would make up an excuse that I was physically unwell, and take a few days off. I would spend hours walking our dogs, as I just wanted to be on my own; it must have been very difficult for my wife and children.

In the late 1990s the strain on my family became too much, I separated from my wife, and with my youngest daughter from my first marriage moved into rented accommodation. The next couple of years were very unsettling and we moved home several times. Then my daughter finished school and started work, I managed to buy a house, and things settled down for a while.

On a visit to my sister in Penzance I met and later married my third wife, and we lived in North Devon for a while. When I was sacked from my job of twenty years in 1999, we moved to Penzance. I was becoming seriously unwell once more. I registered with a doctor in Penzance, who prescribed Prozac. It was probably the worst thing he could have done!

Over the following months I went through the worst time of my life. I was so manic I was borrowing and spending money on ludicrous schemes; at one time I was trying to buy three properties.

But then came the slide from mania into the deepest depression of my life. I was hanging on by a thread.

Then on 30 October 2000, I was admitted to hospital once more as a voluntary patient, where I made a vain attempt on my life. A cry for help, perhaps.

I was put on twenty-four-hour surveillance, until the staff were happy I was no longer a threat to myself. The next few days were a fight within myself to stop unravelling completely; I was not sure what was happening to me, which in itself was very frightening.

After a few days I met Dr Hunter, and became his patient (I still am). Over the next week or so we talked, and he took some blood tests. I was not really aware of what was going on all the time. Then in the second week I went to see him, and he told me I was suffering from bipolar affective disorder. 'What in hell is that?' I asked, and he explained that it is a form of manic depression. 'Good, does that mean I'm not going "Mad"?' He said the illness is caused by an imbalance of the chemical in the brain that maintains normal mood swings. He said he wanted to put me on a course of lithium. Looking back, maybe those were the most significant words ever spoken to me!

Having a diagnosis really helped in my recovery. With the help of the psychiatric team, family and friends I made a steady recovery to some sort of normality, so much so that I was able to move into a flat on my own in March 2001. The cost of this breakdown was my third marriage.

Over the following months I learned about bipolar, its effects and treatment, and tried to find a way forward. I was brought up with horses, but although there were horses available to ride when I was young, I never had one of my own. Ever since I came to live in England I dreamed of putting that right, but because of other commitments was never able to do so. Over the years I often dreamed of trekking with a horse, either with a wagon or a pack. Maybe I had seen too many westerns, or possibly I have itinerant blood, I'm not sure. Anyway, an idea started to grow in my mind: why not make the dream come true?

A few years previously I had been on holiday with my brother in Spain, where we stayed with friends of his in a village in the foothills of the Sierra Nevada near Granada. We did some riding whilst there. I fell in love with the Spanish way of riding; their saddles are so comfortable!

One of the friends was a veterinarian with the endurance riding circuit. The idea of riding between thirty and 100 miles as a race did not particularly interest me, but the thought of riding over long distances did. I asked her how far she thought it was possible to ride a horse if you took your time. She said you could ride a horse as far as physical or political borders will allow you to; as long as you look after your horse, he will take you as far as you want to go. That answer was to prove the spark that, three years later, was to lead to the *realization of a dream.*

The idea of going to Spain to buy a horse, and then trek back to Cornwall, to raise awareness of the effects of mental ill health, became an obsession. At first I was afraid to tell anyone about my dream, in case they sent for the men in white coats!

To cut a long story short, on 27 April 2002 I left Penzance for Spain, I had just over £3000 in my pocket, and with the help of a friend in Spain I got my horse. He was called 'Colina'. We set off from Seville on 14 May, trekking some 2000 miles along ancient pilgrim trails through western Andalusia, Portugal, northern Spain and France, finally arriving in Penzance on 10 September.

Colina became a big part of my life: we did two more treks over the next three years, until he died suddenly of colic on 27 December 2005. He helped me live a dream, and opened many doors for me, for which I am eternally grateful. 'Rest in peace, dear friend.'

Don't be afraid to dream, everything is possible.

To learn more about this extraordinary companion, please see the website www.pilgrimhorse.info

the farmer's tale

Looking back, being twenty-two seems a lifetime ago; the best years of one's life, so they say – not for me though. I'd already been farming for seven years after one year at college. March is a busy time on the farm with lambing in full flow and ploughing to be done, but there was no need for extra help. I was as good as three men then, ploughing, cultivating, planting: I could do it all in my stride – what a buzz from it all – on the go from dawn till dusk, with still enough time to socialize. What extreme energy! I didn't want it to stop, but everything must come to an end. I started analyzing myself too much: maybe I couldn't do that; what if this happened or that; what if I couldn't keep up with work; things were getting on top of me; I was getting upset for no reason. So I reasoned that maybe a few days at the local agricultural show would make me feel better.

Alas, no, too much drinking and merriment. Yet arriving home I could not concentrate on doing anything, I had no enthusiasm, I just wanted to sleep and sleep. I kept telling myself that one day I would wake up and this nightmare would be over, every night praying to be better in the morning – but I never was.

I saw the doctor one day and he gave me an adrenalin injection. Wow, that did the trick, glad rags on and away, only to be met on the stairs by another doctor with a hypodermic to slow me down again – spoilsport! Soon I needed to go into hospital, but I did not understand: I had lost touch with reality; mind not functioning properly. I can remember two stocky ambulance men arriving at the house and trying to manhandle me out of bed – I hung onto it like my life depended on it. They left in defeat. What a shock for my parents the next day when I stood in front of them in the kitchen, holding a suitcase, ready to be admitted to hospital.

Walking in through the hospital doors was a relief – total shutdown, unable to speak and relying on other people to physically feed and wash me. I felt so thirsty but could not drink, so hungry but would rather starve, my mind continually telling me I would be drinking urine and eating vomit. But how nice it was to have my family around me: in the bed opposite was my father – he was always up first, brush and shaving foam in hand, always in that string vest. My brother in that white coat handing out tablets with a smile and a drink of water – why were they all here? Was this my new world?

I found a new machine, a milk dispenser – I can still taste it now, so white, fresh and cold it took away all that thirst. I was coming out of my nightmare – and wanted to phone my mum. What a shock that must have been to the male nurse I approached that I could talk again. How timely this was as the next day I was booked in for some ECT – which was stopped. Every day I gained strength and confidence and within three weeks I was discharged, but what a long road it was before I felt back to normal.

Cut to September 2001 and I was now a married forty-one-year-old man with two children. One night of excess ended in a violent confrontation with someone, resulting in me breaking his ribs. Where did that strength come from, fuelled by an immense pent-up feeling of exhilaration? I then grabbed the nearest object which happened to be a golf club, and attacked the nearest thing, which was a car – try explaining that to the insurance company. I then raced back home unaware that my wife had phoned the local constabulary. They arrived just as I was unpotting all the plants around the house.

I tried to get away but was too late and was tackled by a look-alike from the Welsh rugby squad who brought me down on a gravelled driveway. I was only wearing a shirt and it really hurt. I was now under control with handcuffs in place – they didn't half hurt. I was now experiencing another frightening thing, namely hallucinations. As I was being driven to the police station I could see people's faces changing into what I can only describe as the devil. Where were they taking me? Was it the place for all the bad people of the world?

Those cells are very small and claustrophobic. I remember jumping around and begging them not to shut the door, which they agreed to, and an officer guarded the door. Soon after that I was sectioned, and taken back to the hospital where I had been nineteen years previously. Surprisingly enough, there to greet me at the door was the person who I believed all those years ago was my brother. We recognized each other in an instant; not that mute dishevelled person from the last time we met, but a loud, boisterous, argumentative person who would not stop talking, jumping from one subject to another and unable to stand still. After much persuading I took Haloperidol and soon settled down. This drug is similar to a straitjacket and had the desired effects with my limbs soon feeling like lead and my tongue feeling the size of a cricket bat. I rapidly came back to reality and the remorse and embarrassment were now setting in.

The physiatrist saw me soon after and the words bipolar effective disorder were mentioned. At last there was a name for the illness that I had suffered from for many years.

After release from hospital I was invited to a meeting with the Bipolar Organisation. From this about half a dozen of us set up a self-help group, and with our friendship and support and knowledge of the illness we have encouraged more people to join up, and we are now a strong and established group.

Although the staff were very supportive to me in hospital I felt that they did not have the insight into the illness that I had experienced at first hand. So I volunteered to visit the people that had been diagnosed with bipolar, to give them support and information on what can be described as a very disruptive illness. From doing this I feel I have gained a vast amount of knowledge and understanding about bipolar. I am sure that this has helped me cope personally with this illness that has plagued me for many years.

Although I am still farming, methods have changed considerably. Contractors now help me with ploughing and field preparation, so that we are ready for the new year's crops. This helps me with labour because they usually have new up-to-date machinery to get the job done faster and more efficiently. As well as this, the farm is now in an environmental scheme. I receive payments for fencing both sides of hedges to protect and let the hedgerows regenerate into both food and shelter for wildlife; the farm has already benefited from a number of hares that now occupy the land, and a large flock of lapwings winter here which is quite a spectacle.

Suffering for many years with this illness has given me a greater understanding of what other people are going through, and it gives me immense pleasure and satisfaction visiting the local wards to give people encouragement and hope for the future. With the right medication and education there is no reason why people with this diagnosis cannot lead full and enjoyable lives.

max and the world of tv

I had a comfortable upbringing in suburban Birmingham, with loving parents who only wanted the best for me.

My early opportunities and education were fantastic: I went to a local private boys' school which at that time – the early eighties – was academically the best in the country. I was a bit of a dysfunctional eccentric even then, but I still managed to get good exam results and a place at Oxford.

I took away one very damaging lesson from that school: it's not enough to do well, you have to excel. And to be truly successful you have to do better than everyone else. Combined with mum and dad whispering in my ear that 'the world was my oyster', by the time I left, the school ethos had led me to become pointlessly competitive, full of unrealistic aspirations and expectations.

The crumbling of these expectations – and my manic depression – started at university, where I was pitched into a much bigger pool filled with people more privileged and talented than me. I reacted by showing off, and I found a group of appreciative friends, some of whom became unwitting 'enablers', of both my mania and my use of alcohol and cannabis. On the girlfriend front, feminism had convinced me that as a man I was gen(der)etically compromised, incapable of having a proper relationship with a woman.

Showing off also worked in television – and within a few years of leaving Oxford I was at a small independent company run by a very large man who came the closest of anyone to being my 'mentor'. Despite my worsening mood swings, he believed in me enough to keep on employing me. Besides, I was getting results: a year into my contract, I came up with an idea for a BBC documentary series which I helped to produce and which went on to win a BAFTA.

This long-awaited success provoked my first fully-fledged manic episode, though I didn't know what it was at the time. And when a few other ideas of mine got commissioned I set out to convince the senior management of British TV that I had the Midas touch, not realizing that my over-confidence was fuelled by pure mania rather than actual ability.

But the problem with being manic is that sometimes it *can* work, and in this case the boss of one of the biggest ITV companies fell for my shtick and gave me a high-powered job with a huge salary and expense account. I had arrived! In reality I was actually out of my depth in a macho bullying environment. Forced into another manic cycle, I started going on crazy spending sprees, and the approval on a mortgage for a posh flat had just come through when I was fired as a result of worryingly erratic behaviour at work. For instance, I had been reduced to tears in one meeting but was full of grandiose plans in the next. The end came when I started challenging the authority of other senior managers. Given a week to clear my desk, I came tumbling down and used my generous redundancy to retire for months to fall-back accommodation: a friend's dark, rented basement flat.

It was at this time that my GP and therapist prescribed Prozac, still not realizing that I was actually bipolar and that Prozac could bring on mania. Sure enough, I was catapulted into another manic swing which made me think I could run my own TV production company with very little financial experience.

This turned out to be a green light to giving my manic, self-destructive side full, unfettered reign, and virtually single-handed I tried to make chaotic programmes with the pop-star Prince and a clutch of celebrity criminals, one of whom assaulted me in Rio de Janeiro airport while on speed.

After four years of struggle my company went bust, and I was almost relieved to have to move back in with my parents, even though I was now thousands of pounds in debt.

It was also a kind of relief when an NHS psychiatrist told me for the first time nearly two years ago that I was a manic depressive, even though I didn't believe her at the time and was horrified by the thought that I might have to take lithium for the rest of my life. I agreed to try the alternative Depakote instead, but stopped after a few months.

The manic episode that followed saw me trying to make a documentary about a heroin-addicted pop star who ended up having a fight with me in a hotel room when the deal went bad. The story was splashed in the newspapers and became the subject of a documentary on Channel 4 which caused me to be widely derided as a deluded wannabe.

It took this very public humiliation for me to understand what members of my family knew first hand – I had been in denial about my manic depression for years. I was immediately plunged into a very deep depression, but I started taking the Depakote again as well as a safe anti-depressant and things gradually began to improve.

It was trying to describe my life for this book which made me realize that I was returning to the land of the living. There is something thera-peutic about being able to tell my story without feeling shame or guilt, and even imagining that it might be of use to others.

I also found that I was able to get up the courage to go to a local manic depression help-group, where hearing other people's stories made me feel less of a freak. I joined some great chat forums on line and discov-ered the joys of 'e'-moting to a sympathetic audience. I even started a blog which helped me to monitor and manage my changing moods.

Most importantly, I relied on my family members and close friends to be brutally honest with me about my behaviour, past and present. This process has been a painful one but worth it, because now I'm in a much better position to recognize the triggers of another manic or depressive episode. It's also improved the quality of my relationships.

I'm about to start therapy again, but I've come to realize that there really is no quick fix; my manic depression is something that I will need to carry on treating, probably for the rest of my life. But I don't feel so bad about that any more – if you can control it, being bipolar can bring richness and flavour to your experience that others may never get to taste.

the insider's guide to mental health

a

acceptance

Acceptance is a process by which a person acknowledges something to be true or correct, whether they like it or not. Acceptance requires honesty to face up to things as they really are and to take responsibility.

The opposite of acceptance is fashionably described as 'denial', living in a dream world, whistling in the wind, pretending something isn't happening when it is, or burying one's head in the sand.

Acceptance is a spiritual and mental process practised throughout our daily lives. Bereavement, divorce, serious illness, redundancy and debts are life problems that everybody has to deal with. To ignore something because you cannot face it or because you don't want to believe it or because you are hoping that it may go away, might cause worse consequences later. Acceptance is not an admission of one's approval of a situation or of personal defeat but an admission regarding the truth of a given situation.

The break-up of a relationship or love affair can be very painful, particularly in the teenage and middle years. Anger, insecurity and pride often prevent us from accepting situations. However, when we have fully accepted what has happened, it is possible to move on and start afresh.

Growing up in such an image-conscious society can be problematic in terms of accepting the way that we look. We may feel unhappy that we are too short, too tall, too fat, or born with a big nose or big chin. But unless we find an extraordinary plastic surgeon, the quickest way out of unhappiness is to accept the way we are.

Unfortunately, mental illness does not have any colourful physical manifestations. People suffering from depression or agoraphobia do not wake up one day covered in blue or pink spots, nor do the eyes and teeth of an individual who has become manic turn fluorescent green. Perhaps it would be better if they did – at least friends, family and doctors would be able to tell there was something wrong.

There are five widely recognized stages associated with acceptance and manic depression, death and bereavement which can in part or wholly be applied to any other mental ill health or life crisis.

1 *Denial:* The 'This couldn't possibly happen to me' stage. The doctor must be wrong.
2 *Anger:* The 'Why me?' stage. You are angry at whoever might have triggered this illness; your family, doctor and indeed yourself for behaving in a way that has 'caused' this situation to happen.
3 *Bargaining:* The 'If you do this, I'll do that' stage. I will stop drinking, smoking, going to the races providing this illness is taken away.
4 *Depression:* The 'It really has happened' stage. Perhaps you stop taking the medication, you go out on the town and things go badly wrong.
5 *Acceptance:* The 'I do have manic depression after all' stage. What can I do about it?

Once you have accepted that you are ill, you are in a far stronger position to do something about it.

> God grant me the serenity to accept the things I cannot change
> Courage to change the things I can
> And the wisdom to know the difference.
>
> **Reinhold Niebuhr**

acedia

The name for melancholy in the Middle Ages. Ascetic monks on desert fasts, who were tempted by the 'devil' to melancholic reverie, were deemed to be terrible sinners.

acupuncture

The practice of piercing specific sites on the body, called pathways or meridians, with thin needles in an attempt to relieve pain associated with some chronic disorders.

Based on the ancient Chinese theory of energy fields (meridians), the idea is that Chi, the life force, is rebalanced. The effect of acupuncture can be seen on brain imaging but the likelihood of it having specific benefits in manic depressive illness is not likely. However, the technique can lead to relaxation, and this is important in controlling the symptoms.

ADD/ADHD – attention deficit (hyperactivity) disorder

what is ADD/ADHD?
ADD/ADHD is a sometimes controversial disorder that affects concentration and attention. It is usually diagnosed in childhood and is marked in particular by hyperactivity, impulsiveness, social clumsiness and mood swings.

what ADD/ADHD is not
ADD/ADHD is NOT the result of bad parenting OR an excuse for bad behaviour.

how to get help with ADD/ADHD
Talk to friends, family, other parents. There are some useful websites, support groups (see Websites, page 150) and books available. If you think you, or your child, have ADD/ADHD, the first place to seek help is your GP surgery.

what help you may be offered
You/your child may be offered medication and/or talking treatments (see **Therapists**, pages 298–303) and/or could be referred to you local CMHT (Community Mental Health Trust) or CAMHS (Child and Adolescent Mental Health Services) which may, in turn, offer you and your family support.

medication and controversy
There has been a lot of press coverage about medication for ADD/

ADHD – particularly about methylphenidate (Ritalin). It's well worth discussing these issues with your GP before making any decisions.

top tips
- Stop blaming yourself.
- Speak to your GP/health worker/other people.

websites
NICE (www.nice.org.uk)
MIND (www.mind.org.uk)
ADISS (www.adiss.co.uk)

books
ADHD – The Facts by Mark Selikowitz
Scattered Minds by Gabor Mate

addiction/addictive personality

Is the woman who has been to see *Phantom of the Opera* 2300 times at the theatre an addict, an obsessive or an eccentric enthusiast? She could be all three. What about the man so desperate for a smoke that he stoops down to the pavement to pull out a half-smoked cigarette that someone has dropped into a moist coil of dog excrement?

Whether you are addicted to tobacco, heroin, alcohol, sport, chocolate, porn, gambling, skunk or crack, you will probably only notice something is wrong when you run out of funds to obtain your drug of choice. When does a habit turn into addiction? Primarily when the need for the euphoric effect from the 'drug' starts affecting your mental and physical health and behaviour. Addiction can happen to the nicest of people. Life would be pretty boring if we didn't have things to entertain us, 'give us a lift', 'take us out of ourselves' and 'give us a bit of a buzz', wouldn't it?

A successful stockbroker can be addicted to heroin. A priest can develop an unhealthy dependence on fruit machines. The problem for the stockbroker occurs when he loses that job, cannot get another one and no longer has the funds to feed the habit. The problem for the priest is when he is not caught stealing from the church collection plate to fund his trips to the amusement arcade and continues stealing more. Serious addicts are prepared to get up in the middle of the night and walk miles to satisfy their craving, steal from their families, and ultimately sell their blood and their bodies to raise the cash for their fix. Addiction is like being a slave to something, but you are paying for the privilege and often with your life.

If you are worried that you are unable to function without the enjoyable feeling that a particular substance or activity gives you, then seek professional help.

Somebody with an addictive personality is someone who wants 'more' of everything. Somebody with an addictive personality is most unlikely to resist finishing a bag of crisps or cocaine, box of chocolates or bottle of wine, once already opened.

Famous but unlikely addicts: William Donaldson, the author of *The Henry Root Letters*, was a self-confessed sex addict who in his late sixties became fond of smoking crack. Karen Carpenter, of the Carpenters pop duo, was addicted to fasting and died of a heart attack brought on by anorexia. The American serial killer Ted Bundy, executed in 1989 for murdering up to fifty young women, was addicted to hard-core pornography. Sir Arthur Conan Doyle, author of the Sherlock Holmes stories, was addicted to opium.

See **Twelve Step Programmes**, pages 305–7.

adolescence

The 'Teenage Years' are often considered to be an emotional assault course for all involved. A time of rapid physical development, mood swings and often difficult behaviour in varying degrees. Young people are making the transition from dependence to independence, from childhood to adulthood. This can be a time of rejection and hostility towards parents and carers, interspersed with periods of the opposite – where adolescents need extra love, attention and 'cosiness'. Issues around sexuality, peer group pressures, the 'meaning of life', realizing your carers are not infallible, drugs and alcohol can arise. The time to seek help may be when you notice difficulties around eating, excessive sleepiness and/or extremes of concern over appearance. Adolescents can, of course, pass through this stage with little difficulty – others may require external help at some stage. This could come from friends, family, school-based and voluntary organizations, the GP and/or the Child and Adolescent Mental Health Services (CAMHS).

top tips

Three things not to say to an adolescent

- Why aren't you like Michael/Mary (the 'swotty dork' next door!)?
- You don't know you're born – we had nothing when we were young.
- Why don't you put on a crisp white cotton shirt instead of those baggy dark clothes?

Three things for an adolescent not to say to their parents

- Why aren't you like my friends' parents?
- I don't know when I'll be back!
- I don't care – so what? – big deal.

alcoholics anonymous (AA)

AA was founded in 1935 by Bill Wilson, a New York stockbroker and Dr Bob Smith, a surgeon from Ohio. Having both overcome their own addiction to alcohol, the two men set about devising the now famous Twelve Step Programme that is the foundation of Alcoholics Anonymous. Today AA has more than two million members in 150 countries. There are 3600 weekly meetings in England, Scotland and Wales along with 500 English-speaking meetings across Continental Europe.

Carol Titley, a non-alcoholic trustee of AA, stated in early 2006: 'Alcoholics Anonymous is possibly the most cost-effective means of recovery from alcoholism, with more than 600 meetings a week in London alone. Alcoholism transcends social, economic, age and gender boundaries. People from all walks of life find that drinking is costing them more than money. AA membership figures tell only part of the life-changing stories – behind each alcoholic who stops drinking, there are untold numbers of families, friends, neighbours and employers, as well as healthcare, psychiatric, social and probation professionals who benefit.

'The face of AA itself is changing. Surveys of new members show that half are women and three-quarters are under the age of 45. There have also been recent initiatives to reach out to black and minority ethnic communities; underlining that AA is available to anyone who wants to stop drinking.'

There are those who are put off by references to 'God' within AA literature. However, this reference appears to be optional as there are many agnostic and atheist AA members. The initial premise of AA is that to get well and sober, you need: not to pick up the first drink, acknowledge and accept your powerlessness over alcohol, and try to live one day at a time. Also to accept that there is a power greater than yourself; whatever or whoever that power might be.

AA suggests a codeword for new members to remain sober: HALT. Try and never be Hungry, Angry, Lonely or Tired.

A long-time AA member summarizes what he once thought were the possible pitfalls of AA:

- I was convinced I might be made to play a tambourine and, far worse, sing my life story in the middle of a group of 300 beaming non-drinkers.
- I thought that AA was affiliated to the Freemasons and that I would have to wear my trouser legs rolled up forever more.
- There was a hidden catch in AA involving my bank account.
- That all the people in 'meetings' would either be toothless raging tramps or condescending intellectual types.
- Any sense of fun or laughter would disappear from my life forever.
- I would turn into an anorak-wearing person who had become addicted to AA meetings.

However, on the plus side:

- The only thing AA cost me is the couple of pounds that I place in the 'pot' at meetings.
- AA explained some of the many strange thoughts that had gone on inside my head since schooldays and why certain things had gone wrong in my life.
- AA showed me that there was a good life to be had without drinking.
- AA has supplied me with an invisible handbook on how to cope with life.
- I have a network of extraordinary friends in AA of all shapes and sizes, from all over the world who speak the same language.
- Practising the AA programme and attending regular meetings is a simple but effective way to remain balanced and sane.

the female point of view

Some great things about AA, as related by several female members:

- The feeling that when you walk into a meeting they know you.
- Sobriety
- Opens channels of self-knowledge/healing/recovery
- Gives you back your dignity
- No rules and non-restrictive
- Available worldwide
- Real friendship
- Always having somewhere to go
- Forgiveness – of yourself and others
- Being able to help others/pass on the programme
- Anonymity – if you choose
- Work programme at your own pace
- Say just about anything
- Flexibility

Ten dodgy things I thought might happen to me in AA but didn't:

- It would be too religious.
- It would be gloomy/dreary/boring.
- Men would pester me to hang out with them.
- Women might not want to hang out with me.
- It would be too dogmatic/inflexible.
- I might lose my humour/personality.
- I would find people boring and no fun.
- It would interfere with my 'real' life.
- I would have to wear sandals and eat brown rice.
- All my friends would find out and laugh at me.

best book

Living Sober, available through AA General Service Office, PO Box 1, Stonebow House, Stonebow, York YO1 7NJ

helpline

AA National Helpline: 0845 769 7555

website

www.alcoholics-anonymous.org.uk

Alcoholism is the continued abuse of alcohol regardless of the detrimental consequences to the health of mind or body.

A more popular definition might allude to Jekyll and Hyde, where somebody's personality profoundly changes for the worse as a result of drinking alcohol.

Alcohol is believed to cause around 33,000 deaths per year in Britain. The most common ways to die through alcoholism are:

- Impaired judgement and decision-making process, often resulting in fatal accidents at work and while driving.
- Cirrhosis of the liver.
- Choking to death on one's own vomit.
- Chronic pancreatitis.
- Cancer.
- Atrophy of the brain.

statistics about alcoholism

- One in four admissions to hospital in the UK is alcohol related.
- Sixty per cent of British suicides are alcohol related.
- Alcohol is implicated in forty per cent of domestic violence cases and thirty-nine per cent of fires.
- It is an illness that affects the body and mind, is compulsive in nature and considered to be an addiction. It was first reported by Seneca in ancient Rome as something very close to insanity. The Italian for alcoholic is *alcoolisto*; the French is *alcoholique* and the German is *alkoholiker*.

Many people mistakenly believe that alcoholics are only people who need to have a drink in the early morning or are down and outs sitting on park benches drinking cans of lager. While those examples are likely to be true, there are many 'types' of alcoholic who manage to function within a 'normal' life. The lonely builder who only drinks eight pints of beer at the pub five times a week or the respectable lady magistrate who drinks three glasses of sherry in an evening can both be alcoholic.

Like most addictions, alcoholism comes with practice. The more often you drink the more likely you are to become dependent. Nobody knows why some people become alcoholic while others do not. Many recovering alcoholics maintain they were born that way, wired together differently and that, if it wasn't alcohol, another addictive substance would be their undoing.

Strange fact: The ancient Greeks believed that putting a piece of amethyst in one's glass or in one's mouth while drinking prevented drunkenness. The literal Greek translation of 'amethyst' is 'not intoxicated'.

Obvious fact: Alcohol accentuates your real mood. If you are feeling depressed, alcohol will briefly raise your serotonin level but only briefly, before you feel even worse. If you are feeling euphoric or hypomanic, drinking alcohol will make you higher.

how to tell if you might be alcoholic

- Have you ever felt that you should cut down on your alcohol consumption?
- Do you repeatedly drink more than you intend or want to?
- Can you 'take' or 'hold' your drink? This does not signify that you are not an alcoholic and in some cases can indicate a problem.
- Have you ever felt annoyed when someone criticized your alcohol consumption?
- Have you ever felt guilty about the way you acted or behaved having drunk alcohol?
- Have you been in trouble with your family or spouse, girlfriend/boyfriend, or at work or with the police?

If you have answered yes to more than two of the above questions, it may be wise to talk the matter over with your GP or a close friend. If you have a chronic alcohol problem, it is not advisable to try and stop but to seek professional help as soon as possible.

famous alcoholics

Richard Burton, Michael Elphick, Elizabeth Taylor, Keith Moon, Peter Cook, Ernest Hemingway, Tommy Cooper, Tennessee Williams, Peter Benchley, Truman Capote, George Best, etc.

alternative treatments

See Acupuncture, Homeopathy, Meditation and Yoga.

anger

An American Indian Fable, 'Two Wolves'
One evening an old Cherokee told his grandson about a battle that goes on inside people. He said, 'My son, the battle is between two wolves inside us all. One is Evil. It is anger, envy, jealousy, sorrow, regret, greed, arrogance, self-pity, guilt, resentment, inferiority, lies, false pride, superiority and ego.

'The other is Good. It is joy, peace, love, hope, serenity, humility, kindness, benevolence, empathy, generosity, truth, compassion and faith.'

The grandson thought about it for a minute and then asked his grandfather: 'Which wolf wins?' The old Cherokee simply replied, 'The one you feed.'

The best response to anger is to walk into another room, unless you have strategies to defuse the situation or want to start a fight. Confronting issues when one party is angry is rarely useful. It is better to return to the issue once tempers have settled. This is particularly important in close relationships, which are rapidly destroyed by uncontrolled aggressive outbursts. The only exception is if both parties have equal power in the relationship and are happy using anger as a channel of communication. Anger is not a useful method of communicating with those who have less power than you. You will not raise the IQ or respect of your children or your parents by shouting at them.

In the longer term, difficulties in expressing and acknowledging anger are linked to a number of mental health problems. Suppressing anger through the use of alcohol can contribute to alcoholism, and when that anger turns inwards, over time, it can contribute to depression. Suppressing anger and allowing it to fester can be an exhausting process. Not expressing or expelling this anger over a long period of time can become poisonous and lead to depression and low self-esteem.

You can help avoid the feeling of powerlessness that frequently precedes an outburst of anger by knowing your weak spots and understanding your trigger points. Recognize the changes in your breathing and heart rate that come just before these outbursts and learn to handle the situation differently. The key is to direct the emotion into areas where it can be harnessed constructively.

eight top tips for anger management

1 Relaxation techniques: walk into another room, go outside, count to ten, take ten slow deep breaths, think of something wonderful like your last holiday, have a drink of water and avoid drinking alcohol.

2 Go for a run, use the energy constructively to get fit or clear the garden!

3 Are you thirsty, tired or hungry, and will you think differently in the morning?

4 Think of something funny or ridiculous about the situation. In ten days, months or years will it really be that important?

5 Understand which of your own rules or expectations has been violated, and decide if it was a reasonable rule or expectation.

6 Try to understand the other person's perspective and understand why what they are doing triggers your anger.

7 Punch a pillow or kick box the sofa for two minutes and make them beg for mercy!

8 If you find that you are frequently angry and that your work or home life is being affected, it may be wise to investigate an anger management course.

anxiety

Anxiety is a normal, fear-based emotion – we need a bit of anxiety in situations we find dangerous or threatening. It wouldn't be helpful if one didn't feel a bit anxious when crossing a main road! When your levels of anxiety begin to make it difficult to live your life and you are avoiding significant things because of anxiety, it becomes a problem for you. When you feel as if you don't know what's causing your anxiety and are wondering if it will ever end – seek help. It is widely believed within the medical profession that one in ten people will experience excessive anxiety and many of them will never seek help and 'suffer in silence'.

what is anxiety?

To cope with dangerous or threatening situations, we need to take in more oxygen and our bodies need to be ready for fight or flight. The problems come when you are feeling anxious or fearful much of the time and it's interfering with your everyday life. For example, you might start avoiding activities because of anxiety.

what anxiety is not

Anxiety is not a sign that you are going 'mad'. People with difficulties with anxieties and fears hardly ever have a serious mental illness. It is not a sign of 'weakness'. It's not simply 'stress'. Anxiety does not just go on and on and on even though it sometimes feels like it does – it rises, plateaux and comes down again.

the symptoms of anxiety

In order for our ancestors to run away, say, from a sabre-toothed tiger, they would need to be carrying as little weight as possible, be focused on getting away or fighting, and so on. Some of the symptoms of anxiety, which many people confuse with signs of physical illness include:

- Irregular heart beat (palpitations)
- Stomach problems (e.g. diarrhoea)
- Difficulty swallowing
- Feelings of dread/fear
- Nausea/vomiting
- Sweating
- Shaking
- Numbness and pins and needles
- Difficulty concentrating
- Feeling tired
- Dizziness
- Indigestion
- Breathing difficulties ('I couldn't catch my breath')
- Muscular aches and pains
- Feeling dissociated, 'out of myself', 'as if I'm not there – looking down on myself'

- Worrying all the time
- Experiencing negative thoughts – such as the catastrophic thought: 'EVERYTHING is out of control.'

anxiety, depression and other mental health problems

Many people with manic depressive disorder will experience symptoms of anxiety. Some people have substance misuse problems, including an alcohol problem along with anxiety – they try to cope with anxiety by drinking/taking drugs and often, whilst there can be significant temporary relief, the anxiety gets worse in the long term. Other mental health difficulties occur alongside anxiety – and health professionals call the occurrence of two sets of problems together 'co-morbidity'.

causes of anxiety

Some people are born with a genetic vulnerability to anxiety. Others may have a 'learned' vulnerability. Someone, for example, brought up in a home where Dad 'worries about everything', might get the idea that there's quite a lot to be fearful of 'out there' – that the world is a pretty dangerous place all round. Other people may not be able to identify an underlying cause but, if put under enough pressure, will experience excessive anxiety. Sometimes the cause is very obvious – once the problem goes away so does the anxiety.

types of anxiety

Some types of anxiety are related to specific situations, symptoms and thoughts. You may come to recognize that your anxiety is limited or 'about' only certain things. Anxiety disorders include:

- *Panic disorder with/without agoraphobia:* Panic disorder is a form of anxiety marked by intermittent overwhelming 'surges' of anxiety – panic attacks. Agoraphobia is usually linked to panic attacks and involves fears around and avoidance of being away from a 'safe place' e.g. home. In extreme cases people can become entirely housebound.
- *Generalized anxiety disorder (GAD):* WORRY! Excessive worrying and worrying about worrying, usually over a period of more than six months.
- *Social anxiety:* Anxiety related to social situations and fears of being judged by others.
- *Health anxiety/hypochondriasis:* Anxiety linked to excessive worries

about one's own and sometimes others' health. Marked by, for example, repeated requests for reassurance about your health and hypervigilance for symptoms of illness. Spike Milligan always said that he was a hypochondriac and marked his gravestone 'I told you I was ill'.

- *Post-traumatic stress disorder (PTSD):* Once called 'shell shock' and 'battle fatigue syndrome'. Triggered by reaction to an extreme event, usually involving a fear of dying or being killed. Can come on close to the negative event or sometimes years later. Marked, in particular, by 'flashbacks' and nightmares linked to the triggering event/events. A new treatment called EMDR has been found to be very effective, strangely involving controlled eye movements at the same time as gradually re-experiencing the event. It is not based on hypnosis.
- *Phobias:* Distressing levels of anxiety around a specific event/thing, e.g. fear of spiders, heights, injections, etc.
- *Obsessive compulsive disorder:* A pattern of distressing thoughts (obsessions) that you feel you can't ignore and behaviours (compulsions) designed to 'neutralize' the thoughts, marked by, for example, excessive washing, checking, ruminating and counting.

when to seek help for anxiety

Seek help whenever you think symptoms have been 'going on too long' – more than, say, two/four weeks, and when anxiety is impacting on your ability to live the life you would normally expect.

how to get help

If you can, start by seeking support from family, friends and people around you. If there's no one around, non-statutory agencies such as MIND (www.mind.org.uk) often offer local 'drop-in centres' which offer a space to talk. As with any mental health difficulties, once you and/or those around you have recognized that there's a problem the first port of call should be your GP/surgery who should help diagnose and offer treatment, suggesting self-help measures and offering leaflets and information about non-statutory agencies that may be able to help. (See the **GP** section on pages 209–11 for what he/she might offer.)

a word of warning!

Benzodiazepines – diazepam, lorazepam, temazepam and so on – may be prescribed in the short term for one or two weeks and give quick relief but they are addictive. Take your GP's advice about these medicines, and don't be tempted to continue with them for a long period.

helping yourself

Some ideas to think about include:

- Reading and working through self-help literature (see Books and Websites, opposite)
- Relaxation/meditation/yoga
- Talking to others
- Contacting/joining self-help groups/voluntary/non-statutory organizations (see Books and Websites, opposite)
- Taking time out
- Taking regular breaks
- Structuring your day
- Cutting down/out alcohol – this doesn't have to be forever!
- Adding more pleasurable activities into your day
- Exercising regularly
- Remembering to breathe 'normally' (not deeply – just normally). When you are anxious you tend to 'over-breathe' (sometimes imperceptibly) and lower your carbon monoxide, which leads to symptoms of anxiety
- Eating regularly and well
- Looking after any physical problems
- Recognizing and challenging any unhelpful thoughts.

what to do if someone you know has anxiety problems

If you feel that someone is experiencing difficulties and their anxiety seems to be affecting the way they behave – the best thing you can do is be supportive and talk with them.

- *Don't:* Tell people they are 'being silly' or to 'pull themselves together'.
- *Do:* Listen and offer support. Encourage them to visit their GP if things seem to be getting too difficult to cope with alone.

a final word

As with everything in this book – don't 'suffer in silence'; there's help available out there.

books

Oxford Cognitive Therapy Centre booklets (www.octc.co.uk)

Books in the *Overcoming* ... series published by Robinson, such as *Overcoming Anxiety* by Helen Kennerley

Mind Over Mood by Dennis Greenberger and Christine Padesky

Manage Your Mind by Gillian Butler and Tony Hope

websites

NICE (National Institute for Clinical Excellence) (www.nice.org.uk)

Royal College of Psychiatrists (www.rcpsych.ac.uk)

British Psychological Society (www.bps.org.uk)

MIND (www.mind.org.uk)

The National Phobics Society (www.phobics-society.org.uk)

aristotle

An ancient Greek philosopher who observed the frequent association of the greatest thinkers with melancholy.

'Why is it that all those who have become eminent in philosophy or politics, or poetry or the arts are clearly melancholics, and some of them to such an extent as to be affected by diseases caused by black bile?'

Problematica

autism

Autism affects communication, social and emotional skills. It can be mild to severe but always leads to difficulty in making sense of the everyday world. Often the person may also have learning disabilities; however, there may also be areas of extreme ability, as with the artist Stephen Wiltshire. Mild autism, with average or high intelligence, is known as Asperger's Syndrome. Typically, boys rather than girls are affected.

AUTISM

b

baked beans

Baked beans on toast is one of the tastiest, most nutritional and inexpensive meals you can eat in Britain today. Due to their windy quality, baked beans are the butt of many jokes but are also an excellent provider of protein. A small 205g can contains around 10g, about a fifth or a quarter respectively of the daily protein requirement of men and women. They also provide iron, needed to help prevent anaemia; zinc, required for a robust immune system; folic acid, so vital for good mental health; not forgetting lots and lots of fibre.

balance

A very important skill used by tightrope walkers to prevent sudden death or injury during their working day. It is also important for everyone to maintain a sense of balance about what is important in their lives. Most people with a balanced view would put family, friends and health at the top of their list for personal happiness.

There is also the balance of everyday life. This is about maintaining a sensible proportion of work, play and sleep in our day-to-day lives. Admittedly this can be very humdrum, and it is a good idea to do something different or exciting once in a while. This can range from bungee jumping to attending the world tiddlywinks championships. An erratic and unbalanced sleep pattern can have the quickest effect on mental health.

Admittedly, it is not always easy to sleep when anxious or angry, and unfortunately this can become a self-perpetuating spiral. Exhaustion will often lead to losing a sense of perspective and becoming angry or worried out of all proportion to the original problem. Too much sleep can lead to lethargy and depression. Again, this can spiral into a serious bout of depression. It is very difficult to face the world when depressed and much easier to stay in bed. The more time spent cocooned in bed, the harder it becomes to fight for your sense of self-worth, and so it goes on ad infinitum.

Moderation in all things is a terrible cliché but is an obvious truth. Balance also means that there are times of misery and despair in everyone's life and, to balance this, there are also times when it is really good to be alive.

bereavement

what is bereavement?

Bereavement means literally 'being deprived by death'. The longer you have known someone who dies the more intense the feelings of loss are likely to be. The loss of a child, of a baby through abortion, stillbirth or miscarriage, of a pet, or of a longstanding workmate or friend through illness or accident, will bring long-lasting feelings of grief.

how someone might feel if they have been recently bereaved

Everyone's grief and reaction to bereavement are highly individual. However, in most cases, after a 'major' bereavement, people go through a number of different emotions including:

- *Feelings of denial and disbelief* immediately following the death.
- *Numbness:* often it seems that the person is not recognizing that they have been bereaved. This feeling of numbness is often what carries people through the funeral arrangements.
- *Anger:* towards anyone, even including the loved one for leaving.
- *Guilt:* for not having said enough, 'if only' feelings and thoughts.
- *Depression/grieving:* feeling of sadness, crying, a deep sense of loss. It can also be, conversely, a trigger for hypomania, usually through the intensity of the experience and arrangements for funerals, etc. at a time combined with sleep loss.
- *Acceptance:* accepting that the person is dead and beginning to rebuild a life without them.

how long will it last?

There is no 'normal' grieving period. However, generally a period of around one to two years will be needed to reach 'acceptance'. People who have been unable to grieve or who have delayed grieving for any number of reasons, for example, being too busy looking after others, may take much longer to reach 'acceptance'.

when to seek help

The bereaved person should seek, and be offered, help and support from family and friends from the start. It may also be helpful to think about contacting the GP and/or a non-statutory organization involved in the care of bereaved people, particularly if they feel 'stuck' and unable to move on. If they feel suicidal they should seek help IMMEDIATELY – their first port of call being their GP.

what to do/say to someone who has been bereaved

- Include children and young people in the arrangements.
- Don't avoid the subject.
- Let them talk about the person.
- Don't expect them to 'get over it' quickly.
- Offer practical help.

what not to do/say to someone who has been bereaved

- 'You should be over it by now.'
- 'Never mind – you've still got ...'

top tips

- Bereavement is probably the most painful experience anyone will go through – listen, be patient, be understanding.
- Understand that if you are bereaved you will feel AWFUL but it WILL pass with time.
- Read about grief.
- If you are spiritual contact your spiritual advisers.

website

CRUSE – www.crusebereavementcare.org.uk

books

A Grief Observed by C.S. Lewis

On Death and Dying by Elisabeth Kubler Ross

What to do When Someone Dies by The Consumers Association.

The Tibetan Book of Living and Dying by Sogyal Rinpoche

bipolar disorder

Manic depression is the preferred term for bipolar disorder in this book. See **Manic Depression**, pages 223–34.

blues

- Melancholy spirits.
- Songs of woe and yearning, characterized by a twelve-bar chorus with three-line stanzas of which the third line typically repeats the first.
- The nickname of Chelsea Football Club.
- Popular amphetamine pills known affectionately by their colour.

Most legendary British Blues player: John Mayall

brett, jeremy (sherlock holmes)

Jeremy Brett is best remembered for portraying Sherlock Holmes in a decade-long Granada TV series. He was married to Anna Massey and later to Joan Wilson who died from cancer in 1985 – as a result of which he was distraught and never remarried.

Distinctive for his clear enunciation, Brett was actually born with a slight speech impediment that prevented him from pronouncing the 'r' sound. Years of diction training led to his crystal-clear delivery and pronunciation. He died aged sixty-one in 1995 from heart failure – he was a heavy smoker and also took lithium after he was diagnosed with manic depression.

C

carers

Try and make a 'contract' of care when your loved one is well. It will probably not hold water when the person you care for is unwell, as their thinking will be confused or disordered and they will probably want their own way, feeling you are wrong. But at least you will know that what you are doing is what they agreed to in a good state of physical and mental health. Let them agree that you will talk to others about the condition when you are concerned; and stick to this, it is imperative.

Keep a caring eye, but do not dissect every moment for evidence of illness – a smile, laugh or show of enthusiasm is not indicative of hypomania, neither is a tear indicative of a depressive crisis.

Most of all, you must look after yourself during a very stressful time. This will mean keeping your outside interests and responsibilities going even though there may be misery at home. The old adage is true that you can't look after someone else if you can't look after yourself.

Remember to forgive yourself if you can't make everything right. You cannot *change* people; you can only offer your help and do your best. After that you must say you've done what you were able to do, and feel your love for them.

chocolate

The food of the gods and something that is poisonous to cats. Chocolate is a psychoactive food made from the seeds of the tropical obroma cacao tree. It was a favourite food of Jeanne Calment, super-centurian (1875– 1999). Dark chocolate contains phenols, which help purify the fats in the blood. Apparently, fifty per cent of women prefer chocolate to sex! (According to Dr Tony Hughes' secretary Jane.)

churchill, winston

Our great wartime hero suffered from what he described as his 'black dog'. He was a depressive despite his courage, strength and charisma. It was even mooted that he might have suffered from a mild form of manic depressive illness. In his biography, *Churchill's Black Dog*, psychiatrist Dr Anthony Storr alluded to the concerns of his staff that if they had gone ahead with some of Churchill's more excessive ideas disaster might have ensued. However, with his past grandiose personality and expansiveness perhaps this was a character trait rather than a psychopathy. As with another example of a warrior leader, Alexander the Great, how does one ascertain the 'norm' for these monumental figures from history? As a painter and brick-laying wall-builder Churchill attested to the value of quietly reflective, healing pastimes.

cobain, kurt 1967–1994

Founder member, singer and guitarist of the grunge band Nirvana. A talented and creative child, Cobain was diagnosed as 'hyperactive' and prescribed the amphetamine derivative Ritalin. Deeply affected by his parents' divorce at the age of seven, Cobain is alleged to have said that he never felt loved or secure again. After a series of relocations, and staying with various relatives, Cobain eventually settled in Seattle and channelled his energies into music. Troubled by continual insomnia and an unidentifiable stomach complaint, Cobain began self-medicating with drugs. By the late eighties, Nirvana were up and running and had released their first album *Bleach* and become recognized as the pioneers of the grunge sound that characterized the rest of the nineties, paving the way for other bands such as Pearl Jam. In 1992, Nirvana released the hugely successful album *Nevermind* and the single 'Smells like Teen Spirit'. Mass media attention followed with Cobain's photograph adorning numerous front covers of newspapers and magazines all over the world, and the album selling several million copies. The band rapidly became the voice of a disgruntled generation with many fans idolizing Cobain. Distinctly uncomfortable and depressed with the demands of such sudden and intrusive fame, Cobain turned increasingly to heroin. Despite marrying and having a child, the continuing rollercoaster success of the band placed Cobain under even greater stress, and in March 1994, he was admitted to hospital in a coma having attempted suicide. A week later, he enrolled in a Los Angeles psychiatric drug recovery centre. Thirty-six hours after admission, he bolted and ended his life with a single shotgun blast to his head. Heroin and valium were found in his bloodstream.

sad facts

- Two of Cobain's uncles had also taken their own lives.
- One of Cobain's favourite Nirvana songs was 'Lithium'.

cohen, leonard

A late starter (by today's youth-obsessed standards), Leonard did not enter the world of music until his mid thirties, after he had already established himself as a novelist and poet. Born into a middle-class Jewish family in the Montreal suburb of Westmount to progressive parents, the young Leonard was encouraged to express himself from an early age. He graduated from McGill University in 1955, where he majored in English. He then embarked upon a successful career as a poet and writer, and became as well known for his free lifestyle, involving many women and experiments with LSD (when it was still legal!), as for his writings.

A sufferer from depression since early adolescence, when a sadness which Cohen attributes to an unexplained 'biological reason' afflicted him, he experimented with an impressive array of drugs, from prescription to illegal. This culminated in 1993 with a decision to devote his time to the Buddhist faith, and live at the Zen Center on Mount Baldy in California. He stayed there until January 1999, when he came down and settled in Los Angeles.

Of his decision to move to Mount Baldy: 'I was interested in surrendering to that kind of routine. If you surrender to the schedule, and get used to its demands, it is a great luxury not to have to think about what you are doing next.' (www.observer.guardian.co.uk)

On his realization that the 'veil of depression' had lifted: 'There was just a certain sweetness to daily life that began asserting itself ... I said to myself, "wow, this must be like everybody feels." Life became not easier but simpler. The backdrop of self-analysis I had lived with disappeared.

It's like that joke: "When you're hitting your head against a brick wall, it feels good when it stops."' (www.observer.guardian.co.uk)

On depression: 'Depression and melancholy are the worst kind of sleep and although we have to have experience with these kinds of emotions, they do cripple if they become chronic. So it's our responsibility to ease ourselves out of those conditions and the conventional methods are indicated. Conversation, wine, entertainment, a friend who flatters you – anything to break the gloom is valuable.' (www.observer.guardian.co.uk)

comfort zone

For those not in a crisis period, pushing oneself out of the 'comfort zone' can be very healthy. Try and go a little further than usual to test your limits. Jump out of a plane – preferably with a parachute on – go rock-climbing, bungee-jumping (God forbid!) or do an outward bound course. These things stir up the system and hold off depression. For those less physically inclined, join a theatre group, especially if you are terrified of performing! But if the stage fright really is too much, join to do the stage management, help with the costumes, the makeup, the lighting. Or learn a musical instrument. Anxiety, fear and depression are all interlinked. As they say Down Under, 'Go for it'!

co-morbidity with alcohol and other drugs

There is a considerable overlap with addictive behaviour. This may be in terms of individuals trying to self-medicate, feeling that alcohol will lift their mood in depression and their reduced sense of worth, or the excitement of adding further 'liberation' in hypomania from alcohol, cocaine, ecstasy, etc. While there are plenty of manic depressives who do not need alcohol or drugs to see that raw mania is a totally clear-cut malady in itself, the combination can lead to the over-diagnosis of manic depression, especially where admission to hospital is necessary and insurance involved. (See **Insurance and Employment**, page 217.)

'You're such a control freak!' An accusation that covers a whole range of behaviours from insisting on hospital corners when making the bed to behaving like a tin-pot dictator of a small South American country.

Do you recognize yourself in any of the following?

- Someone who can't live with crumbs in the kitchen.
- Someone who can't be driven in a car by anyone else.
- Someone who must have charge of the TV remote – 'Herr Flick'.
- Someone who develops a baleful expression when their plans might be altered.
- Someone who wants to ring and not be rung.
- Someone who not only thinks but deep down knows they will make a better job of barbecuing the sausages/cleaning the windows/speaking to the bank manager than absolutely anyone else.
- Someone who HAS to be right.
- Someone who continually interrupts or finishes other people's sentences.

It is easy to confuse the need to be in control with feeling one is right. It can mask deeper issues such as fear of uncertainty and unpredictability, having fragile self-esteem, having a low tolerance to perceived stress, or simply being a perfectionist. Control and perfectionism in many ways are from the same stable – and the sad thing is that perfectionism is often the enemy of an enjoyable life/job/relationship. On some levels being a 'control freak' is a very effective characteristic. If there is a job to be done and someone's got to be in charge – a film needs to be made or a wedding planned – then sometimes this is often the only way the deadline is going to be met. However, if in the process all the actors vow never to work with you again, or the parents-in-law feel insulted and sidelined – then clearly being a control freak comes with a rather negative price.

coping mechanisms

Coping mechanisms are the methods that we use to manage the discomfort and difficulties that result from the complexity and contradictions that are part of being human. Everyone uses coping mechanisms of one sort or another. Some are more effective than others. The best coping strategies are flexible, adaptable and sensitive to what's going on in our surroundings.

Coping mechanisms include talking to friends; displacement activities such as going to a film; compensating for a weakness in one area by developing skills in another; imagining how someone else might deal with a situation and copying them; idealizing one thing in order to avoid looking at the limitations of something else; fantasizing in order to escape grim reality; denying that there is a problem; making jokes about something serious; projecting one's own weaknesses and unpleasant emotions onto others.

The trick is to become aware of which strategies you use most often; assess how effective they are; and if necessary develop strategies that help reduce stress and also support your own well-being and the well-being of those around you.

counsellor

A counsellor (who is sometimes also a psychotherapist and vice versa) is usually someone taking a non-judgemental, empathic stance, who helps people think through and move towards making decisions around how to solve difficulties. They may work using different models of counselling practice (see **Therapists,** pages 298–303)

how to find a counsellor

Your GP practice may have an in-surgery counsellor and you may be referred via your GP.

ANYONE can call themselves a counsellor, so personal/professional recommendations should be taken and/or professional bodies consulted, as training levels may vary considerably.

website

British Association of Counselling and Psychotherapy (www.bacp.co.uk)

depression

what it is

'The black cloud', 'I just feel so sad', 'It's like wading through mud', 'A feeling of utter hopelessness', 'Everything seems pointless', 'It's all such a struggle', 'I'm useless'.

Everyone feels a bit low or 'down' once in a while but depression is quite different, often making it a struggle to get on with even the simplest tasks in your life. It is a recognizable illness marked by a prolonged period of low mood, sadness and feelings of apathy that has a significant impact on day-to-day life and its enjoyment and that lasts for more than a month. Sadly, untreated depression can be a killer disease with the major proportion of the 4000 suicides a year in England being attributed to depressive illness.

what it isn't

Depression is often called the 'common cold' of psychiatry. ANYONE can experience depression – even your GP! However, it is a condition that can be difficult for others to understand. People who have not experienced depression may tend to dole out platitudes – such as 'Pull yourself together', and so on. Depression is NOT a passing feeling of low mood or sadness. NEITHER is it a sign of 'weakness' or lack of 'machismo'. It is not a sign of 'madness', whatever you think 'madness' is. Depression is sometimes referred to as 'clinical' depression – this just means depression needing treatment. The good news is that, in the vast majority of cases, depression is highly treatable.

how depressed people think, feel and behave

Depressed people typically have a negative view of themselves, people around them, their environment and the future. They have often stopped enjoying things that they used to like. A depressed person might ask you, 'Why does everything bad happen to me?', they may tell you that they're a 'failure', that everything is 'meaningless' or that everyone else is awful or that there is no hope for the future and everything looks bleak. Depression colours your thoughts – painting them shades of grey/blue right through to black. These negative thoughts keep the depression going and part of many treatments and/or self-help is likely to look at ways of recognizing and challenging patterns of negative thinking. Depression influences the way you behave – if everything is pointless and hopeless and everyone is awful, what's the point in doing anything, seeing anyone? Depressed people often tend to do very little – although sometimes they will overdo things in order to avoid thinking. Depression 'takes' everyone in different ways.

the symptoms of depression

Typically the symptoms of depression, as identified by medical professionals and mental health team workers include: changes in appetite; suicidal thinking; hopelessness; lack of motivation; sleep difficulties; early morning waking – e.g. waking around one to two hours earlier than usual and not being able to get back to sleep; feeling sad; loss of self-worth; loss of interest in other people; loss of interest in sex; difficulties in making decisions; memory difficulties; feelings of guilt, worthlessness and emptiness; difficulties concentrating; unexplained physical symptoms; a change in alcohol intake (ideally don't drink alcohol if you're depressed – it can seem like a good idea at the time but remember it's actually a depressant! That's why we lose our inhibitions when we're a bit 'tipsy'!); feeling anxious; taking street drugs to excess.

types of depression

Depression is thought of as having levels of severity and causes. Some people refer to 'reactive' or 'exogenous' depression which is usually directly related to an external event. 'Endogenous' depression is a term for a depressive episode for which, initially at least, no clear precipitating factors can be identified. Depression is often classified by professionals as being mild, moderate or severe with one of the major defining factors being the impact of the illness on a person's life and relationships. Some people experience dysthymia, a mild form of depression, usually lasting two years or more, marked by a pervasive feeling of low mood and general unhappiness. Many people will experience just one or two episodes of depression over a lifetime. Others may experience more than three episodes of depression over a lifetime – which may be considered as 'recurrent' or 'chronic' depression. Depression is also part of what is called manic depression which is marked by significant mood swings – cycling through periods of mania and depression. Depression with periods of mania is often called bipolar depression. Occasionally people can experience an episode of psychosis with depression, particularly with severe depression.

confusion!

People are often confused about depression in that it can be associated with other psychological disorders – you can, unfortunately, for example, be depressed AND anxious, have alcohol problems AND be depressed and so on. Sometimes one difficulty keeps another one going.

triggers for depression

Triggers for an episode of depression might include: the loss of a job; extended grief following a bereavement; stress; the birth of a child (post-natal depression); work stress; lack of social support (for example, following a house move); relationship difficulties; physical illness; and the weather (Seasonal Affective Disorder (SAD)). Sometimes the trigger is not clear and the depression just seems to 'come out of the blue'. There are a number of factors that may make certain people vulnerable to depression.

what makes some people vulnerable to depression?

At present, it is considered that there is a genetic as well as a learned element to depression and a glance through one's own family tree might show a pattern to depression – which may indicate both genetic and learned factors. 'Grumpy Old Grandpa' may well have been suffering from depression which may have had a genetic element but may also have given his child a pervasive feeling that 'the world is rather a miserable place', and so on. All is not lost – it's quite possible to break the cycle! Other factors considered to render one vulnerable to depression include: poor social support; difficult/abusive early experience; and low self-esteem. It is well recognized that disturbances in the action of neurotransmitters contribute to triggering and maintaining, and in turn are maintained by, depressive illness and the majority of anti-depressant medications work on neuro-transmitter action.

lifespan, gender and depression

It can be useful to think of lifespan, gender, transitional and development issues when thinking about depression. Postnatal depression is linked to the period after the birth of a child and can be a debilitating and upsetting illness, at a time when most people would expect to be feeling particularly happy. Difficulties negotiating times of transition and hormonal changes can both contribute to triggering a depressive episode. Some illnesses, such as Alzheimer's disease, kidney disease, low thyroid function and viral illnesses, for example influenza and herpes, cause depression and it is always worth considering other illnesses when making the diagnosis. Many medications cause depression as a side effect (always read the accompanying literature with prescription drugs). This is why your GP may consider a physical examination and perhaps blood tests before recommending a treatment package. Whilst it is commonly known that a greater number of women present with depression, there is some evidence to suggest that this may be because men are less likely to present to professionals with depression for a number of reasons.

Unfortunately, for many people the idea that their depression is other than a physical illness treatable by anything other than medication, or indeed needing no treatment at all, is difficult. It should be noted that the National Service Framework recommends that the optimum treatment package for depression would be a course of medication alongside a course of cognitive behavioural therapy.

when to get help

If you have been feeling low in mood for more than a month, are finding that your mood is impacting significantly on your life and are experiencing symptoms of depression as described above (nobody will by any means have all of them!) you should talk to someone else about it and consider contacting your GP. Some professionals, confusingly perhaps, refer to some of the symptoms as 'biological' symptoms which serve to help to confirm a 'definite diagnosis' of depression. Certainly, a pattern of early morning waking, loss of libido, sleep difficulties and change in appetite would indicate to most professionals that their client is unwell with depressive symptoms. You should seek help immediately if you are experiencing suicidal thoughts, with your GP being your first port of call. (See **Suicide**, pages 295–7.)

how to get help

It's true that many people with depression get better without intervention. Nevertheless, it's important that you don't feel you have to 'grin and bear it' or 'put on a brave face' – there is help available and nobody should feel they have to go through this debilitating illness alone.

People with depression will need varying degrees of help. The NHS has recognized the importance of timely and appropriate interventions for depression. The NICE (National Institute for Clinical Excellence) guidelines (www.nice.org.uk – a website well worth looking at) recommend a stepped care approach with the initial three (of five steps) right up to moderate and severe depression being primary-care based (e.g. GP-surgery based). A Community Mental Health Team referral is recommended at Stage 4 for, for example, 'atypical' depression, complex difficulties, a high level of risk (e.g. of killing yourself or harming others), psychosis with depression or 'treatment-resistant' depression.

Often the thing to do is to talk to someone close to you – they might even have recognized changes in you and be worried about you already.

Once you, or those around you, have recognized that you are ill and have plucked up courage to seek help, there is an excellent chance that you will get better a lot quicker than if you left it to 'Old Father Time'. Remember, many GPs, film stars, shop assistants, company directors will have had, or will experience, an episode of psychological illness in their lifetime – it's just that, perhaps unfortunately, not many people talk about it.

Your first port of call should, ideally, be your GP. Remember a GP has around seven minutes per consultation and you need to be clear about exactly how bad you feel and what your symptoms are. Try to give him/her all the information you can, maybe bringing a list of symptoms to the meeting. It might be helpful to take someone along with you to the surgery. If the initial consultation doesn't go quite as you planned – maybe your GP doesn't seem to understand – don't worry or lose hope; make another appointment or, if there is one, try another GP in your surgery. Some GPs are much more psychologically minded than others and it may be worth finding one you feel you work well with. But remember, GPs are trained to recognize and treat the symptoms of depression so you should be able to get the treatment you need.

what kind of help is available?

You and your GP can consider the options which may include medication and/or psychological therapy, a referral to the Community Mental Health Team, or perhaps, initially, a brief 'wait and see' or 'watchful waiting' approach. A referral to the CMHT would normally be offered after a period of GP-based treatment and consultation, if things are not moving forward for you after some time of surgery-based treatment. In very severe long-term or chronic cases you may be offered ECT – electro-convulsive therapy – following onward referral from your GP. This was once the stuff of *One Flew Over the Cuckoo's Nest* nightmares but times have moved on. Whilst nobody knows precisely how it works, ECT has been shown to have a positive effect in ninety per cent of cases. Much more typically, you may start on a course of anti-depressant medication. It's important to note that anti-depressant medication takes a few weeks to take effect. Be cautious as always when responding to press articles about medications and discuss these with your GP before making any decisions.

onward referrals – what else might happen after a visit to your GP

If you are lucky enough to live in an area with in-surgery psychological help or counselling available you could then be offered a short course of counselling/psychotherapy to help you look at ways of understanding and working your way out of/coping with depression. Alternatively, you may be referred to your local Community Mental Health Team. Your local CMHT can make onward referrals if necessary, for example for highly specialized psychological treatment. The referral from your GP surgery will usually be allocated to an appropriate member/members of the CMHT who are all likely to have been trained in mental health issues, regardless of their title. Normally you would then be 'assessed' by a member/members of the team and the most appropriate care package (referred to as the Care Plan Approach (CPA)) would be worked out between yourself, your carers (if appropriate) and members of the team. This may include 'talking treatments'/psychotherapy. It is possible, also, that at any stage various types of self-help literature might be recommended to you to work through (either on your own or with support) and in some areas there are opportunities to use computer-based self-help programmes. Sometimes, group psychotherapeutic treatment is offered. In cases of severe depression the norm is to use hospital as a last resort and to work towards building a care programme for you in the community.

help outside the statutory services – i.e. the NHS

There are, of course, non-statutory agencies that you can involve in your care either in addition to or, sometimes, instead of the care you might be offered within the NHS. You can also seek private psychiatric and psychological treatment. Again, you should think about discussing a private referral with your GP. On another note it is important to check what will and will not be paid for before doing this if you have health insurance – some insurers put a limit on psychological treatment. In terms of psychological help there are many private psychologists, psychotherapists and counsellors available with varying levels of fees. You can also consider a referral to a private psychiatrist after a discussion with your GP.

complementary medicine and 'helping yourself'

You may also think about complementary medicine such as taking fish oils or St John's Wort, visiting an acupuncturist, and so on. Again, it is worth discussing these interventions with your GP.

St John's Wort is a mild herbal anti-depressant available from pharmacists without a prescription in the UK. It can be useful, but nonetheless it can still lead to hypomania and it does interact with a number of other medications.

It can be hard to have good insight into depression. Long-standing depression can be as unremarkable as the wallpaper; some people just feel a bit low all the time and like to try to help themselves. By all means try St John's Wort, but remember that you will not be able to get it on prescription. It is still important to have some experienced input into your mental health, possibly from your GP, your psychiatrist or your community psychiatric team. Finally, you will have to pay for St John's Wort but for some people it is worth the price so they *feel* in control.

Certainly, there are many ways you can improve your chances of a speedy recovery including:

- Taking exercise
- Cutting out/down alcohol/street drugs

- Building positive activities into your day
- Eating well
- Cutting down caffeine intake
- Drinking plenty of water
- Talking to others
- Seeing other people
- Sorting out any physical problems
- Taking care of your appearance
- Taking up yoga, etc.
- Recognizing and challenging negative thought patterns.

depression and those around you

Depression is a difficult illness both for those experiencing the debilitating effect on their physical and mental well-being and for those around them. It is, for example, sometimes difficult to even think of a time when you felt happy. Others may feel they have forgotten what you are like when you do not have depressive symptoms. It is important for those who are spending long periods of time with someone who is depressed, as well as offering understanding, patience, listening and support, to make time for themselves – to nurture themselves and to remember that depression is an illness that, in the vast majority of cases, will pass. If the person you care for has been referred to a CMHT, you can also request a carer's assessment which may be helpful.

keep trying

The first step in fighting depression is recognizing it and deciding to seek help. Sometimes getting help can be difficult in itself and you may need to keep trying. You are not alone. Depression is, in the majority of cases, eminently treatable, and the sooner you can begin to access help, both social and professional, the shorter this debilitating illness is likely to last.

the depression alliance

The Depression Alliance provides relief from and prevention of depression by providing information, support and understanding to those who are affected by it.

contact
35 Westminster Bridge Road, London SE1 7JB
Helpline 0845 123 2320

email
information@depressionalliance.org.uk

website
www.depressionalliance.org

the depression alliance may help by:

- *Local support:* They have a national network of self-help groups, which help people affected by depression to share experiences and coping strategies with others in similar situations. Group meetings are not the same as therapy but many people find they gain from the support and understanding of fellow members. New people are always welcome. To find your local group there is a list of addresses and contact email and telephone numbers on the website. Groups vary in size and frequency of meeting. Some may meet weekly or monthly and in various locations. Most groups operate an introduction system where each member gets about five minutes to introduce themselves. However, you don't have to speak if you don't want to. Each group has an organizer. It is important to know that the Group Organizer is not a trained therapist and may be suffering from depression themselves.
- *Publications:* Their website has a range of leaflets, posters, tapes and videos.
- *Pen Friend Scheme:* You can write to someone who understands. The Depression Alliance can put you in touch with someone through this scheme, details of which are on their website.
- *DA Talk:* This is operated through yahoo! and is a membership-restricted forum, which serves as a self-help group. You can join this scheme through their website.

diagnosis

Diagnosis is the smart medical term for working out what's wrong with a patient and giving it a label. Technically, it is the act or process of identifying or determining the nature and cause of a disease or injury through evaluation of patient history, examination and review of laboratory data. From the patient's perspective, having a diagnosis means that the doctors know what is going on, which brings with it hope of treatment and cure. Diagnosis authenticates illness. By comparison, without a diagnosis, there is no rational treatment; a lack of credibility; and without other patients to identify with, it can be difficult to make sense of the experience of illness. The relief of getting even the direst diagnosis frequently outweighs the uncertainty of the unnamed symptoms. Finally, just about every insurance and state benefit depends on getting a recognized diagnosis.

Essentially, a diagnosis is a label. In physical medicine a large number of tests and investigations help confirm and track the progress of an illness. In psychiatry, there is not a single diagnostic test, or an objective way to confirm or refute a diagnosis. A psychiatric diagnosis depends entirely upon the opinion of one or more psychiatrists. This is in contrast to the way that a blood test confirms anaemia or a swab from a wound or sore throat can help decide which antibiotic is best.

Psychiatric diagnoses are defined within a large book called *DSM IV*, which is an internationally agreed catalogue of symptoms and behaviours. A psychiatric diagnosis describes a pattern of symptoms and behaviours but it does not explain how the individual came to have those particular symptoms or behaviours. Given our present understanding, it seems likely that each psychiatric diagnosis covers a number of conditions; for example, the diagnosis of manic depression is attached to people with a variety of precipitating events including stress, head injury, medical and non-medical drugs, family tendency, a wide range of symptoms and of behaviours and experiences.

diary

Keep a diary yourself and suggest to your closest carer that they do so as well. You can discuss it with your therapist/psychiatrist/group at meetings. You will then not have forgotten incidents, feelings and questions as they arise out of the blue.

DIARY

Writing a diary has a long and honourable tradition. It is a place to safely explore moods and emotions. By tracking one's daily mood, it is possible not only to learn better how one feels but also what causes those feelings and how to manage them more effectively.

Even if you are not suffering from any mental health issues, keeping a diary is a good way of recording and expressing your dreams, inner fears and hopes. Writing things down can often be an excellent way of shedding light on psychological or emotional problems that appear to baffle us.

In either situation, it is also a good way to monitor one's progress as one's confidence returns and understanding of what has happened grows.

diet

When we are depressed we either eat too much or too little. We eat for comfort, or we have no appetite as we are so miserable.

If you can face up to it, even feeling so wretched, try eating at least some 'healthy' things – go and buy some fresh vegetables, fruit, fish. In general, if you can train yourself to eat well when you feel well it will help carry you through the bad times. Don't just go for the tinned food, the take-away, the snacks. Go to the market, where you will get better value. Try and get local produce, the stuff the supermarket won't buy because it isn't round enough, or flat enough. Go to the market at the end of the day to get reduced prices. 'Organic' carries the stamp of health but is expensive, and may not be relevant; after all, it is a stamp of diminished value now – with the 'organic' take-away, the 'organic' bar of chocolate. Tinned foods and pre-packaged foods are a damned sight better than no food, but they usually contain too much salt and sugar, not enough of the vitamins fresh foods would provide and artificial taste enhancers to make you want more.

It is easy to get overweight if you're depressed and the two then inter-weave – low self-image leads to eating and eating leads to low self-image.

Try and break the cycle. Sometimes it's easier to DO something rather than STOP doing something. Go to the gym and start getting fitter and then eat better when you've started feeling the benefit. It doesn't take genius to eat better, prepare wholesome food or cook something halfway healthy, and, once taste buds have readjusted, it tastes much better anyway … what you call a win-win situation.

quick nutritious and comfort meals

- Bananas and custard
- Rice pudding with strawberry jam
- Porridge oats with brown sugar/maple syrup/honey and milk
- Ham and mushroom omelette with buttered toast
- Baked beans on fried bread or toast

meal ideas to boost serotonin and protect against stress

Tryptophan is an amino acid (protein-building block) which, amongst other functions, is converted into serotonin. Tryptophan-rich foods include meat, fish, eggs, cheese, milk, yoghurt, nuts and vegetables such as peas, beans and lentils. Particularly rich sources are turkey, cottage cheese and game. Marmite, bananas and chocolate are good sources of tryptophan, which is important in fighting off depression. Eating whole carbohydrates such as wholemeal bread, brown rice, brown spaghetti, jacket potatoes and porridge oats alongside tryptophan-rich foods helps to force the tryptophan to turn into serotonin. Foods which do not contain tryptophan are fats and oils, sugar and alcohol.

Breakfast

- Wholemeal toast with poached egg and grilled tomatoes
- Live yoghurt with chopped fruit and sunflower seeds
- Porridge with maple syrup, milk and fruit of choice
- Yoghurt with rice puffs and berries
- Grilled bacon with mushrooms, onions and tomatoes

Light meals

- Mixed green herb salad with crumbled feta cheese and walnuts
- Baked jacket potato filled with sweetcorn and salmon bound with hummus
- Thick lentil and vegetable soup
- Beans on rye toast
- Sardines on wholemeal toast

Main meals

- Kedgeree – smoked fish, rice, peas and onions
- Beans in spicy tomato, garlic and onion sauce with couscous
- Pasta or noodles with mushroom and seafood sauce

- Salade Niçoise with tuna, egg, salad, olives, herb olive oil dressing
- Chicken and coriander curry with brown rice
- Grilled mackerel, gooseberry sauce, chips and peas
- Grilled salmon with cooked spinach
- Sausage casserole with tomato sauce

Snacks
- Crackers with pâté/hummus
- Oatcakes with nut butter and strawberry slices
- Mixed fruit and nuts

website

www.foodandmood.org.uk

disinhibition

Disinhibition is literally the opposite of inhibition, and a state where normal social restraints of behaviour are lost. People grow merry with alcohol as the alcohol first anaesthetizes their inhibitions, then their ability to hold a conversation, before finally it removes their ability to stand upright or make their way home unassisted.

One of the early signs of hypomania and mania is loss of inhibition. The personality of the person with manic depressive disorder changes, as they at first become the life and soul of the party. As hypomania progresses there is further disinhibition; the individual may engage in extremely frank conversations with colleagues and complete strangers, and become over-familiar with people he or she would normally be highly respectful of. The individual will then most likely spend extravagantly, run around starting numerous tasks, act on every impulse, become sexually promiscuous, irritable, and unable to concentrate for more than a couple of minutes as thought processes become increasingly disorganized.

drake, nick

The acclaimed singer-songwriter Nick Drake was born in Burma in 1948 and brought up in England in the Vale of Coventry. Educated at

Marlborough, he attended Cambridge University for two years before dropping out to pursue a career in music.

Discovered and nurtured by British producer Joe Boyd, Drake was signed by Island Records. During his short career, Drake's three albums received some critical acclaim but had disappointing sales. His music was compared to Van Morrison, Tim Buckley and Leonard Cohen.

Drake was intensely shy and prone to depression, and his reputation rested on his outstanding guitar playing, personal and poetic lyrics and the intimacy of his vocal performance.

By late 1974, Drake was so disillusioned by his lack of success that he abandoned his last set of recordings, including the bleak premonition of death in 'Black-Eyed Dog' and decided to give up music and live in Paris. Having started to learn French, he tragically took an overdose of anti-depressants and died on 25 November. Some say he took the overdose by accident. 'I always said that Nick was born with a skin too few,' actress Gabrielle is alleged to have said about her brother.

Nowadays, Drake is recognized as a hugely influential artist and his catalogue contains some of the era's most accomplished music, including *Five Leaves Left* (Island 1969), *Bryter Layter* (Island 1970), *Pink Moon* (Island 1972).

dreams

Dreams can be a valuable tool in the awareness of our mental health – and can be used to probe our unconscious minds. They are often a way in which we can stand inside our minds. Some people believe they can provide a direct route to the source of our true wishes, desires, worries and vision of the truth. They were a basic tool of Freud in his psycho-analytic theory at the beginning of the last century, and are still used by analysts for exploring the unconscious.

Even if you think you don't dream, or don't remember your dreams, by trying to recall your dreams each day they will become more vivid and more easily remembered. Waking up and immediately writing down as much as you can remember of a dream will activate this particular pathway to the unconscious with practice.

Keep a dream diary by your bed to write in the moment you wake up in the morning.

book

Dreams, Memories and Reflections by Carl Gustav Jung

website

www.sleeps.com/dreams.html

drugs (pharmaceutical)

Three main types of drugs are used in manic depression: drugs to stabilize the mood; drugs to calm and lower mood in hypomania and mania; and drugs to improve and raise mood in depression. The number of drugs available for treating manic depression increases year on year, either as new drugs are specifically developed to treat mental illnesses, or as a result of discovering mood-altering properties of existing drugs. A number of anti-epilepsy drugs have proved particularly useful in manic depression.

There are three main types of drugs used in treating manic depressive disorder, as well as other, less common ones:

1   Mood stabilizing drugs
2   Mood lowering, anti-psychotic drugs
3   Anti-depressants
4   Sleeping tablets

1. mood stabilizing drugs

Three mood stabilizing drugs are prescribed for the majority of people with manic depression. These are lithium, valproate or depakote and carbamazepine.

These drugs are well established in treatment, relatively safe and almost certainly do not hold any unpleasant surprises for the future. Other newer drugs are constantly under development and review and can be used if a person has frequent further episodes whilst on standard treatment or the standard treatment is causing too many side effects.

For more information on lithium, see the **Lithium** section on pages 219–20.

Valproate, like carbamazepine (opposite), is used to treat epilepsy. However, it is also a mood stabilizer as well as having anti-manic properties. As with lithium, it not yet clear how valproate works. It can be effective when lithium has not been, either instead of, or in combination with, lithium. Side effects include weight gain and tremor.

Carbamazepine has mood-stabilizing properties and can be used together with or instead of lithium and valproate. Side effects include dizziness, intestinal upset and drowsiness, though it does have fewer side effects than most of the other drugs prescribed for manic depression. However, one rare side effect is a severe skin reaction and loss of white blood cells known as Stevens Johnson syndrome.

Newer mood stabilizing drugs include lamotrogine, and gabapentine. Lamotrogine and gabapentine were, like carbamazepine and valproate, originally prescribed for epilepsy and were found, like carbamazepine and valproate, to additionally reduce mood swings in patients with both epilepsy and manic depression.

2. mood lowering, anti-psychotic drugs

There are two types of drugs that lower mood and reduce mania. The first are the group of drugs variously known as 'major tranquillizers', 'anti-psychotics' or 'neuroleptics'. These drugs include haloperidol and chlorpromazine as well as the more modern, atypical anti-psychotics, such as olanzapine and quetiapine.

Major tranquillizers work by calming and lowering mood and reducing the delusions and hallucinations associated with mania and psychosis. Because there are fewer side effects with atypical anti-psychotics, generally people are more prepared to take them, particularly long term. However, there are two serious side effects associated with all of these groups. First, they are associated with significant weight gain, both because they increase craving for food and because they seem to have a direct effect on the metabolism, which makes people more susceptible to type 2 diabetes. It is important to be aware of this possibility and to avoid sugar and sweet foods as much as possible, whilst starting or continuing an exercise plan. Secondly, they can cause uncontrollable movements, such as chewing or facial tics. This is called 'tardive dyskinesia' and is extremely distressing. It may disappear when the drug is stopped but not always, so it is important to be aware of this and, if it happens, to stop the medication as soon as possible.

The second group includes all other drugs known to reduce mania. This includes lithium, valproate, and more unexpected candidates such as tamoxifen. For some people, benzodiazepine drugs such as diazepam and lorazepam help reduce mania, although benzodiazepines can equally well remove a person's last few remaining inhibitions and make mania and hypomania worse.

3. anti-depressants

Anti-depressants are designed to make someone feel better by improving their mood and energy levels. There are several different types of anti-depressants and if one is not helping, then it is worth trying different ones as they may be more effective. Anti-depressants take between two and six weeks to work and so patience is needed – they are not an instant cure.

There are a number of different types of anti-depressants.

- Tricyclics (TCAs)
- Selective Serotonin Reuptake Inhibitors (SSRIs)
- Selective Noradrenaline Reuptake Inhibitors (SNRIs)
- Monoamine Oxidaze Inhibitors (MAOIs)
- Others

Not everyone is helped by anti-depressants. In most studies, forty per cent of people respond to a placebo or dummy pill, whilst a larger proportion, between fifty and sixty per cent, respond to the active drug. This still leaves forty per cent or more of people with no benefit from anti-depressants. Some of these people will respond to a different anti-depressant, others will get better on their own and a few are extremely difficult to treat. Overall, many people do greatly benefit from anti-depressants. Other people experience significant side effects without a lot of improvement in their mood. In general terms, the best results come from a combination of drugs and psychological therapy, such as cognitive behaviour therapy.

TCAs (Tricyclic anti-depressants): 'Tricyclic' refers to the chemical structure of the drug. Tricyclic anti-depressants include amitryptyline, dothiepin and trimipramine.

Tricyclic anti-depressants are not often prescribed nowadays. Their main benefit is that they can be prescribed in small doses which can be helpful when someone is having a lot of side effects with SSRIs or other anti-depressants. Also, if someone has found a particular tricyclic anti-depressant helpful in the past, it can be useful to prescribe it again. In small doses at night, they can be helpful as painkillers, especially for chronic (long-standing) pain.

SSRIs (Selective Serotonin Reuptake Inhibitors): 'Selective serotonin reuptake inhibitor' refers to the chemical activity of the drug. SSRIs block the nerve cells from taking up serotonin, thus leaving more serotonin lying around so the person feels better. Or so the theory suggests. However, the actual effect of SSRIs is now thought to be more complicated than initial studies suggested. It almost certainly depends, at least in part, on nerve cells developing new connections and new serotonin receptors.

SSRIs include fluoxetine (Prozac), paroxetine and cipramil. SSRIs have largely replaced tricyclic anti-depressants as first choice for the medical treatment of depression. They are more effective, safer and seem to have fewer side effects. They are prescribed at a standard dose, which ensures adequate treatment. In general terms, anti-depressant treatment is generally more effective if it is combined with psychotherapy or counselling rather than relying only on medication.

SNRIs (Selective Noradrenaline Reuptake Inhibitors): SNRIs include venlaflaxine and reboxetine. These are another type of anti-depressant that act in a similar but different way to SSRIs. They can work when SSRIs have not. In general terms they are thought to be of more help in people who are slowed by their depression whereas SSRIs seem to deal better where depression is combined with anxiety.

MAOIs (Monoamine Oxidaze Inhibitors): MAOIs include mianserin (which does not have food restrictions), mobenclamide, phenelzine and isocarboxid.

MAOIs, like SSRIs and SNRIs, are named after the chemical effect they are thought to have. MAOIs increase the concentration of monoamines, which like serotonin make a person feel better. Although these drugs are effective, with comparatively few side effects, they are rarely prescribed, because they react with certain foods that contain tyramine. These foods include beans, cheese, red wine, chicken livers and preserved meat products, soy sauce and chocolate.

How long should I take anti-depressants for? This is a twenty million dollar question (or billion dollar question if you are a pharmaceutical company!). Medical teaching suggests that anti-depressants should be continued for at least six months and where depression is chronic or

DRUGS (PHARMACEUTICAL)

recurrent, for two or more years. However, in practice, a number of people who are prescribed anti-depressants probably don't need them. Their symptoms recover spontaneously within a few weeks and there is no good reason for them to continue anti-depressant therapy once their crisis is over. For those people with significant depression who are prescribed anti-depressants for a good reason and find them helpful, continuing anti-depressants for six months is reasonable. The brain needs to regain its equilibrium and learn to stay with a normal mood. It is best to come off anti-depressants when you are feeling as well as possible and able to face the challenges that changing medication might cause, rather than at the first possible opportunity.

Stopping SSRIs: Although anti-depressants are not technically addictive, even the most hardened drug company is now prepared to admit that there is a 'withdrawal syndrome' or 'anti-depressant discontinuation syndrome' that some people experience when they stop taking anti-depressants. The 'withdrawal syndrome' includes dizziness, sickness, feeling faint, balance problems, tingling and strange sensations in the muscles, flu-like symptoms, hallucinations, blurred vision, irritability, vivid dreams, electric shocks, anxiety and nervousness. To all intents, these symptoms can feel like a recurrence of the original depression, as well as the new problem of the person feeling completely dependent on their tablets.

It is important to realize that these symptoms are not the same as depression. The symptoms can be eased by changing to an SSRI with a longer 'half-life', such as fluoxetine (Prozac). Fluoxetine stays in the body longer so that there is a less abrupt jolt to the nervous system as the dose of drug is gradually reduced. The brain gets used to drugs and when the dose is reduced, initially the brain finds the change difficult to manage. However, the brain is adaptable and gradually, with perseverance and support from your doctor, it is possible to reduce and then stop SSRI medication.

4. sleeping tablets

Good sleep is a crucial part of self-management (see **Sleep**, page 291).

Lack of sleep causes hypomania. There may be a number of reasons for not sleeping which are not all related to manic depression, for example, too much caffeine, anxiety, impending exams, changing time zones and shift work (not recommended). Sleeping tablets can be invaluable, especially if sleep is the only change and there are no other signs of impending hypomania.

However, disturbed sleep is also one of the earliest signs of impending hypomania and mania. It may be possible to avert a hypomanic episode at this stage by restoring a normal sleep pattern using sleep and other self-management strategies. The need for sleep is urgent when there are other warning signs and triggers present that threaten an imminent relapse into hypomania.

Ideally, everyone with sufficient insight into their illness should carry their own stocks of sleeping tablets and major sedatives, for use when self-management techniques alone can no longer hold back impending hypomania.

Mild non-addictive sleeping tablets are available without prescription from the pharmacy. Unfortunately, the more effective a sleeping tablet, the more addictive it is and the more reluctant doctors are to prescribe them. Doctors not infrequently fail to understand the critical importance of sleep in manic depression and do not take insomnia seriously enough. This can make it more difficult to manage the condition at this stage.

The most effective sleeping tablets for people with manic depression are probably zopiclone and zolpidem. These have what is known as a 'short half-life', which means from a pharmacological perspective they are metabolized quickly by the body, so causing fewer problems in the morning. Sleeping tablets are never anything other than a short-term solution, as physical and psychological addiction can appear within four to six weeks. Within a very short period of time, the brain starts to think 'Why make the effort to go to sleep, when I can take a tablet that does the work for me?' This is along the same lines as 'Why walk when you can ride? Why stand when you can sit?' Put simply, if you don't keep exercising the skill of falling asleep it won't be long before your brain is no longer bothered to do it and has reached a state of addiction.

At this point, although it is enough to try a sleeping tablet for the first night, the best plan may be to add in an antipsychotic drug such as olanzepine or even haloperidol sooner rather than later. It can be difficult, as after weeks or months of monotonous lows a little bit of high can seem like a welcome and well-earned break. It is not easy to deliberately take a tablet that will extinguish the final glimmer of hope in a desperate, dull, grey world.

drugs (recreational)

The misuse, abuse or dependence on any recreational drug can seriously damage your mental health. Although an argument exists that anything taken in moderation can't be harmful, using drugs to pump yourself up, anaesthetize feelings of depression, shyness or lack of confidence, can often delay a diagnosis of the real problem and make you feel worse. Anyone who knows they have a mental illness or an addictive personality should exercise extreme caution where taking *any* recreational drugs is concerned.

amphetamines *(speed, whizz, uppers)*

Amphetamines were originally introduced into the UK in the 1930s as a treatment for colds, flu and hay fever.

The most common is speed – one of the most impure drugs in circulation – often mixed with talcum powder or bicarbonate of soda. Amphetamines were distributed during the Second World War among English, German, Italian and Japanese soldiers as a supplement to war rations. At the end of the war, the surplus flooded the streets and caused many addiction problems.

Medical use: Ritalin is an amphetamine-related drug used in the treatment of ADHD (Attention Deficit Hyperactivity Disorder). Amphetamines were used for weight loss but are no longer commonly prescribed.

Effects: Last for several hours – like an adrenalin rush, with breathing and heart rate increasing. Appetite is suppressed and users feel increased energy and confidence. Risk of dehydration with body temperature rising. It is most commonly found in the form of powder which is sniffed up the nose. Usage does not cancel fatigue and hunger but merely postpones them until the following day, when the user can wake up feeling lethargic, ravenously hungry and deeply depressed (the speed blues).

For obvious reasons, anyone suffering from a manic depressive condition should not consider taking speed.

amyl nitrate *(liquid gold, poppers)*

Originally, highly popular in the 1960s and within the gay community. It became quite popular again in the 1970s disco culture, and the rave culture of the 1980s and 1990s.

Effects: Gives a powerful burst of energy that lasts for a few minutes. Risk of strong headache, faintness and nausea, flushed upper body and relaxation of sphincters.

anabolic steroids

They affect growth and physical development, and are used to develop muscle tone.

Effects: Increased capacity to exercise or train, increased competitiveness. Aggressive feelings can continue up to twenty-four hours after consumption, and the use of anabolic steroids has been known to lead to violence and sexual abuse. There are many other side effects connected to long-term use: depression and paranoia; liver failure and erection problems amongst others.

barbiturates *(e.g. tranquillizers and sleeping tablets)*

Popular over thirty years ago as sleeping tablets, these were highly addictive. They were also claimed to have worse withdrawal symptoms than heroin and to carry an increased risk of accidental overdose when inebriated – which is quite possibly what happened to Marilyn Monroe.

cannabis

This was first documented as an herbal medicine used by the Chinese in the first century AD. Today its properties have been claimed to ease pain, nausea and vomiting in advanced stages of cancer treatment, AIDS and other serious illnesses.

With tetrahydrocarbinol the active ingredient, the drug has a disorienting effect that is either pleasurable, and may lead to the odd joyous giggle or even continued giggling, or very distressing, often due to excessive dosing in the unfamiliar, leading to unpleasant paranoia. It has recently been the subject of questioning as to whether this paranoiac effect will tip an individual susceptible to psychosis into frank schizophrenia. Professor Robin Murray at the Maudsley Hospital in London is an advocate of caution in this respect.

It is medically a very bad idea for anyone, but an even worse one for people with any mental health problems. The evidence for this is well documented, despite the present government's decision to downgrade this substance. The psychiatric wards are full of individuals who have taken a joint too many and found themselves joining the ranks of the

DRUGS (RECREATIONAL)

long-term mentally ill. Too much use, which for some is not very much at all, can lead to depression, psychosis, paranoia and anxiety.

Thanks to the entrepreneurial drive of some horticulturists there are new strains of cannabis/marijuana available known as skunk. These strains are much more powerful than those that were available just a few years ago. For added effect these are sometimes mixed with other illicit smoking materials, which are very addictive and may lead to using class A drugs. Even if users don't end up as inpatients on a psychiatric ward, they can become seriously addicted.

If this happens, then life becomes an exciting whirl of trying to beg, borrow or steal enough money to feed the addiction. Any spare time is spent waiting for hours on the local pushers who seem to enjoy treating their customers like dirt. This may lead to other problems and the life of a social outcast living on the streets. Sounds exciting and romantic when aged sixteen and first experimenting with drugs. The reality can be rather different. Frightening, lonely and cold are the adjectives most often used by those who have managed to survive.

Effects: Can make user feel relaxed, leads to increased appetite known as 'the munchies'. Other physical symptoms include decreased blood pressure, increased pulse rate and dry mouth. It heightens the senses and can produce a greater enjoyment of being with people, or conversely a deep introspection and often bouts of hilarity over the smallest things. Risks include impairment of short-term memory and concentration and tobacco damage from deep inhalation. An increasing body of research suggests long-term use can contribute to various mental health problems and the inability to live an effective life.

cocaine *(charlie, coke, snow)*

Extracted from the leaves of the coca plant in South America. Up until 1916, cocaine was openly on sale at Harrods under the label 'A welcome present for Friends at The Front'.

The long-term use of cocaine can cause serious mental health problems ranging from mild depression to the extremes of cocaine psychosis, in which the user has symptoms similar to schizrenia.

Effects: Increased confidence and energy, increase in body temperature, pulse rate and blood pressure – lasts around half an hour. After effects last quite a long time with depression and tiredness over a couple of days.

crack cocaine

Mix of powder cocaine, baking soda and water. It gets its name from the cracking sound it makes when it is being smoked.

Effects: Similar to effects of cocaine but more concentrated and shorter. Crack is highly addictive and will eventually lead to fatal heart problems, convulsions and damage to lungs. Heavy regular use will seriously affect mental health, making users restless, confused, paranoid and desperate.

DMT

Also known as businessman's lunch, it is a powerful hallucinogen in the form of crystals or oil. Usually smoked, it has fast-acting effects, an intense trip of up to half an hour. Blood pressure and pulse increase.

ecstasy

Also known as E and disco biscuits amongst others.

Man-made drug causing combined effect of amphetamines and hallucinogens.

Effects: The effects will last up to six hours, with an initial adrenaline rush followed by calm energy. Colours, music and emotions will be more intense with an increased feeling of empathy for people.

Affects body temperature and brings a serious risk of dehydration and overheating. Later flashbacks can occur, leading to great anxiety.

According to government statistics, about twenty people a year die from taking ecstasy, usually as a result of hypothermia and dehydration. Evidence also points to the fact that death can be caused by excessive consumption of water, diluting the body's essential minerals and salts in the process.

gamahydroxybutyrate or GHB

This is a colourless liquid with no distinguishing smell that is usually sold in small bottles, or in powder form as capsules. GHB has recently become popular in dance and rave culture and there is growing concern over its use as a 'date rape' drug.

GHB is also known as liquid ecstasy, liquid X and GBL.

heroin *(gear, smack, china white)*

Effects: Heroin is extremely addictive both physically and psychologically. A small dose will give an instant feeling of well-being; higher doses cause

DRUGS (RECREATIONAL)

drowsiness or unconsciousness. It suppresses pain, but causes a lack of concentration, sometimes anxiety and fear. Long-term use means more is needed for the user to just feel normal, and withdrawal symptoms (cold turkey) are unpleasant: hot and cold sweats, aches, vomiting, sneezing and spasms. These will pass after around three days.

Most of the heroin that is smuggled into the UK comes from Afghanistan. It is a very costly habit – up to £10,000 per year can be spent on the drug.

ketamine *(K, Special K, Vitamin K)*

An anaesthetic for use on humans but mainly by vets on animals. Street ketamine is sometimes sold as an alternative to ecstasy in tablet form.

Effects: Hallucinatory experiences lasting up to three hours, can also temporarily semi-paralyse the user. Suppresses pain.

LSD *(acid, trips)*

Aldous Huxley died after two deliberate overdoses of LSD (he had throat cancer). A powerful hallucinogenic drug, it is derived from a fungus found growing on rye and other wild grasses. In 1943, after accidentally swallowing some of this chemical, a US scientist documented the first LSD 'trip'.

Effects: The 'trip' (lasting up to twelve hours) is different each time and also depends on the individual taking it. Alters and distorts perception, movement and time. Trips can be enjoyable, but a bad trip can occur and there is no way to stop it once started – users can experience great fear, paranoia and disorientation. Later flashbacks can also strike without warning long after the drug was taken. In some cases, people have been known never to recover from a trip (acid casualties), and it can complicate depression and anxiety states long term.

magic mushrooms

Their use dates back thousands of years. They contain hallucinogenic chemicals – psilocybins – that distort sensory perception. They commonly cause nausea, but the user will either feel content or paranoid and anxious.

narcotics

Literal meaning is 'numbness or stupefaction'.

solvent abuse

Glues, aerosols, paint thinners, butane and propane gas.

Commonly believed to have originated in the punk era, glue sniffing actually started in the mid 1960s as a cheap form of intoxication amongst teenagers. Interest in solvent abuse can develop in children through something as simple as sniffing their mother's nail varnish or father's paint remover. Currently in the UK, there are thirty kitchen and bathroom products that can be legally abused. Similar to alcohol, addiction to solvents becomes greater with increased use. Some sniffers may become drowsy after indulging but others become aggressive and take more risks than they would ever take normally. Accidents are therefore common and sometimes fatal. The majority of deaths occurring from solvent abuse are due to inhalation of gas lighter fuel.

dual diagnosis

This is not a fight to the death between competing medical specialists; rather it describes a state where two diagnoses are believed to contribute to the patient's mental state. The other term is **co-morbidity** (see page 171). Some diagnoses seem to go together more than others, for example, alcoholism and manic depression, personality disorder with manic depressive disorder and/or an eating disorder. It is not clear why particular disorders are associated together.

eating disorders

anorexia

There are few people with completely healthy eating habits. The commonest eating disorders are anorexia, bulimia and compulsive overeating. (See also **Overeaters Anonymous**, pages 254–5.) Anorexia is a condition where individuals starve themselves. The Eating Disorders Association estimates that about 165,000 people in the UK have eating disorders with one in ten dying from their disorder or its complications and only sixty per cent recovering. Overall, eating disorders cause more deaths than any other psychiatric illness, if we include overeating resulting in obesity.

The modern fashion for ultra-skinny models may have affected the incidence of anorexia, and altered the way in which people perceive themselves. However, eating disorders are complex, with a number of likely causes including feelings of low self-worth; a dominant, over-protective and critical mother; a passive or withdrawn father; a tendency to perfectionism; a strong desire for social approval and overvaluing appearance; a need for order and control; an attempt to gain control over a chaotic world. Nonetheless, for each individual at some stage the beliefs and behaviours of anorexia gave them the means to cope with their environment.

Depressed young women are at risk of anorexia and anorexic women do get depressed. Any condition that leads to emotional exhaustion will lead sooner or later to depression.

Anorexia has both physical and psychological effects. Physically, lack of calories, vitamins and nutrition causes an emaciated appearance, with muscles wasting, prominent bones with fine downy hairs on the face and arms, cessation of menstruation and thin bones as a result of the loss of oestrogen. There are also heart and bowel problems.

The individual develops ritualistic food habits, becoming preoccupied with food, for example cooking but rarely eating; excessive chewing; denying hunger; exercising excessively; choosing low calorie food, especially diet foods; and finding a multitude of ways to conceal the extent of their self-abuse.

Even when the individual has determined to become well, treatment may not be that successful. It can include admission to a hospital unit for eating disorders, very rarely force feeding; group therapy; family counselling; psychotherapy; and anti-depressants. Around one third of patients recover fully; another third improve significantly and the last third do not recover. Without doubt it is hard to change deeply ingrained beliefs around food and survival. The mental and physical scars remain and the condition may flare up when the individual is stressed.

bulimia

Bulimia nervosa is a type of eating disorder, two to three times more common than anorexia, but physically not as dangerous. Nonetheless, laxatives and self-induced vomiting and starvation can cause rupture of the oesophagus, bowel problems, stomach disorders, mineral deficiency and dehydration, metabolic problems, irregular periods and polycystic ovaries. Excessive vomiting causes tooth decay, bad breath, mouth ulcers, sore throats and stomach problems.

Bulimia was only officially recognized in the 1970s and is characterized by a cycle of bingeing and starving. It can occur at any weight from the obese to the anorexic. People with bulimia have many of the psychological characteristics of those with anorexia but without their physical appearance. It is thought that up to half of anorexics also suffer from bulimia and some forty per cent of bulimics are reported to have a history of anorexia. People with bulimia tend to be older than anorexics, take a longer time to recover and are more likely to commit suicide.

Treatment for bulimia includes the use of anti-depressant drugs (there are often concomitant depressive symptoms), counselling which examines the cause of bulimic behaviour, and behavioural modification, including education about healthy eating.

book

Overcoming Anorexia Nervosa by Christopher Freeman

electroconvulsive therapy (ECT)

ECT is a physical procedure used to treat severe, treatment-resistant depression and, more rarely, extremely suicidal patients and patients with treatment-resistant mania. It is not known how or why it works, but it does. Approximately 100,000 people are treated each year. ECT consists of giving electrical shocks to the brain under an anaesthetic. It sounds far worse than it is. It is usually given in courses of six to twelve treatments. The risks of treatment are related to the anaesthetic, memory loss and confusion following treatment. Anti-depressant treatment is usually started before and continued after a course of ECT.

It seems to have an effect similar to rebooting a computer: at some point the depressive pathways are bypassed and a normal mood takes over. The worst long-term side effect is memory loss. This has three parts: a number of existing memories seem to be lost beyond recall; memories of the course of ECT and surrounding events are often not stored; and, subsequently, it is harder to remember things than before. This does improve with time. It also improves as the depression lifts.

Despite its bad reputation, it is an effective therapy, and for those with severe depression it can be a lifeline. For some people, it is the only treatment that seems to work. There are now well-defined guidelines to help decide whether ECT is suitable for an individual, so if your psychiatrist recommends it, then consider the offer.

It is, however, likely to become a treatment of the past in the not-too-distant future as more focused treatments become available. An example of this is 'direct brain stimulation' which is being researched now, involving focused energy targeting areas of the brain relevant to the problem, according to what is being revealed by neuroimaging (see pages 249–50).

esquirol, jean-etienne

Pupil of Falret (see page 205) in the 1800s in France who observed the frequent association of the greatest thinkers and manic depression.

There are those for whom the instinct for the horizontal life remains immutable … those for whom repose is the raison d'être … the physically unchallenged … the apotheosis of the Type B personality. The problem is that life has its own inexorable way of bringing on 'stress' … and one of the methods of counteracting this is by *moving*. There was always something in that law of Isaac Newton's, equal and opposite forces and all that, that implied a reaction was normal, rather than the absorption of stimulus into the adiposity of the soul.

Running down the front in Brighton at 7.30 on a cold January morning, the grey winter's light yet to come, in the blustery south westerly periodically bringing with it squalls of rain, I smiled at the thought of that as I felt a small slurry of seagull excrement coursing down my cheek. It brought back memories of rugby, playing on the wing at the age of fourteen, in the arctic wind, the lack of passes, the lack of will to break the ice with a tackle, the pathetic crossing of arms to harbour warmth, the inefficacious swinging of arms to engender it in the first place, through to the New Year's plunge in the North Sea at sixteen, well-hung-over, nowhere else though, with the water half a mile out … all the imposed or self-imposed discipline and pain of youth. TH

It's not that bad going to the gym, or going for a run or a bike ride or a game of football.

Exercise is NOT for other people, it's for YOU!

Do whatever you can. If you're feeling desperate walk up and down the stairs ten times or go six times round the block.

Put on an old pair of shoes or trainers and go for a run. If you're physically able, do it.

Go for a bike ride, a swim or to the local gym.

Go first, think later! You may not want to – it's irrelevant – go and do it. By the time you've started you can have a little think, but hopefully by that time it's too late and you might as well carry on.

Aerobic exercise, where you get hot, sweaty and out of breath is what you need to do if you're going to use this method to keep depression and anxiety at bay, and achieve a sense of well-being. It gets rid of the toxins and releases one's own endorphins (opiates from within that make you feel good). It oxygenates the mind and body.

Exercise with others if you can, but if you can't it's not an excuse! It's easier to arrange with just yourself.

Do it when you're well, in order to stave off future bouts of depression.

Do it when you're unwell (but not if you have a fever) and you'll probably feel better afterwards. Go *especially* at the most difficult times of your life – during unemployment, cancer, the outrageous office hours, the bust up of your marriage.

Integrate deep breathing exercises. They re-oxygenate the system, open the lungs fully, massage the bowel, suffuse the brain. There are three areas of the lungs to work on. Abdominal breathing can be practised with a towel tightly wrapped around the abdomen and forcing the abdominal wall against it. Use this when you breathe in. The diaphragm moves down and the abdomen *protrudes more during inspiration*. It is drawn *in* to exhale. The next is for the lateral chest wall and done by raising the arms to the sides (like chicken wings!) to create a bellows effect. The third is for the apex of the lung and can be achieved by short sharp breaths with the hands clasped above the head. These exercises are taught in martial arts, and included in yoga and Tai Chi.

There are scientific studies to support the value of exercise. A well-known one was that of James Blumenthal, published in 1999 in *Archives of Internal Medicine*. It was a comparison of exercise against anti-depressants. If you are considering stopping anti-depressants and taking up exercise it is important to talk this through with your doctor as many people have a better response from medications, and the two forms of treatment can be combined. A more recent study found benefit from exercising either three or five times a week.

Do it!

f

falret, jean-pierre

French psychiatrist who in the mid-nineteenth century described 'la folie circulaire', observing the simplistic swing between the high of mania and the low of depression.

family

'Can't live with them – can't live without them.' 'You can choose your friends but you can't choose your family.'

what is a family?

A family is any group of people who refer to themselves as a family and who care about and for each other.

Your family is an integral part of the system you operate in. How it works can be both helpful and unhelpful. Difficult family issues are likely to be affected by, and affect, the mental health problems of a family member. Families can be highly supportive.

A family's love and goodwill can be severely tested by the behaviour of a manic depressive sibling or parent. Enduring the anxiety and worry regarding repeated manic depressive episodes with the often disastrous financial and socially damaging consequences can cause irreparable rifts in families. Conversely, the recovery of such a family member can bring about a tremendous healing quality to a family as well.

help for families

GPs, CMHTs, non-statutory organizations and hospitals should always make themselves aware of the family situation when considering an individual's

FAMILY

problems. Your family may, with your permission, be asked to attend meetings with you. You and your family may also be offered specific family support/therapy.

top tips
- Remember this is a difficult time for your family too.
- Families of people with mental health difficulties are often entitled to additional help, so ask your GP, Citizens' Advice Bureau, MIND or CMHT.

book
Families and How to Survive Them by Robin Skynner and John Cleese

websites
Institute of Family Therapy (www.instituteoffamilytherapy.org.uk)
Association of Family Therapy (www.aft.org.uk)
MIND (www.mind.org.uk)

fear

> 'If we let things terrify us, life will not be worth living.'
>
> ***Seneca***

Fear doesn't just mean a dry mouth, sweaty palms and a beating heart. Fear can be so deep rooted within us, we are barely aware that it is there. Sometimes we have lived with fear for so long it has become part of our psyche and personality, and we have moulded our living habits according to its presence. Fear of uncertainty, commitment, the future, being hurt, taking risks, failure, being ridiculed, being seen, being alone. Fear is often the root cause of our addictions, mental ill health and unhappiness.

books
Feel the Fear and Do It Anyway by Susan Jeffers

Fish are a fantastic source of protein and good oils. White fish (plaice, cod, skate) are good but don't have the advantage of plentiful Omega 3 oils (see pages 253–4). The 'oily' fish are salmon, trout, mackerel, herrings, anchovies, sardines and pilchards. Tuna is a rich source, but being the top of the food chain receives all the accumulated impurities in its diet, such as mercury, so should not be eaten more than once a week.

Farmed fish have the advantage that they are not diminishing fish stocks, but they are open to contamination from infection in the farm, pesticides, etc. This may be to some extent a theoretical risk and the levels, for example, of dioxins in farmed salmon are not likely to cause cancer. Some farms are more eco-friendly with rotation of pens, etc.

The abuse of the oceans is going to be another of our planetary tragedies unless more care is taken. River estuaries are being destroyed by pollution. Overfishing is leading to species' survival being threatened. There are deep sea fish that should be entering our markets but not enough pressure is being brought to bear by the public to change supermarket acquisition. We must take care of our heritage!

g

gambling

Government research published in 2006 confirmed that British people are currently spending £1 billion every week on gambling and that at least 300,000 people are addicted to it. This situation has been attributed to the relaxation in British gambling laws, the opening of many more casinos, high pay-out slot machines and online gambling opportunities. Gambling is highly compulsive and differs from other addictions in so far as there is, however remote, the constant possibility of gaining a financial reward. One definition of insane behaviour is someone who keeps doing the same thing while expecting different results.

For those who find themselves betting far too often on an internet poker site, casino table, fruit machine, greyhound or horse racing track and discovering their finances and lives are being devastated as a result, Gamblers Anonymous offer a solution. (See **Twelve Step Programmes**, pages 305–7.)

genetics

Studying the life code we receive from our parents throws light on many psychiatric illnesses. Though unipolar depression does not have a strong genetic link, manic depressive illness does. There is strong inheritability in manic depression. Of a group of monozygotic (identical) twins, one of whom has manic depression, sixty per cent will also have a twin similarly affected. This is a high rate for an inherited condition (though there are conditions that are 100 per cent inherited) and many conditions would be regarded as having genetic inheritance with much less than this. One asks, 'Well, what of the other forty per cent?' This shows that even if you start life with exactly the same genetic recipe you have a good chance of NOT having the condition. What does this mean? It means that *environmental* influences are paramount in development.

One of the most important new findings in the world of genetics which has a huge relevance to us all is that every time the genes reproduce themselves, when the cells divide to produce the billions of our cells, they are affected at *each* stage by their *environment*. This does, in effect, hand back part of the key to our destiny to ourselves – WE CAN INFLUENCE OUR GENES. This is so important: if one can arrange one's life in a way that is healthier it will *reinforce* itself. So, even if a life has been torn apart by the ravages of severe mental disorder the individual can still pick up the pieces and move forward.

Interestingly, in a study performed by Nick Craddock, Professor of Genetics at Cardiff University, asking families if they would wish to test their children for manic depressive illness during childhood, *before* the onset of symptoms, the majority said yes, if a genetic test were available. It is quite likely to be available soon. The benefit of this knowledge in advance of the problem becoming apparent is that one can prepare for it by lifestyle modification and being alert for symptoms and behaviour patterns. The earlier a diagnosis is made the better.

gordonius

Fourteenth-century physician who made an early case study of bipolarity. He observed that a man whose skull had been fractured by a sword would become manic whenever the wound began to close, and return to his 'normal' state when the wound re-opened (though one must assume he remained a little aggrieved!). This is an early example of how physical causes were recognized in the study of the illness.

GP

your GP
Your GP is likely to be your first port of call if you are experiencing mental health problems. Everyone in Britain has a right to access a GP. If you are experiencing any illness, perhaps even more so with mental health-related illness, your relationship with your GP is one of the most important factors in your care.

visits to the GP for mental health difficulties

Thirty to thirty-five per cent of people on a GP's 'books' will require treatment for a mental health problem, such as anxiety. That can be anybody – your child's school teacher, your vicar, the local builder – anyone! Lots of people don't actually present with mental health problems – they'll present with physical symptoms for which no clear physical cause can be found. Fifteen per cent of people will visit their GP with what are termed 'hidden psychiatric' problems.

Depending on your GP's training and level of interest in psychiatric problems the outcome for this group of people can be very different. Ideally, your GP would be able to 'spot' signs of psychological distress early on.

when to visit your GP

Make an appointment whenever you and/or those around you think that the way you feel is getting on top of you and you are finding it difficult to carry out your day-to-day tasks.

what to do when you visit your GP

Tell him/her what the problem is. He/she will have seen loads of people with mental health problems – he/she might have experienced them personally. Don't be afraid to take someone else along with you and to take a list of symptoms. Remember your GP's typical consultation time is between six and eight minutes – if you've got a lot to discuss it might be worth asking for a double visit. If you feel the visit didn't go well you can ask for another appointment, ask to see another GP or ask to see a specialist in mental health problems.

how to access GP care if the patient refuses

It is difficult to get a GP to see someone against the patient's wishes. However, if you think the person is becoming very unwell, behaving in a way they would not wish to when they were well, seems unaware of being unwell or particularly if they seem to be a danger to themselves or unable to care for themselves adequately, you can contact your GP for a home visit. The GP may visit alone or he may ask a social worker/mental health worker and/or psychiatrist to visit with him (or without him). This is because he may feel the case warrants a second opinion and because it may, in some circumstances, be necessary to take the person to hospital under a section as outlined in the Mental Health Act (see **Sectioning**, pages 284–5).

what you can expect from your GP

Your GP may offer you treatment which will be likely to be medication and/or a referral for talking treatment which may be based within the surgery. You and he may, initially, decide to adopt a 'watchful waiting' approach to see if things get better on their own over a few weeks. Depending on the Primary Care Trust in which your GP is based you may be offered at the surgery: written or computerized self-help material; group therapy (see **Therapists**, pages 298–303); and counselling or psychotherapy (usually brief). Should you and your GP decide that it would be more appropriate for you to be referred to the CMHT and/or more specialized care he/she can arrange a referral. Your GP can also discuss how you can help yourself, and issues around complementary medicines, and can make referrals for private psychiatry and/or psychotherapy.

what to do if things aren't working with your GP

Some GPs are great with mental health problems, some not so great. Some are more interested in more physically based medicine and some lean towards an interest in psychiatric problems. Some seem to think that only medication works, some think only psychological treatment works. You probably need someone whose opinions are somewhere in the middle. If you are experiencing problems with your relationship with your GP talk to him/her about it. You can always ask for a different GP. It's worth speaking to other people to see who they recommend locally as a GP who is sympathetic to mental health problems.

Remember, though, that your illness may be clouding your judgement of the situation and it's well worth thinking about this. It could be helpful to take someone else with you to check out your opinions of the way you are being cared for.

groups

Groups such as the ones run by the MDF and AA are often really helpful, and can be vital. Don't allow the arrogance of thinking you are special or different from others to stop you from going.

h

hemingway, ernest

Hemingway's early life was spent in the Great Lakes region of Illinois, and this was reflected in his first collection of short stories.

Rather than going to college he became a newspaper reporter. This style provided 'the best rules I ever learned for the business of writing. I've never forgotten them.'

Hemingway fell in love with Cuba and moved there in 1939. He owned up to fifty cats – one was a six-toed cat given to him by a ship's captain – and their descendants live on at the Hemingway museum at his home in Key West.

Married four times, Hemingway had been a very heavy drinker throughout his life and suffered periodically from depression. In 1960, his dark mood was compounded by what he saw as his failing physical and artistic powers. He was hospitalized in Minnesota for treatment of depression, and released in 1961. During this time he was given electric shock therapy for two months. On 2 July Hemingway committed suicide by shooting himself at his home in Ketchum, Idaho.

recommended works

A Farewell to Arms, For Whom the Bell Tolls, The Old Man and the Sea, Islands in the Stream and short-story collections *In our Time, Men Without Women* and *Winner Take Nothing.*

hendrix, jimi

More superlatives have been heaped upon Jimi Hendrix than any other rock guitarist. One of music's most exciting and influential figures, he brought a unique vision to the art of playing the electric guitar. Few rock musicians have anything dedicated to them after their death. Thanks to the admiration of a computer magnate, the Experience Museum in Seattle, Washington, is dedicated to Jimi Hendrix. The legendary left-handed guitarist who played a right-handed guitar christened his first band Jimmy James and the Blue Flames and went on to play for Little Richard and the Isley Brothers. Moving to London in 1967, Hendrix formed the Jimi Hendrix Experience with Mitch Mitchell and Noel Redding. They went on to record three albums: *Are You Experienced?* (1967) which included the acclaimed 'Purple Haze'; *Axis: Bold as Love* (also 1967) and *Electric Ladyland* (1968), which included his version of Bob Dylan's 'All Along the Watchtower'.

The band broke up in 1969 but Jimi's star kept shining right up to his memorable appearance at the Woodstock music festival. Tragically, two weeks after that, he died in London from ingesting too much wine and sleeping pills. No evidence has ever been uncovered to show whether his song 'Manic Depression' held any special significance or not.

coincidence?

- Jimi Hendrix was born in Seattle, the same town as Kurt Cobain.
- Both musicians died when they were twenty-seven years old.

hobbies

Hobbies are a vital ingredient of mental health. The word hobby originates from 'hobyn' meaning a small horse, hence 'hobby horse'. The purpose of a hobby is to do something you enjoy, something that takes your mind off things, off you, and off whatever the rest of the world thinks.

Here is a list of favourite hobbies supplied by various manic depressives around the UK:

- Doing the crossword and solving puzzles
- Swimming and playing squash
- Collecting old tins and bottles
- Gardening and growing indoor vegetables such as tomatoes
- Beachcombing and selling discoveries on eBay
- Knitting and pottering round bookshops
- Cinema and writing film scripts

- Chess and Scrabble
- Fishing and walking
- Loud rock music and watching old comedy films.

homeopathy

This is based on the idea of treating 'like with like' that arose at the same time as Jenner did his work discovering the vaccine to prevent smallpox. This was taken further by the theory of serial dilutions, i.e. that the more dilute a treatment is the stronger it is. It is not the same as herbalism, in which extracts of plants are given in significant quantities and may indeed have physiological effects. Many of orthodox medicine's treatments arose from plant study.

Homeopathy should not be used for serious depressive or manic depressive illness (particularly bipolar 1). The consultations themselves, however, with homeopaths who have experience with mental problems, can be supportive as they usually can offer time to a patient, which is, of course, an invaluable commodity in caring for patients. If a patient is going to a homeopath because he/she is unhappy with their doctor, it is that relationship which should be examined, and if necessary a different medical team should be found, with better rapport between them and the patient.

hope

In both manic depressive illness and depressive illness there will be great progress over the next few years in treatments. This offers hope to the many sufferers who feel a sense of despair that there is little out there to help them, and such as there is has not worked. Several key areas of research include **hormones** (see page 215) and the neurochemical imbalances of brain cells involved in both illnesses, **genetics** (see pages 208–9) that will offer new diagnostic guidance and treatments, and **neuroimaging** (see pages 249–50) that will give new insights into areas of the brain particularly relevant to these illnesses. These will help sufferers regain control in areas of their lives, giving fresh starts. There will always be the need to face up to the responsibilities of having vulnerabilities, like everyone; they will not pay our rent or mortgages but the future holds promise, and mental health, historically the poor relation, will begin to consolidate the fruits of research and medieval attitudes will begin to change … the brain, and mental health, are the new frontiers.

hormones

Where neurotransmitters may act almost instantly to effect an action, hormones act more slowly by comparison. They may be seen as the background 'stage-set' for the body. They affect, for example, the speed of the body's metabolism (in the case of the thyroid), or support and control the female menstrual cycle (oestrogen and progesterone). There is a hormone that is known as the fight and flight hormone, adrenaline, which is released in situations demanding alert response.

Another hormone that has its own daily (circadian) rhythm is cortisol. One of its roles is in the system of defence against infection and response to stress. Its level goes up in times of stress. Normally, hormones have what is called a feedback cycle, whereby if too much is present in the bloodstream this level is registered and causes a reduction in its production. In 'chronic' (in other words long-standing) stress or depression the normal 'feedback' ceases to work and the levels remain high. This is an active area of research at present. Two hormones from within the brain itself that control the level of the cortisol in that cycle are called ACTH and VP. It appears that a problem with this mechanism can develop, and that the raised level actually damages the brain, not only being involved in the depression itself but also affecting 'executive' function and memory. Trials of blocking drugs are being done currently.

hypomania

Hypomania comes from the Greek words *hypo*, below, and *mania*, meaning to rave in anger. The Mania in Greek mythology were the Furies who pursued those who had committed unavenged crimes and drove them to madness. This is illustrated by the view of 'Those whom God wishes to destroy, he first makes mad,' Euripides (*c.* 485–406 BC). Thus from the Greek perspective, madness can be seen as punishment.

Hypomania is characterized by raised energy, increased spending, disinhibition, sexual promiscuity, a sense of importance and grandiosity.

i

incest

Incest is often at the root of shame-based mental illness and is still one of the biggest and yet unspoken about problems in our society today. Incest is defined as sexual relations taking place between a brother and sister, father and daughter, mother and son, uncle and niece, grandparent and grandchild, or half-siblings.

This type of 'sexual abuse' occurs in secret and is often kept secret by a family, thus denying aid or help to the molester or victim.

Incest is gaining sexual satisfaction from a relationship that is traditionally based on trust and instigated by someone associated with a protective role.

- Incest is an offence under sections 10 and 11 of the Sexual Offences Act 1956.
- Incest is more likely to occur where alcohol or drugs have dismantled the normal inhibitions in the individuals concerned.
- Incest can be an expression of psychosis, psychopathic disorder and organic brain disease (including senile dementia).
- Incest is most likely to occur where poverty and overcrowding compel families to live in intimacy; and where there is a breakdown of the sexual relationship between a husband and wife.

website

Sexual Recovery Anonymous (USA and Europe) (www.sexualrecovery.org)

insurance and employment

For those persons with private medical insurance, whether through their work or as an individual, there will usually be limitations on policies, for example there are pressures by private health insurance companies not to recognize 'alcoholism' treatment. This may be obviated by psychiatrists diagnosing 'depression' and the cover may be secured. In the NHS this is obviously not a problem – only the overall problem of insufficient funding for mental health.

Where an individual has insurance for a work project, of course a definitive diagnosis can be helpful rather than the unhelpful terms 'breakdown' or 'lifetime crisis', in order to receive compensation. If a manic depression sufferer has a first episode this can have major work consequences if as a result he/she were to lose their job (or were self-employed) and need to look for a new position. New employers would look upon a prospective employee in a poor light if he declared this. Of course, not declaring is against the law if a pre-employment declaration is signed, but it is obvious why some are economical with the truth.

Employers are not allowed to decline (in law) a prospective employee who is 'able to do the job', despite having a medical impairment, but it would be hard to challenge the employer on this. If an employee has time off work during their employment, obviously medical certification would be applicable – but after several months off, as sometimes happens, the employer's position may become stronger and 'settling' an unfair dismissal may be easier for them.

life insurance

Where a manic depressive sufferer seeks life assurance if he/she has been well for a year, it is unlikely an insurer would decline them but loading is to be expected.

jamison, kay redfield

Kay Jamison suffers from manic depressive illness herself, and is a leading researcher and probably the world's best known exponent in the field. She co-wrote a defining text on the same subject with F. Goodwin in 1990 (see *Manic Depressive Illness* in Recommended Reading). Being an English scholar herself she writes in a lyrical and beautifully crafted language about her own illness in *An Unquiet Mind*. She has also written a study of affective (mood) disorders in creative people in *Touched with Fire*; a suicide study *Night Falls Fast*; and *Exuberance*, balancing the dark with the light of human emotion. She holds the Chair of Psychiatry at Johns Hopkins University, USA.

1

Lithium was discovered in Melbourne, Australia, in 1948 by a pioneering psychiatric researcher, Dr John Cade. Its purpose is to help control the excessive mood swings of manic depression. It has been a godsend to thousands of sufferers over the last thirty-five years since it became an accepted treatment. Dr Cade had the idea that mania was caused by the excessive build-up of the body's waste products. He injected guinea pigs with the 'active' ingredient of urine – urea – and used lithium to form the injecting solution, only to discover the animals sedated. While some argue against 'drugs' this is, in fact, a naturally occurring salt.

Lithium remains one of the most frequently prescribed and useful mood stabilizing drugs. There is no longer any doubt that lithium benefits large numbers of people with manic depressive disorder. For some it works like a dream, it is almost as though they had a lithium deficiency. However, other people put on weight, feel awful and develop side effects.

In general terms, lithium is very safe as long as its level in the blood is closely monitored. Side effects include tremor, weight gain and gastrointestinal problems, and over the long term, possible memory loss, unsteadiness, tremor and kidney damage, as well as hypothyroidism. An early sign of kidney problems is getting up in the middle of the night to pass urine, because the kidneys are no longer able to concentrate urine overnight.

Unfortunately, there is no way of knowing who will be helped by lithium and who will suffer serious side effects. Experience suggests that those most likely to benefit are those with a strong family history of manic depressive disorder and who are relatively well between episodes. Doses may have to be increased considerably to achieve the required effect and this puts some patients off. Often those needing it the most are the least likely to comply with the treatment. The wide range of responses to lithium supports the idea of manic depression as a label for a number of conditions, rather than one condition.

People taking lithium need regular (six-monthly) blood tests to check lithium levels, kidney function and thyroid function. Lithium levels can increase if someone becomes dehydrated through, for example, diarrhoea and vomiting. Excessively high levels of lithium cause tremor, unsteadiness, lack of coordination and drowsiness.

coming off lithium

If you decide to stop taking lithium, this should ALWAYS be done in consultation with your doctor and lithium should NEVER be stopped suddenly. This is because eighty per cent of people who stop lithium suddenly are ill again within a year, yet by comparison only thirty per cent become ill when lithium is stopped more gradually over two months. Ideally, people should take six months to a year to come off lithium, taking other drugs as appropriate.

loneliness

Loneliness is not just about being alone. It is just as possible to feel lonely, even amongst a group of friends. Rather, loneliness reflects separation from other humans. We are a social species and constantly need to make contact with members of our own species; of our own tribe. Some people are more social than others, but we all have a need to connect and communicate with others like ourselves. Unfortunately, all too often, someone can be left feeling they are from a different planet.

Relationships and a feeling of being in control are the keys to managing loneliness. The worst triggers for loneliness are loss of an important relationship or relationships. One of the worst times can be the first term at university, or the first week at your first job when social skills may still need polishing and familiar relationships have been left behind. Being lonely despite the presence of lots of people frequently reflects a poor relationship with self (low self-esteem), and less efficient social skills.

Loneliness can occur when:

- You are facing changes in your life – a new school, town, job, or other changes;

- You feel there's no one in your life with whom you can share your feelings and experiences;
- Your self-perceptions are that you're unacceptable, unlovable, not worthwhile even if others don't share those perceptions.

One of the best ways to counteract feeling lonely is to try to get involved with other people by offering to *help*. Imagine the world is a big party where you don't know any of the other guests, but by offering to hand round the sausage rolls, drinks or sandwiches you feel useful and stand a better chance of getting to know people and vice versa.

However badly you feel about your situation, make a positive choice to not isolate yourself from the rest of the world but to somehow join in.

m

Initially, a state of mind reminiscent of how you felt as a child waking up on Christmas day, multiplied by the power of five. Being hypomanic is like having endless energy, along with wonderful enthusiasm and self-worth. The world around you seems brilliant and a kaleidoscope of opportunities. You feel so multi-talented you are able to complete daily chores in a fraction of their normal time, and to keep occupied you concentrate on learning to speak Russian and play the piano whilst becoming a grandmaster of roulette. It's possible to believe you are Superman, Napoleon or Jesus Christ, where you see everyone's problems and potential, flaws and beauty, and make grand plans to turn the planet into a better place.

Yet as hypomania accelerates into mania, it is like an express train travelling with no brakes, quite slowly at first but gathering speed. Ultimately, you have no fear, and each day you remain high, and any sense of danger diminishes. You may normally be afraid of heights, but you take part in a skydiving event and then sign up to a course to learn to become an instructor. So many brilliant ideas keep coming into your head, you consider hiring an assistant to keep track of them, or creating a company called Brilliant Ideas Ltd. Your confidence is so sparkling and powerful, your point of view so tangible, you are able to convince friends, family, work colleagues and complete strangers of anything. Those that you cannot quite convince, you temporarily lie to, until the time is right to explain the truth.

Everything you once dared to remotely fantasize or dream about doing now seems within your grasp. How could you have *ever* been depressed? You need very little sleep and feel capable of achieving anything providing there is enough time. You've become super combative and ready and willing to take on anyone in court, the boxing ring or even the three abusive louts shouting down the street. Outlandish but possible business schemes are galloped into with loans from banks or acquaintances. Property acquisition, artistic and charitable endeavours can also be launched with gusto, and often funded by the money borrowed for the business scheme. *It's all the same, isn't it? Anyway, it's all my money and I'll balance the books later with a hundred times more.*

As the train speeds up, so does your spending and uninhibited sex drive. You don't mean to spend five times more than you have but you do because *you know* one of your schemes will soon be making millions. You are making two hundred calls and sending the same amount of emails per day. No one got anywhere without taking risks and by not thinking big. Consequently, you now only travel first class, dress first class and have champagne and caviar for breakfast. Mindful of others who are less fortunate, you buy up the stock of a sweet shop and have it delivered to a children's hospital ward. As a reward you test drive three Ferraris, but instead of being extravagant, settle on only leasing two. Your sex drive is so high it's gone completely off the dial. You meet people in bars, stepping out of cabs, buying milk in a shop and after a moment's conversation invite them back to your place.

Your train is heading off the rails with all its speed and pressure gauges about to explode. The incredible energy coursing through your veins can turn into a massively negative charge of paranoia and anxiety but you try not to notice because you don't believe anything is wrong. You believe that you are omnipotent; you are Mozart, Bowie, Rumpole, Casanova, Geldof and Clint Eastwood rolled into one.

From the outside, mania is the stage after hypomania. As a person's energy and stress levels rise higher and higher, the mind disintegrates. The person stops sleeping and becomes involved in a tireless series of activities. Manic individuals can become aggressive if challenged or stopped from doing what they want or need to do. Mania, unless reversed by drug or other physical intervention, can lead to death as the individual exhausts him- or herself through lack of sleep and ever-increasing activity.

manic depression (bipolar disorder)

the diagnosis of manic depression

Manic depression is described as a 'pattern of illness due to an abnormal mood', which means any time a person feels abnormally happy or sad.

Mood disorders include two general categories. The first category of mood disorders is straightforward Major Depressive Disorders where the individual has times when s/he is abnormally unhappy. The second category of mood disorders is Manic Depressive Disorders, where the individual experiences times of abnormal elation, in addition to experiencing times of abnormal unhappiness.

Depression is defined as a period lasting at least two weeks, where the person feels depressed, unable to enjoy life, has problems eating and sleeping, guilt feelings, loss of energy, trouble concentrating and thoughts about death (which includes just about everyone at some stage in his or her life).

Mania is defined as a period of at least one week, where the individual feels elated or irritable, grandiose, talkative, hyperactive, distractible and happy but shows poor judgement and difficulty functioning in their work and/or social environment.

People with Manic Depressive Disorder have episodes of mania, hypomania or mixed episodes, with or without episodes of depression.

A number of different types of manic depression are described in the *DSM IV*:

- **Type I** There has been at least one manic episode with or without major depressive episodes. Type I people tend to run into trouble with repeated episodes of mania.

- **Type II** There has been at least one manic or hypomanic episode to make this diagnosis. However, Type II people tend to have a preponderance of depressive episodes, rather than manic episodes.

- **Type III** Manic Depression Not Otherwise Specified. This is a rag-bag collection of conditions that do have symptoms of manic depression but do not meet the criteria for full-blown manic depression.

- **Cyclothymic Disorder** where the mood swings between depression and hypomania but without fulfilling the criteria for major depressive or manic episodes.

In bipolar illness everyone has their own different presentation. The most clear-cut is florid manic behaviour, but often the picture is more obscure. Sufferers may have had years of depressive episodes, or episodes of 'mixed' symptoms, where for example agitation is more manifest than the sense of overwhelming well-being normally associated with mania. People's 'personalities' are wrapped in this heady mix. Adolescent behaviour may look remarkably similar. Use of stimulant drugs such as cocaine and ecstasy may appear like hypomania with excitement, insomnia, irritability, excessive confidence, even euphoria. If these persist after drug use is stopped M-D illness will be a more likely diagnosis. But often the two are intertwined – someone with hypomania will gravitate towards alcohol and drugs; and someone heavily into drugs will not necessarily stop for the convenience of a diagnosis.

The psychosis of schizophrenia may be very similar to that of mania, with paranoia (feeling you are being watched) or distortions of the sense of 'self': not knowing who you are any more or even the conviction of being someone grand or preordained such as Christ. There are patients whose diagnosis changes after years from one to another, as the picture may be quite unclear to even careful and experienced psychiatrists.

other relevant terms

- *Mixed State.* This means a state where some features of the 'high' hypomanic state occur at the same time as features of the 'low' depressive state. In addition, there may be a mêlée of other symptoms such as anxiety or irritability which further confound it. It is often, thus, difficult to treat.

- *Rapid Cycling.* This describes a person who, within one year, has at least four episodes of either depression or mania. However, the cycle can vary in extremes, from extreme daily changes in mood, to weekly or monthly cycles. With such rapid shifts, normality is impossible and damage is cumulative, as the repeated damage to social relationships and cognitive function takes its toll.

- *Without Full Interepisode Recovery.* This describes a person who goes from depression to mania without a stage of being symptom free.

Mood symptoms are common in a number of other mental health disorders. However, the diagnosis of manic depression is only made when mood symptoms predominate. In addition, for reasons that are not fully understood, manic depression is independently associated with physical illnesses such as thyroid problems and epilepsy.

causes of manic depression

Genetics: Parents with manic depression have a one in ten chance that their children will develop manic depression; if both parents have manic depression the odds increase to four in ten. These figures also show that a significant proportion of people with manic depression do not have any family members with manic depression.

Despite decades of research, no one has yet found the cause of manic depression. It is known that manic depression, along with some other major mental illnesses, runs in families. When identical twins are brought up in the same environment between forty and seventy per cent of twins both have manic depression. By comparison, where the twins are non-identical, on average, there is only a ten per cent chance that both will have manic depression. So without doubt, some kind of vulnerability is inherited. However, research is littered with papers claiming to have identified a specific gene associated with manic depression, only to be disproved the following year by other researchers.

A different approach may be to compare manic depression with sunburn. Fair-skinned people are at risk of sunburn, and frequent sunburn leads to wrinkles and rarely skin cancer. There is no specific gene for sunburn, wrinkles or skin cancer, although skin colour itself is genetically controlled. Furthermore, only fair-skinned people who are exposed to excessive sunlight get sunburned, whilst some, by careful planned exposure and diligent use of sunscreen, can develop beautiful tans and those who stay inside can avoid it altogether. In addition, even dark-skinned people with no fair-skinned genes get sunburned if they are suddenly exposed to extreme sunlight after, for example, a European winter.

So to extend the analogy, perhaps the time has come to stop searching for a gene for sunburn, wrinkles and skin cancer and look at those factors that make people vulnerable to manic depression and mental health difficulties. It is well established that the close relatives of those with manic depression, but who themselves do not have the condition, are above averagely successful in life.

Manic depression occurs in all groups of people, whether separated by race, colour, creed or geography. It happens right across the world and has been known for centuries.

Clues as to the mechanisms of manic depression: Although the actual mechanics of MD are not known, studies of the brain are yielding fruit that will give a fuller picture in time. Studies of **hormones** and **neuroimaging** are helping (see pages 215 and 249–50). Studying the micro-anatomy is starting to show results. The gap between the neurons (brain cells), called the synapse, is being analysed to see if there are significant differences in sufferers and non-sufferers. It is again the problem of the 'chicken and the egg' as to whether any differences are caused *by* the illness or the cause *of* the illness. On a larger scale, injuries to the brain, tumours and strokes can lead to MD, demonstrating that there are important pathways in the brain that are interrupted.

Though brain function is not understood, Susan Greenfield, in her book *The Private Life of the Brain,* provides evocative images when speaking of the kaleidoscope of neurochemical activity and neuronal 'arousal'. She proposes that during different states, such as the intense focus of children, amphetamine use or in mania, there are small, highly active focuses of brain activity; whereas in depression or anxiety, with 'too much' information causing the state of malaise, there are much broader areas of brain activity that correspond to the state.

The fact that schizophrenia, a related (though clearly different) illness, appears to occur throughout humanity at roughly the same prevalence as MD has led some scientists to question whether both conditions came about due to genetic changes in tandem with our defining features, perhaps our unique brain asymmetry or the ability to self-reflect, arising together before we spread out from the Cradle of Africa (somewhere in the region of 100,000 years ago). Maybe some of the genes of hypomania, shared with those of exuberance, confidence and leadership, have been a genetic advantage over the millennia?

other causes

Drugs, prescription and non-prescription: Treatment with anti-depressants is known to cause hypomania and mania in up to a third of patients who are known to have manic depression, depending upon the dose and type of anti-depressant used. This is not a reason not to use anti-depressant treatment as long as it is monitored carefully and anti-depressants are taken in conjunction with a mood-stabilizing drug.

However, anti-depressants can also cause hypomania, even in patients who have no history of manic depression. This is more common with the older tricyclic anti-depressants, such as amitryptyline, but will occur with Selective Serotonin Reuptake Inhibitors such as fluoxetine and paroxetine, when it is thought to occur in less than three per cent of cases. However, the likelihood of an individual developing mania or hypomania with anti-depressants depends a lot on the individual. If they already experience significant mood swings, and/or have other family members with manic depression, then the risk will be much higher than with an individual who has a more depressive temperament.

Manic depression has also developed after treatment with a number of unrelated drugs, including Lariam, an antimalarial drug; after severe illness and toxic shock; after head injury; and from taking cannabis, especially the stronger street drugs, such as skunk. Research leaves us in no doubt that taking large doses of non-prescription drugs increases the number and severity of episodes of manic depression, thereby damaging one's mental health.

Stress: A number of studies have shown that the initial episodes of manic depression at least are precipitated by stressful events. With time, the stress required to trigger an episode becomes less and less and episodes seem to appear spontaneously.

the diagnosis of manic depression and its impact

The reaction to receiving the diagnosis varies. Some patients are even relieved that at last a cause for their disturbed behaviour and mood has been found. 'At last, it is no longer my fault,' may be felt. Parents may feel this way, especially having blamed themselves for years of unhappiness. More commonly though there are fearful emotions, of denial, shame and regret that may take years to overcome.

Personal impact: The diagnosis of manic depression is not like a physical diagnosis. When someone is given the diagnosis of manic depression it tells the rest of the world who they are, how they behave, what to believe about them and what to expect from them. And as long as they are who they are, it is a label that will define them for the rest of their life. They do not deserve the label, and they should not be blamed. Other people have worse problems, and live worse lives, and yet other people's sanity is never questioned. From the moment of diagnosis, the illness can explain that person's thoughts, their moods and their emotions and from the moment they are diagnosed, just in case they become unwell again, their judgement is never to be fully trusted again. Everyone close to them will be entitled to check up on them at any time, or so the story goes.

To be diagnosed as a manic depressive goes to the core of who you are as a person. It is difficult to feel good about a diagnosis that reaches into your very soul. Furthermore, there are no external signs to mark the condition out as special, to get the ordinary sympathy for illness or to provide even a hint of what you experience. Suddenly, medication becomes a permanent part of daily routine, doctors and psychiatrists become privy to every personal fact and able to judge each personal experience.

The first reaction to mental illness is often denial, 'Obviously the hypomania was a response to stress. Anyone can have such a reaction, hardly surprising under the circumstances.' At this stage, relatives and friends will usually collude, explaining away the destructive behaviour with phrases such as 'always a bit excitable'. It is only as episodes keep happening that everyone's patience gets exhausted. But in the beginning, it is easier not to talk about it. Shame follows denial. Words do not describe the awfulness of losing your mind. There are other losses: energy, excitement, a thousand different meanings, a hundred new friends, where did everything go? Mania, almost as inevitably as night follows day, is followed by depression. And although psychiatrists proffer anti-depressants, in truth the depression feels nothing worse than that person feels that he or she deserves. Tablets cannot remove shame, repair relationships, replace lost careers, repay the overdraft, restore savings, refund wasted money and remake lost opportunities. Only time can separate you from the disgrace of mental illness. Life has changed beyond all recognition. Depression is the wages of mania. Lack of energy reflects exhausted mental batteries left for dead after the multi-millennial light-shattering firework display that was the preceding days and weeks.

It is doubtful whether the brain ever truly recovers from an episode of mania; the world never looks quite the same again.

At the point of diagnosis, traditionally an individual has two choices. The first choice is to reject the psychiatrist's explanation, to refuse to believe that this is an illness. After all, everyone knows that an illness makes you feel ill. You never felt better in your life, there are no broken bones, no abnormal blood tests and you don't have a temperature. It is impossible to believe that the incredible feelings of being high were wrong; to believe that the experience was one of illness not expansion; to believe that the insights that flowed through your being like a stream in spring were just tricks of a disturbed mind; to give up the knowledge of oneness with the universe and forget that it provides whatever you need in abundance.

For those who believe they are free thinkers, it is easy to reject the psychiatrist's explanation, to reject the identity of a psychiatric patient and to reject the prescription drugs that stop the universe opening up and pouring out its secrets. Yet as time goes by, the refuseniks' ability to live in the ordinary world, instead of an extraordinary universe, and to construct an ordinary life from the dry bones of reality, deteriorates: their minds slip into a state of perpetual change, where each day is swept by a new tide of moods and emotions. Their concentration, their memory, their ability to solve the problems of everyday life deteriorate. They fail to fulfil their early promise. And just as with any addict, they lie in wait for the next fix of mania, which has become the only way to hold at bay the progressive waves of depression that flood the plains of a sinking mental landscape. Admissions become more frequent, medication is given forcefully in higher doses and the individual loses more and more of the totems of social acceptability.

Few people follow the first choice exactly, and they become increasingly isolated and eccentric as fewer and fewer people can enter their world. More people make this choice secretly: on the outside they appear to be following psychiatric advice (the second choice – see below) whilst on the inside they desperately hope to preserve what remains of their shattered self.

The second choice is to follow psychiatric advice, take regular medication and report regularly to the psychiatrist, community psychiatric team, therapist and general practitioner. It is in part a surrender to the medical model of illness, that of a doctor making a diagnosis and applying treatment. The system sets up appointments and the individual is left to rebuild what remains of their life. All aberrant behaviour is accounted for under the umbrella of illness for which the person cannot be held responsible.

For the lucky ones, this approach works. They take their medication and their life continues more or less as it did before their world was turned upside down. However, it is a passive approach, which leaves the individual at the mercy of a mental health system that frequently fails. It doesn't allow for the possibility of growth and learning or the possibility of improving their mental and physical health.

Recently a third choice has appeared. This choice is based on acknowledging and accepting the condition and taking responsibility for one's behaviour, well or ill, learning to manage oneself, one's moods and emotions, and living a life that supports health. It is based on learning strategies to help stabilize one's mood from within; on learning about other people's experience of manic depression; on learning better ways to meet one's needs; on gaining self-knowledge and insight. The third choice is about making changes and abandoning beliefs and behaviours that do not support health and well-being; it's about learning to make changes as well as learning to accept one's self and knowing when to do which. It is also about being constantly self-aware and mindful.

Healthy living means not smoking, abandoning alcohol, eating a healthy diet, taking nutritional supplements, especially multiminerals, multivitamins and vitamin B complex, together with essential omega 3 and 6 fatty acids, as well as taking regular exercise and enjoying plenty of sunlight that helps to stabilize moods.

The third choice is also about being responsible for one's illness. It is not about feeling guilty, or blaming oneself for what happened. Rather, responsibility is about seeking to understand and change the pattern of one's illness. This includes understanding and accepting the diagnosis, finding out what happened, what led up to the episode of illness and how it might have been handled, and asking the central question, 'What have I learnt about myself, about other people and about the world as a result of this episode of illness?' Responsibility is about explaining to people who were involved, what happened, why it happened and, where possible, making amends. It is the first step in teaching one's subconscious mind to behave differently. The third choice is about learning to manage moods and emotions; about raising self-esteem; about learning to look at events from a number of different perspectives.

By these means, the third choice seeks to improve mental and physical health and minimize the impact of manic depression. People usually reach this position after they have tried and failed with the first two approaches. They are generally more mature and have more experience of the impact of the illness and have found that medication alone or even medication and psychotherapy together are not giving them the quality of life they want.

it's not all bad: the benefits of illness

It always surprises people without handicaps or health problems that those with challenges would not necessarily wish them away. Without doubt, this is true of many people with manic depression. The illness provides experiences and a view of the world that those who have not been there can never appreciate. Moreover, empathy, wisdom and acceptance can come from the suffering of depression. Nietzsche's muse was undoubtedly, at least in part, his manic depression, which enhanced both his creativity and vision and his ability to look into the void to see the world in all its awfulness.

A recent survey from the Doctors Support Network (a self-help group for doctors with mental health problems) graphically described the suffering and difficulties associated with mental illness. However, ninety-five per cent of doctors found something positive in their experiences; they found they were more empathetic with their patients; had developed greater self-awareness and maturity; had a better work–life balance. Their comments included: 'I am a humbler person now. I like this version of me as a doctor.'

managing manic depression

There are four strands of management:

1. Drug therapy: There are four main types of drugs used in manic depression: mood stabilizers; mood-lowering drugs; mood-improving drugs; and a rag-bag group of drugs that includes things like sleeping tablets. No one wants to take drugs, least of all to prevent something that isn't happening at the moment, but might happen again in the future. However, it is possible to see medication as the trainer wheels you need for your mental bicycle as you teach your brain to ride straight again. In the meantime, whilst gaining the extra stability offered by drug therapy, you can begin to understand what happened and gain insight into your experiences.

2. One-to-one psychological therapy: Psychological therapy aims to improve mental health. The approach depends on where the problems lie and where support is needed. It can be based around a one-to-one relationship with a therapist, which is psychodynamic therapy, where someone explores the underlying tensions from an emotional perspective, or cognitive behaviour therapy, which is a more structured rational approach to emotional management. Dialectic cognitive behaviour therapy is a form of cognitive therapy that emphasizes coming to terms with the contradictions in life. However, the most important part of any kind of therapy is the relationship with the therapist: generally the more interactive the approach, the more likely it is to succeed. It may take several attempts to find the right therapist for you – the person with whom you can do your best work.

In terms of therapy, studies are being done to confirm the value of cognitive therapy. It is highly unlikely that this will reveal anything other than its great benefit. This may help swing government funding. It is much cheaper, after all, to keep a patient well in the community with therapy and back-up than to admit them to an expensive hospital unit.

3. Group-based activities: It is always a seminal moment when you read about someone with manic depression or talk to someone else with the condition for the first time. What seemed strange, shameful, unique and personally unbearable can be seen in perspective. It is then possible to begin the process of understanding and getting to grips with the experience.

There are a number of organizations through which it is possible to meet other people with manic depression. This includes the Bipolar Organisation (also known as the Manic Depression Fellowship), MIND, as well as a number of online groups on the Internet. For medical practicioners there is the Doctors Support Network.

Meeting other people who have had similar but different experiences is a fundamental part of the recovery process. It is key to coming to terms with the condition and learning methods of coping and self-management.

4. Self-management strategies: There are a large number of self-management strategies. The key is to finding the ones that work for you, make you feel better and help you cope better with the situation and life you live and fit in with your commitments. Cognitive behavioural therapy does cover most areas of psychological management, and will include self-help. A first-class book on this, including work plans and sheets, is Jan Scott's *Overcoming Mood Swings*. She is a leading psychiatrist and researcher in this field.

These strategies need practising daily. Self-management is about doing ten things 10,000 times and not doing 10,000 things ten times. Find out what works and stick with it, and if you do nothing, nothing works.

The Manic Depression Fellowship runs self-management courses. These developed from the experience of people with the condition coming together and discussing what worked for them and then putting together a course to pass on their knowledge and experience.

care plans

These are plans, developed in consultation with the community health team, community psychiatric nurse and psychiatrist to help manage psychiatric care in the community. Everyone leaving hospital should leave equipped with a care plan.

advanced directives

The purpose of Advanced Directives is to enable someone to make decisions ahead of a crisis, at which point they may no longer have the capacity to make appropriate decisions. For example, an Advanced Directive can include information about where you might be admitted or what kind of treatment you want.

It encourages a long-term view and planning, so that if the worst happens, you and those close to you are prepared. It does not have any legal force; just because something is in the Advanced Directive, it doesn't mean it will happen. However, since most people (including psychiatrists) want to please and to help people, if you make your wishes known, it is more likely that things will happen the way you want.

manic depression fellowship – MDF bipolar organisation

MDF Bipolar Organisation is a user-led charity working to enable people affected by manic depression to take control of their lives.

contact details

MDF Bipolar Organisation, Castle Works, 21 St George's Road, London SE1 6ES
08456 340 540 (UK only)
0044 207 793 2600 (Rest of world)

email

mdf@mdf.org.uk

websites

www.mdf.org.uk
www.mdfwales.org.uk (Wales site)
www.pendulum.org.uk (*Pendulum* journal site)
www.steady.org.uk (STEADY self-management course site)

membership

You can become a member of MDF through the website. As a member you will receive the following benefits:

- *The organization's quarterly journal, **Pendulum***. This is full of current debate about manic depression, overseas news, forthcoming events, etc.
- *Advice.* A twenty-four-hour line providing legal advice, employment advice and advice about benefits and debt. Your questions will be answered by qualified solicitors.
- *Travel insurance and life assurance schemes*. MDF offers travel insurance to its members which covers manic depression as a pre-existing condition, something most insurers will not cover. For further details contact MDF on 08456 340540. Members can contact MDF and get practical advice on applying for life assurance and avoiding common pitfalls.
- *Self-management training*. SMT (self-management training programme for adults) or STEADY (self-management for young people aged between eighteen and twenty-five). These courses are delivered either as a face-to-face residential course or as an online course. Training is designed to give you a thorough understanding of the concepts, tools and techniques involved in learning to self-manage extreme mood swings. It is based on a six-module course with two facilitators. The course includes identifying triggers and warning signs, strategies for coping and complementary therapies. There is a small administration charge for participating. As this is an independent organization there is no link between the project and psychiatric services. Remember, this course is run by a user-led, independent organization.
- *Self-help groups*. You can find your closest self-help group through the website. MDF describes these groups as a safe space for mutual support with people in similar situations to your own.
- *Information*. Comprehensive website content and all information and publications provided by the organization. You will also gain access to a number of fact sheets which cover information on diagnosis, medication and information for families.

Membership costs vary. You can become a member online or by telephoning 08456 340 540.

Without membership, the website offers brief information on diagnosis, including medical criteria (DSM IV & ICD 10), NHS services, information about day-to-day issues such as driving, finances, benefits and nutrition, and advice for friends and family.

marijuana

See **Cannabis**, pages 195–6.

martial arts

You can look at the cause of frustration and work it out, and you should, but sometimes you're just left frustrated. If that's the case, and you're young(ish) try a martial art. Men, women, let it out. There is discipline. They won't let you get away with it. It is tough, uncompromising. If you're mean you'll be punished by someone better than you. It teaches self-respect and respect. It's not about fighting – it's about mental attitude. It teaches us positivity.

Many things in life aren't fair – you can't change them and you have to come to accept them, but along the way, if you feel angry and frustrated, use it positively; it is an energy. Maybe when you're physically fit you'll find a direction to focus the frustration in, something really constructive for yourself, and it'll help you get mentally fit too. It hasn't been a way of life in the Orient for thousands of years without reason.

meditation

The inner calm induced by this is an ideal counter to the stresses of life. Recent studies by neuroimaging on monks, trained in the art for many years, have shown areas of the brain responsible for creative thinking are more active during meditation.

Meditation is brain training for relaxation.

The ability to relax is an essential part of good mental health. It lowers the pulse rate, lowers blood pressure, lowers the level of stress hormones and leads to a more relaxed mental state and greater mental flexibility.

Just as with any other kind of exercise there are many ways to do it and it needs to be done regularly. One trip to the gym will not get you fit. There are different types of meditation, some based in the mind, others in the body. For example, Transcendental Meditation is mind based. It involves repeating a completely meaningless mantra over and over again, whilst not falling asleep, and learning to let go of thoughts that inevitably bubble up during the meditation. It helps to show that a thought is nothing more than a thought. It shows that the mind produces thoughts just as a biscuit factory produces biscuits. Overall, one biscuit is very much like any other biscuit and only rarely does a biscuit or thought have any significant consequences.

Being able to let go of thoughts is a key step in developing a healthy mind. Meditation is a mental exercise that helps develop that particular mental muscle. Other ways to meditate can involve concentrating on a single object, contemplating a single word such as 'peace' or using body-based methods such as concentrating on breathing in a particular pattern, or relaxing parts of the body. The purpose of meditation is to allow the brain to reach deep states of relaxation, whilst at the same time becoming intensely aware of the present moment.

Unfortunately, the very people who most need to learn to meditate find it most difficult. For people with very high anxiety levels, meditating for even three or four minutes a day can be a struggle, an achievement and the first step in learning to manage the mind.

melancholia

The term derived from the Greek *mela* (black) and *cholia* (bile), which described the temperament of the melancholic. The ancient Greeks described four 'humours' – yellow, red, green and black bile – which were thought to cause the different personality types.

memory loss

As time goes by, more and more people begin the day by asking questions, such as 'Where did I leave my toothpaste?' One common and distressing feature of almost all mental health problems, as well as ageing, seems to be memory loss. Patients often come in fearing they have dementia, whereas in fact most often they have far more treatable conditions.

Recall requires attention and concentration, and high levels of anxiety prevent the memory from functioning adequately. In severe depression and mania the brain often fails to store memories. It can be very disconcerting when someone describes a conversation they had with you two hours earlier and you know for a fact you have never seen them before in your life. It also makes life very difficult when there are a large number of gaps in a day. This is one very good reason to treat depression in old age. Resolution of the depression can lead to a remarkable increase in cognitive function, memory and get-up-and-go! It is also a very good reason to try and resolve severe anxiety, where the preoccupation with ruminative thoughts severely disrupts memory function.

To work properly, memory inputs data, stores it and then recalls it. Unlike a computer, human memory does not accurately store and reproduce data; instead, over time, memories tend to adapt to fit with what we would like to believe; hence nostalgia and the popularity of memorabilia.

Although it won't make you a genius, Gingko Biloba can improve mental function and memory, and don't forget plenty of omega 3 and vitamin B complex.

menopause

The menopause is the time of cessation of periods for women, which means fertility also, and is usually between the ages of forty-five and fifty-five. It may be greeted gladly by some but for others it is a reminder of the passage of time. Some will feel no mood change at this time, others mild and a few severe.

Concurrent depression should be evaluated and background factors looked into with management following a 'holistic' approach looking at lifestyle changes, exercise and exploration of problems perceived at the time.

Some women with low mood state post-menopausally will elect to try HRT (others continuing it as they have a sense of well-being) despite the slightly increased risk of breast cancer or cardiovascular problems. Release of progesterone into the uterus to protect its lining by an IUS (intra-uterine system) as well as oestrogen administration can be a successful treatment. With oestrogen treatment being so controversial advice will continue to change. Certainly current advice is not to use oestrogen as prevention against bone loss after periods cease. Psychiatrists and gynaecologists have not reached a common agreement and once again there are grounds for more links in research in the two disciplines.

Many women see the advantage of being unhindered by a monthly cycle in their approach to family, sexual intimacy, profession and interests as a more liberated time of life.

the mental health foundation

The Mental Health Foundation is primarily an independent research organization that helps to develop services, design training, influence policy and raise public awareness about mental health. The organization does not provide any direct services and does not have membership. However, their website has a lot of useful, up-to-the-minute information about how and where to get help, and about problems and treatments.

contact details
Mental Health Foundation, 9th floor, Sea Containers House, 20 Upper Ground, London SE1 9QB
020 7803 1100

email
mhf@mhf.org.uk

website
www.mentalhealth.org.uk

mentality

Mentality, founded in 2000, is a national charity dedicated solely to the promotion of mental health. The Mentality team is part of the Sainsbury Centre for Mental Health. Whilst not offering direct services, the website offers information, advice and free publications about mental health promotion and positive steps towards it. The concept of mental health promotion is relatively new and is mainly about promoting positive concepts and well-being, rather than focusing on the negative aspects of mental illness. Mentality works with user groups, mental health professionals and voluntary agencies. The website offers further explanation.

contact details
Mentality, 134–138 Borough High Street, London SE1 1LB
020 7716 6777

email
enquiries@mentality.org.uk

website
www.mentality.org.uk

milligan, spike

If British humour is characterized by being the best in the world for self-deprecation and zaniness (coming from these islands in the clouds), Spike has to be responsible for the origin and supremacy of such crazy, lateral-thinking comedy. His Goons gave birth to the celebration of the absurd and acted as a beacon for the future of comedy. His humour rode on hypomania and he used his wild creativity in his highs but suffered for it in frightful depression. He was the Patron of the Manic Depression Fellowship.

mind

MIND is the largest mental health charity. Its mission is to improve life for everyone with experience of mental distress. MIND endeavours to advance the views of people with mental health problems, challenge discrimination and promote inclusion. It influences policy through campaigning and education.

contact details
15–19 Broadway, London E15 4BQ
Information and Helpline 0845 766 0163
Fax: 020 8522 1725

MIND has a helpline, which offers confidential help on a range of mental health issues – 0845 766 0163. There is also a special legal service for the public, lawyers and mental health workers – 020 8519 2122 Mon, Weds and Fri 2–4.30.

email
contact@mind.org.uk

website
www.mind.org.uk

local mind networks
MIND has a network of over 200 local associations. These local groups offer supported housing, crisis helpline, drop-in centres, counselling, befriending, advocacy, employment and training schemes. To find out where your local MIND network is, contact the helpline or look on the website.

MIND's befriending schemes put people in touch with volunteers who have received training and will offer support and friendship on a one-to-one basis.

Many local networks have an advocacy service. This may include providing information to help you make informed choices, explaining your rights relating to the Mental Health Act and the Patients' Charter and Community Care Act, and assisting you in contacting other agencies, solicitors, etc. Advocates can support and prepare you for forthcoming Care Plan meetings, Mental Health Review tribunals, ward rounds, etc. Some networks offer forensic advocacy too.

As well as providing a lot of information about the range of supported housing available and useful links, MIND also runs its own supported housing in some areas. All this can be found by contacting your local MIND (details on the main website).

Many local networks run a counselling service with trained counsellors on a one-to-one basis. Local networks vary but many ask that you pay a small contribution to costs.

Some local networks provide employment and training schemes for those who are unemployed with mental health problems. Schemes often relate to community activity, for example in Hammersmith and Fulham there is a Cleaning Hit Squad and Community Repaint Scheme. Westminster MIND

(WAMH) runs Birthday Bakers, a catering business and training scheme for those with long-term mental health problems. These schemes and others involve a referral process which is explained on the local website.

Drop-in centres are what the title says! Centres may vary from area to area but may include opportunities to get advice about welfare, money worries, etc. There may be a programme of activities, including relaxation and group work. Again, look on your local MIND website to see what is on offer.

MIND link

MIND has another network called MIND Link, which is a service for users of mental health services who can offer each other support and share experiences.

information

MIND's website is vast. MIND produces a wide range of publications, including factsheets about anxiety, depression, schizophrenia and other mental health problems.

It also has factsheets that promote ways of coping and strategies for living. There is comprehensive information about the range of mental health services available and how to access them. It provides thorough explanations about who's who in mental health, from psychiatrist to occupational therapist to volunteer.

There are further factsheets about employment, employment rights, training opportunities, etc. Each factsheet is accompanied by lists of useful organizations and related links.

These are all available in full on the website or you can email publications@mind.org.uk or telephone MIND Publications 0844 4484448. There is also a monthly magazine called *Openmind*.

membership

As a member you will receive a ten per cent discount on MIND publications, £3 off the annual subscription rate to *Openmind* magazine and a concessionary rate for MIND's annual conferences. Members also have the right to vote at the annual general meeting. There is a membership form on the main website.

MIND operates in England and Wales, but not Scotland and Northern Ireland.

The old idea that the brain is somehow fixed and doesn't change because the number of brain cells is already present at birth is wrong. How we think and approach our lives affects how our brain grows. The 100 billion brain cells (neurons) we have, counting on a clear day, are constantly re-shaping and developing new connections.

We can effectively make our brains grow in the directions we wish. For example, violin players have an enlarged area of the brain related to this skill.

New studies have shown taxi drivers' brains grow as they study the 'knowledge', i.e. all the streets and locations they have to learn. Over a three-year period the 'hippocampus', the part of the brain involved in this process, was demonstrated to grow.

It is now thought that some 5000 stem cells migrate from one area in the base of the brain (the cerebellum) to do repair work each day.

By trying to learn new things we expand the mind. The new connections allow the mind to grow. The wider the skill base, the greater innovative thinking we can do: Michelangelo and Leonardo had broad-based minds from which to draw together their talents, and ordinary mortals like us can increase our own abilities by learning different things, by thinking and cross-referring in different ways.

Try something new, like Sudoku, the saxophone, singing, chess, sand-yachting, computer study, or ancient Egyptian astronomy.

music

'If I were not a physicist, I would probably be a musician. I often think in music. I live my daydreams in music. I see my life in terms of music.'

Albert Einstein

'There is no feeling, except the extremes of fear and grief, that did not find relief in music.'

George Eliot

MUSIC

Whether your taste in music is for the Beatles, Bach, Copeland, Abba, Baroque, Pink Floyd, Tchaikovsky, Coldplay, Nine Inch Nails, Erik Satie, Duke Ellington, Led Zeppelin, Delibes, Sex Pistols, Stravinsky, Speed Metal, Coltrane, Debussy, James Brown, Mozart, Joni Mitchell, Drum and Bass, Jazz, Funk, Kaiser Chiefs, Mahler, Nick Drake, Madonna, Elgar, Hip Hop, Green Day, Rolling Stones, Handel, Disco, The Killers or Leonard Cohen, it is good to remember what a difference music can make to our lives.

Music can often express things we feel in a way that words cannot. We can use music to lift our moods and better articulate how we actually feel. Music can help to unblock and express anger, shame or grief. It can take our minds away from our own troubles, sometimes into a far more profound joyous world or sometimes into a superficial and disposable one. Above all, music can make us feel alive.

Here are some suggested classical, pop and rock charts, compiled with that particular black sense of humour associated with manic depressives. (Please feel free to make up your own lists and send them to the publisher for possible inclusion in an updated guide.)

ten classical tracks to reflect upon the darker side of life to

Some of these tracks often have such sad and painful beauty that one cannot help but feel better; others are just plain dark!
1 BEETHOVEN: Symphony #7 – second movement
2 BARBER: Adagio for strings
3 PERGOLESI: Stabat Mater
4 MOZART: Requiem
5 PUCCINI: La Bohème – heroine's death aria
6 BACH: Toccata and Fugue in D minor BWV 565
7 VAUGHN WILLIAMS: Fantasia on a theme by Thomas Tallis
8 BENJAMIN BRITTEN: Four sea interludes from Peter Grimes Op 33a (especially Movement III, Moonlight & Movement I, Dawn)
9 SCHUBERT: Symphony #8 'Unfinished' – first movement
10 RACHMANINOFF: Piano concerto #3

ten classical tracks to unwind to at the end of your day

1 BACH: Air on a G String – orchestral suite #3 in D BWV 1068
2 PACHELBEL: Canon and Gigue
3 MOZART: Anything by Mozart is generally beautiful and relaxing, a few favourites being: Serenade in C min K388 – andante; Piano Concerto #21 in C mj K467 – slow movement; Clarinet concerto – adagio
4 SATIE: Gymnopedie #1 – lent et douloureux (all three Gymnopedies are lovely!)
5 DEBUSSY: La Mer
6 DELIBES: Flower Duet from 'Lakhme'
7 ELGAR: Enigma variations – variation IX (Nimrod), adagio
8 SAINT-SAËNS: Carnival of the Animals Mvmt 13 – The Swan
9 BEETHOVEN: Piano concerto #5 'Emperor' – second movement – adagio un poc mosso
10 GRIEG: Peer Gynt Suite #1 – Morning

ten classical pieces to fill you with the joys of spring

1 BEETHOVEN: Symphony #6; Piano concerto #5 'Emperor' – Movement III: Rondo allegro; Symphony #9 – Movement 5: Allegro Assai (Ode to Joy)
2 MOZART: The Marriage of Figaro – Overture
3 VIVALDI: Nulla in Mundo Pax Sincera (trampoline scene from the film *Shine*), The Four Seasons
4 BACH: Brandenburg #3 in G
5 HANDEL: Zadok the Priest – Coronation anthem
6 COPELAND: Appalachian Spring
7 SCHUBERT: The trout piano quintet in A – Andante
8 ELGAR: Pomp and Circumstance March # 1
9 TCHAIKOVSKY: Symphony #4 – finale
10 BRAHMS: Symphony #4 – allegro giocoso

ten rock/pop songs to make you want to get up and get going

1 ROLLING STONES: You Can't Always Get What You Want
2 BILL WITHERS: Lovely Day
3 FREE: All Right Now
4 RAM JAM: Black Betty
5 KC AND THE SUNSHINE BAND: That's the Way I Like It
6 SCISSOR SISTERS: Take Your Mama
7 STEVIE WONDER: Don't You Worry 'bout a Thing
8 THE WHO: Won't Get Fooled Again
9 GLORIA GAYNOR – I Will Survive
10 ROBBIE WIILIAMS – Let Me Entertain You

ten rock/pop songs to calm down with

1 BOB MARLEY: Three Little Birds
2 ISLEY BROTHERS: Summer Breeze
3 KRAFTWERK: Autobahn
4 LOU REED: Walk on the Wild Side
5 LOUIS ARMSTRONG: Wonderful World
6 PAUL SIMON: African Skies (from *Graceland* album)
7 SIMON & GARFUNKEL: Scarborough Fair
8 STEVIE WONDER: I Believe When I Fall in Love
9 PETER GABRIEL and KATE BUSH: Don't Give Up
10 VAN MORRISON: *Astral Weeks* (album)

thirteen rock/pop songs to wallow in gloom and misery with

1 LEONARD COHEN: Suzanne
2 BEATLES: Eleanor Rigby
3 BOBBIE GENTRY: Ode to Billy Joe
4 TERRY JACKS: Seasons in the Sun
5 DEL AMITRI: Driving With the Brakes On
6 PINK FLOYD: Comfortably Numb
7 JOHNNY CASH: Hurt
8 RADIOHEAD: Pyramid Song
9 THE SMITHS: How Soon is Now?
10 REM: Everybody Hurts
11 NIRVANA: Lithium
12 BILLIE HOLIDAY: Strange Fruit
13 PORTISHEAD: Wandering Star

narcotics anonymous

Founded in 1953 in Los Angeles, Narcotics Anonymous now has a network that stretches from the Western world to Islamic societies, with more than 20,000 meetings in ninety countries every week.

Like Alcoholics Anonymous, NA uses the twelve steps as the central precept of its recovery programme. The organization emphasizes the therapeutic value of members working with each other to become free of drug addictions, rather than employing professional therapists with no personal experience of drug or alcohol problems. Those who commit to the rehabilitation process are encouraged to stay off drugs and alcohol as the best means of achieving recovery. Due to the dramatic increase in drug addiction in our societies, Narcotics Anonymous currently offers the most inclusive and cost-free way to tackle the problem.

Fact: Four million of Iran's seventy million people are addicted to drugs, with opium being one of the most prevalent in the country.

contact details

Narcotics Anonymous, 202 City Road, London EC1V 2PH
020 7251 4007
Helpline: 020 7730 0009
Fax: 020 7251 4006

email

ukso@ukna.org

website

www.ukna.org
For advice, information and counselling on drug addiction.

nature

It is possible that the contemplation of nature in all its savage beauty and being a witness to the world may be the only valid reasons for our existence. It certainly gets us out of ourselves and allows healing of our minds. Genetics may have the answer as to how we got from an atom to a human, a butterfly or an oak tree but it cannot stop the sense of wonder, with the continual force of chaos, that we are reflecting on this at all. Surely anything is possible?

nervous breakdown

'Nervous breakdown' is not a medical term but a popular one. It implies that the individual has reached the 'end of their tether' and can 'no longer carry on': a crisis point. As with all crises there are different possible outcomes – the tragedy of suicide or the opportunity to address an illness or look at the life issues causing such a strain.

neuroimaging

Neuroimaging means looking at the brain with tools such as X-rays, CAT scans and MRI scans (the latter being done by powerful magnets not using X-rays).

There are various techniques with MRI at present, including 'structural' imaging which looks at the brain in a static state and in a 'functional' state (which looks at it, as the word implies, actively, as it functions). There are few consistent findings, which is partly due to the fact that the studies are relatively new. One apparently consistent finding is that the system that bathes the brain, called the ventricles, does appear enlarged in manic depressive illness. In very unwell patients there may be a difference in an area with a tongue-twisting name: the subgenual prefrontal cortex in the anterior cingulate gyrus. However, the relevance of these findings has not yet been determined. One of the problems is that the brain 'normally' varies, therefore it is difficult to ascertain the relevance of individual differences. Large groups iron out some of these problems. So the answer to the question, 'Can you see a difference in the brain of an individual sufferer compared to someone who is not?' is 'No'. Researchers at the Maudsley Hospital in London are currently studying 'discordant' identical twins (identical twins, one of whom has the problem and the other does not) to see if it reveals sites of different brain activity. 'Dynamic' studies are being performed where tasks are given in order to identify different reactions. In time such studies of groups of patients will give helpful information.

Difficulties for those scientists undertaking studies are, apart from getting enough people to study, questions such as how long the illness has been present, the severity of the illness, whether the patient has had treatment, and whether there are co-morbid factors such as drug abuse (e.g. alcohol). The question of 'Is it the chicken or the egg?' has not been resolved, i.e. 'Is the difference caused by the illness or has it caused the illness?' Studies done over a period of time (called longitudinal studies) are underway and these should eventually give the answer to this.

neurosis

A persisting inappropriate condition of mind causing distress to the individual, that involves a degree of insight, i.e. the person realizes at the time that the perception or mood state is not healthy. Typical examples would be unremitting anxiety or obsessive-compulsive disorder. The cause usually appears to relate to unresolved psychological conflict.

nicotine

If you have to, then smoke. But don't if you don't have to. One of despair's friends in times of crisis, grief and pain is a cigarette. But give up when you can. It will change the world when there is no fug in the jazz club, no Gitanes in the French bar, no cigar smoke in the restaurant, no biddies in India, no clove-scented cigarettes in Indonesia. Nicotine masks the pain and it is a 'little pleasure', but it's better to breathe in deeply the fresh air, face up to it, because you need every bit of fresh air you can get to beat mood swings.

The best advice that no one ever takes is not to start smoking. Nicotine is perhaps the most addictive drug known to man or woman. Its addictive power can be measured first by the extent to which people will go to get their fix: discreetly picking butts out of ashtrays; begging from complete strangers, especially late at night after a bad party; driving miles to the twenty-four-hour garage; being nice to all fellow smokers regardless of how little you like them, in case you need a cigarette. Secondly, the addictive power of nicotine can be measured by the extent smokers lie to themselves: 'I need my cigarettes,' (no one ever died for lack of a cigarette); 'They are my only pleasure in life,' 'I could stop if I wanted to,' and 'I am only harming myself' (of course you are only harming yourself – and your newborn baby; anyone in the same room; kids who see you smoking and think it's okay; providing the cigarette companies with a profit so they can run more adverts, etc).

cold turkey, cut down or nicotine patches?

Cold turkey is the only effective way for the truly determined. And if you are not yet determined, then now is the time to get determined. With determination and a copy of Allen Carr's book *The Easy Way to Give up Smoking* under one arm, the process can be virtually painless.

Cutting down is fine until you don't, and then you are back where you started.

Nicotine patches no more match up to the early morning hit of the first cigarette of the day than swallowing a dose of methadone matches up to jacking up a decent dose of smack. Nicotine patches and methadone have a lot in common. They keep the addicts off the streets, stop them injecting/inhaling and keep them in thrall to their drug of choice.

nursing assistants

Possibly the most undervalued workers in the NHS. They carry out the basic day-to-day routine on the wards, serving meals, doing the laundry, getting shopping for clients and other mundane tasks. However, despite their lowly status they are the backbone of the ward. They often form the relationships that are valued the most by patients. Good nursing assistants are as skilled as any therapist; this skill is intuitive and they speak with the common sense and normal syntax that often get lost by the academically qualified therapist or nurse.

ogden, john

John Ogden was a prodigiously talented musician born in Manchester in 1937. Large of stature, but known as a 'gentle giant', he amazed listeners and critics with his musical mastery and panache at the piano. His physical and musical stature matched the enormous repertoire he played through – much of which was played from memory. He also managed to compose over two hundred pieces, and taught and wrote extensively on music. His was creative genius in full flow.

However, at the peak of his hectic playing schedule in 1973, Ogden suffered a major breakdown – perhaps in part triggered by his lifestyle. He was hospitalized for several years and diagnosed with mania and schizophrenia like his father before him, though there is also speculation as to whether his illness was a form of manic depression.

Ogden resumed playing in public where he still managed to wow audiences – but not with quite the same consistent shine as before. There were notable exceptions like his four-disc recording of Sorabji's 'Opus Clavicembalisticum', which revived the vigour and genius of his earlier performances. Ogden was clearly physically compromised by a life lived at full throttle, and died from pneumonia brought on by undiagnosed diabetes – he was fifty-two.

The BBC film about his life, entitled *Virtuoso*, is based on his biography written by his wife and fellow-pianist, Brenda Lucas Ogden.

old age

Manic depressive illness does not go away as one gets older. However, many patients learn successful methods of controlling symptoms and how to manage their illness better so that its effects are less. Medications may have increased side effects as one grows older, as metabolism and excretion are less efficient, so lower doses of drugs may be used. Bipolar illness may commence after fifty, and an increasing number of people are diagnosed for the first time after this age, but 'physical' causes should never be excluded in the older age group (for example, a brain scan may be more readily recommended). Depressive symptoms in bipolar patients can be accentuated as they can be generally in older people.

Depression amongst the elders of society is very common when there are reduced prospects, often ill-health and loneliness. Despite these being obvious results of circumstance, anti-depressants can have a remarkably rejuvenating effect. Genuine interest in life can become startlingly apparent and there should be a low index of suspicion of depressive illness clouding limited circumstances. Who would not wish to enhance the later years of life if there were the chance – even if in a slightly artificial manner – real value from life can ensue?

omega 3

Omega 3 essential fatty acids cannot be easily formed by the body but, as well as their potential benefit for the heart and circulation, they appear to be an important component of our diet for their effect on brain growth and function. Do not forget the brain is a powerhouse of activity; continually reforming, growing new connections and even new brain cells. It is hardly surprising. For six billion years DHA (docosahexaenoic acid – one of these compounds) has been a building block of the most primitive sensory systems. Forty per cent of the dry weight of the brain consists of phospholipids, with essential fatty acids in their structure. However, it has to be stressed that just because something is essential it does not mean that taking excessive amounts is of value. We can see this in vitamins, where excess is just flushed out of the body.

The difficulty is getting evidence of the appropriate intake, through diet or even supplements. None of the big pharmacological companies have any real interest as the potential for profit is too small to warrant large trials. Past trials have been either small or poorly conducted. Trials have to be 'double-blind' – where the administrator and the recipient are both unaware of whether the 'capsule' being taken is the 'active' ingredient or a placebo. Improvements were shown in reading and attention deficit in studies in Northern Ireland and County Durham, and a small benefit in manic depressive illness was discovered by Sophie Frangou, Consultant Psychiatrist at the Maudsley Hospital recently, though other studies have given equivocal results. It does seem of benefit during pregnancy and for children to make sure there is adequate intake. If a pregnant woman does not have enough in her diet, she depletes her own stores of Omega 3 for the baby.

Bernard Gesch, a researcher in physiology at Oxford University, did a prison trial and showed that supplementation (with vitamins as well in this case) reduced aggressive behaviour. There have been anecdotal reports of high doses helping drug-resistant depression and schizophrenia (anecdotal meaning not enough to be able to really interpret the meaning in larger groups).

On balance, with the current information available, it does seem beneficial to the body as a whole to have a good intake. Two meals of oily fish a week are probably enough, but if you can't do that take a supplement. If you don't like the fishy taste, try flaxseed oil, which if swallowed with a meal considerably reduces the indigestion potential.

overeaters anonymous

Compulsive overeating has only recently been recognized as a distinct condition, while obesity and unhealthy eating habits have been acknowledged as serious problems in Europe and America for some years. According to a recent medical report, over half the UK population is either overweight or obese, and what we feed ourselves and our children is the subject of constant public debate.

OA aims to offer support and advice for anyone who eats compulsively and wishes to stop. OA views overeating as another form of addiction, and treats this accordingly with the Twelve Step method. (See **Eating Disorders**, pages 200–201.)

contact details
PO Box 19, Stretford, Manchester, M32 9EB
07000 784985

websites

www.oagb.org.uk

The National Centre for Eating Disorders (www.eating-disorders.org.uk)

The International Eating Disorders Centre (www.eatingdisorderscentre. co.uk)

Eating Disorders Association (www.edauk.com)

Anorexia and Bulimia Care (ABC) (www.anorexiabulimiacare.co.uk)

Eating Addictions Anonymous (USA) (www.eatingaddictionsanonymous. org)

paediatric manic depression

In children manic depression is rarely diagnosed in the United Kingdom; in the United States it is diagnosed quite frequently. Cardinal symptoms used to support a diagnosis of manic depression are insomnia and grandiosity (where the child has a persisting and genuine belief in his own self-importance – as opposed to temporary play acting which is of course normal). There is often co-morbid drug use which can obfuscate the picture. The area is of major importance as parents may wonder if their adolescent mischief-maker is 'organically' sick or just going through the growing pains of youth in a disorderly manner. There is value in early diagnosis of manic depression, though it is often only made retrospectively, and early management is important. In reality, the older the youth is the more likely manic depression is to be the correct diagnosis. There is an increasing incidence into the early twenties (being the maximum age of onset).

The adolescent should have a careful evaluation by an experienced psychiatrist. Differentiation from ADHD (Attention Deficit Hyperactivity Disorder), 'personality disorder', drug use and behavioural disorders in a healthy child brought up in a dysfunctional manner are key. An accurate and careful diagnosis is important. Clear diagnosis may not be possible where there is a combination of these elements initially.

The danger of over-diagnosing as a society is that everyone ends up being 'sick' with something that needs 'treating' with medication. That doesn't mean manic depression does not exist; it just means we have to be on the look out for over-diagnosis.

There are studies suggesting that children/adolescents going on to have manic depressive illness have a higher IQ than the average but if this is true it may be only a small difference. Highlighting the potential of manic depressive sufferers can have a backlash in the frustration of those unable to focus their energy and intelligence into a successful outcome.

paranoia

A feature of a mental state generally characterized by delusions. Usually marked by a heightened state of suspicion, persecution beliefs, or ideas of grandeur.

parenting

The issue of parenting has been the subject of unprecedented focus in recent years. We now have numerous support groups, services, experts and laws; all contributing to the debate on what makes acceptable parenting. With an increasing body of research on the demonstrable link between adequate parenting and adult mental health, much of it points to the first three years of a child's upbringing as having the greatest impact on his or her later mental health and happiness. Research points to the fact that, invariably, psychopaths have had childhoods of astonishing neglect or maltreatment. On a less dramatic scale, early traumatic or painful experiences can be echoed later in adult depression and anxiety states.

It was in the 1960s that the paediatrician Donald Winnicott wrote of the concept of 'good enough mothering' – meaning that being a perfect parent – whatever that is – is an impossible task. He meant that for a baby to receive good enough attention, nurturing and love would set good early foundations for later in life. Good parenting is enabling a child to feel strong within him/herself. If he/she fails at something you still hold them in your arms and you love them; it is fundamentally important that you allow a child to be loved for their failures as well as their successes. Trying not to set unrealistic goals, or to have unrealistic expectations, is the aim. Instead of only being an absorber of information the child should learn by his or her own experience, being one who contributes. It becomes a problem if the television is left on for hours. With Britain having the highest rate of teenage pregnancies in Western Europe, these are perhaps more challenging goals than ever.

Whatever age parenting is embarked upon, many testify that it changes your life in a way they could never have predicted.

- *Family Caring Trust:* A traditional value base, with material banded in age groups with videos. Training offered.
- *Parenting Education and Support Forum:* Offers information on parenting courses around the country and other local parenting activities. Also parenting materials and information on training.
- *Trust for the Study of Adolescence:* Information for parents of young people and for professionals working with both parents and teenagers.
- *Parentline Plus:* Offering parents support both on the site and via their twenty-four-hour helpline: 0808 800 2222.
- *National Family and Parenting Institute (NFPI):* An independent charity working to support parents in bringing up their children, to promote the well-being of families and to make society more family friendly.
- *Young Minds:* Help and information for parents who are concerned about their child's mental health. Helpline: 0800 018 2138.

phobias

what is a 'simple' phobia?

A phobia is an excessive and/or irrational fear experienced when thinking about, confronting or imagining an object, place or situation which would not normally trouble most people. People with phobias experience problems with anxiety around the object/situation they are afraid of and often go to excessive lengths to avoid it. Phobias are VERY common. It is thought that many phobias have an evolutionary basis; after all it is sensible to be afraid of snakes. (Studies with monkeys have shown that fear of snakes is 'hard-wired' into their brains; in other words they are born with a fear of snakes – you don't need your mum to tell you – which is not a bad thing as one snake bite may be your last one!) Nowadays, certainly in the UK, these fears are, thankfully, not quite so relevant.

what kind of phobias are there?

A phobia can be about anything: heights, hospitals, injections (blood injury phobia), rats, snakes, enclosed spaces (claustrophobia), thunder, spiders, wasps, clowns, lightning, cows – absolutely anything can become the subject of fear. In fact, the myriad different names of phobias can even become the subject of pub quizzes.

when do phobias start?
Phobias usually start in childhood but they can start at any time.

when to seek help
If your phobia is preventing you from carrying out activities that you would like to take part in and/or affecting your life significantly, i.e. you are avoiding activities for fear of activating your phobia, then you should seek help.

what help is available?
Unfortunately, it can be difficult to get help for a simple phobia within the National Health Service unless it is impacting very significantly on your life and on those around you. If you are offered help it is likely to be either in-surgery cognitive behavioural therapy/counselling, or via the CMHT (Community Mental Health Trust). Therapy may involve de-sensitization techniques, for example seeing a photo of a spider and gradually increasing familiarity until at the end of training one might even be touched. You may wish to seek private cognitive behavioural therapy (see BPS or BABCP websites – see **psychotherapists**, page 300–303) or hypnotherapy which some people find helpful. There are a number of good self-help books available and The National Phobics Society offers helpful advice.

book
Overcoming Phobias – Diana Sanders (www.octc.co.uk)

websites
The National Phobics Society (www.phobics-society.org.uk)
The Hypnotherapy Association (www.thehypnotherapyassociation.co.uk)

pink floyd

In 1966 five Cambridge friends, Roger Waters, Rick Wright, Nick Mason, Bob Klose and the late Syd Barrett, formed a band called Sigma 6. Inspired by two blues musicians, Pink Anderson and Floyd Council, they then changed their name to The Pink Floyd Sound. By the end of 1967, the band had changed their name again to Pink Floyd, guitarist Bob Klose had left the band and was replaced by David Gilmour. On 6 April, the following year, Syd Barrett's departure from the band was announced.

For many people growing up in the 1970s and 1980s Pink Floyd represented the best mind soundtrack on offer. Listening to early albums such as *Saucerful of Secrets*, *More* and *Ummagumma* was said by some to be like taking a hallucinogenic trip without the actual LSD or mescaline. Loathed by most of the British music press for representing uncool progressive rock, Pink Floyd's music remains popular all over the world. Their album *Dark Side of the Moon* has sold over thirty-five million copies to date, only slightly less than Michael Jackson's *Thriller*, the all-time biggest seller. Listening to those early Pink Floyd albums, it would seem that mental health and drug issues were closely entwined with the band's music. Indeed, its founder member and composer of the band's two early hits, 'See Emily Play' and 'Arnold Lane', Syd Barrett had his battles with LSD and his mental health made public by the media; possibly explaining why the band wrote and recorded a song in his honour: 'Shine on You Crazy Diamond'. But it was Roger Waters, bassist, singer and composer of the majority of the songs on *Dark Side of the Moon* and *The Wall*, who seemed best at encapsulating the pressures of modern life pushing people over the edge into madness. Songs such as 'Careful With That Axe Eugene', 'Brain Damage', 'Welcome To The Machine', 'Money', 'Comfortably Numb', 'Run Like Hell', and 'Another Brick in the Wall' explored themes such as hypocrisy and greed, stress and alienation, displacement, fear of dying, childhood and abandonment.

fact
One in four UK households owns a copy of *Dark Side of the Moon*.

plath, sylvia

Sylvia Plath was born in Boston in 1932 into a middle-class family. She attended Smith College and suffered a breakdown at the end of her junior year. She went on to receive the Fulbright scholarship and spent two years at Cambridge University where she met and married the British poet Ted Hughes. They settled in England and had two children.

A record of her encroaching mental illness can be seen in the three volumes of poetry, *Ariel*, *Crossing the Water* and *Winter Trees*, that were collected after her death from suicide in 1963 at the age of thirty.

plato

The original exponent of the idea of creative mania or divine inspiration, Plato was a hugely influential philosopher. According to Aristotle (his contemporary) Plato experienced depression in a polymath life full of creative genius.

PMT

PMT stands for pre-menstrual tension and is an unpleasant cyclical mood change around the time of periods. For some women the monthly onset of menstruation is a relief (the natural flow of the fertility cycle, with the fall off in the level of progesterone; even the absence of an unwanted pregnancy). For others it is a burden (the physical inconvenience and discomfort; perhaps the absence of a wanted pregnancy).

Some whose symptoms are marked may have relief during pregnancy, where, though there is build-up of hormones, it is not fluctuating. Physical symptoms such as pain may be helped by anti-prostaglandins (e.g. mefanamic acid) or combined oral contraceptives. There may be contributing influences relating to family or historical emphases (e.g. 'the curse'). A careful evaluation by a doctor/nurse is important, exploring background factors, though in a small number of women disability is difficult to treat.

If there is evidence of background depression, management should follow appropriate lines. Lifestyle changes such as exercise and diet can make a huge difference. Some women find vitamin supplements helpful, particularly vitamin B6, and some Omega 3 essential fatty acids of value. Many complementary treatments can be beneficial, such as acupuncture and massage; and yoga helps the body function better overall. These should be first line approaches.

Poetry is a great way of soothing your soul, following an emotional cross-word puzzle and bringing a smile to your face. Good examples: Dylan Thomas, John Donne, Dorothy Parker, W. H. Auden, Philip Larkin, Sheamus Heaney, Adrian Henri and R. S. Thomas.

In *Touched with Fire*, her study of manic depression and its links to the artist's temperament, Dr Kay Jamison established that 'Two aspects of thinking are pronounced in both creative and hypomanic thought: fluency, rapidity and flexibility and the ability to combine ideas or categories of thought in order to form new and original connections.'

The following poets suffered from mental illness during their lives.

- William Blake
- Lord Byron
- Emily Dickinson
- Gerard Manley Hopkins
- Samuel Johnson
- Vachel Lindsay
- Sylvia Plath
- Ezra Pound
- Percy Bysshe Shelley
- Dylan Thomas

- Robert Burns
- Samuel Taylor Coleridge
- T. S. Eliot
- Victor Hugo
- John Keats
- Boris Pasternak
- Edgar Allan Poe
- Anne Sexton
- Alfred, Lord Tennyson
- Walt Whitman

rapid cycler

Here I am then –
poised in the arena,
The Velodrome
that is my circular theatre,
my cycle begins ...

Again.

Like some strange
Olympian athlete
with ergonomically designed head gear
(but no other protection)
grasping handlebars in fear, I glide

from top
to bottom
in the direction
of the identical Other Me,
free-wheeling down the S

                       L

                          O

                             P

                                E

                                   S

and whizzing up the opposite side,
chasing Sane Me in the distance,

Welcome to the velodrome ride
that is my Dis

                ease,
overtaking shadows –
where every nuance of friction is enhanced,

                                          and the
cheering-of-the-crowd-covers-every-sound-of-the-brakes –

F A I L I N G.

A climax of sparks –
leaving only burnt rubber tyre marks
on the sloping surface,
And the Sane
Insanely watching Me

'Hey, She could race!'
they say,
'Did you see her pace
against the clock?
Rapid cycler,
or what?'
Katie Southall © 2006 (used by kind permission of the author)

postnatal depression and mania

Childbirth is a momentous time. It can lead to mild or even severe instability of mood, both high and low. Part of this is felt to be due to sudden hormone change and part to sheer fatigue. It is often difficult to sleep after a birth. Hypomania or even mania can arise, and a woman with a family history of manic depression must be carefully monitored as there is a much higher risk. Manic depressive illness may begin at this time and then recur, independent of pregnancy.

Severe postnatal depression may occur quite separately from manic depression and both of these conditions can be life-threatening.

Milder forms of mood swing are being studied and may give valuable information for management of more severe illness. Treatment of manic depressive illness in pregnancy and the puerperium (the first postnatal month) requires care by experienced psychiatrists, particularly as mood-stabilizers can be injurious to the foetus and infant.

prayer

'Searching the self I find little but questions. But asking them, I guess, is a beginning. I turn to you, whom many have described as "the being who is there", and I hope.

'I hope in silence and in words and in thoughts. All these are here in the reality of this moment and me. I am with them now. So listen, O Listener, and let me breathe with faith and murmur with expectation. I am because I am. Make me, if you may, make me, just make me grasp anything that is real and lasting.

'I hold on to the faith and hope of others and make it my own. Their prayers make mine and accept just these random mutterings. I hope, if I do not then at least I wish to.'

Dom Antony Sutch

'In prayer it is better to have a heart without words than words without a heart.'

Mahatma Gandhi

The best-known anti-depressant, chemical name fluoxetine, was introduced in 1988, bringing controversy in its wake. It is one of a generation of drugs, known as the SSRIs (see **Drugs (Pharmaceutical)**: anti-depressants, pages 190–92), that came after the tricyclics that were well known for unpleasant side effects and, being much freer of them, it became effectively a major event in mental health worldwide. Millions of prescriptions have been written and the willingness of the medical profession to prescribe caused a public backlash against doctors who were felt to dole out the pills without consideration of their appropriateness to the specific condition. Many people considered that depression is an illness that should be dealt with by looking at the circumstances causing it – a much more involved and time-consuming approach.

Peter D. Kramer's book *Listening to Prozac*, the landmark book about anti-depressants and the remaking of the self came out, suggesting that people's whole personalities were altered by the drug – the timid became confident, businessmen's transactions were improved, the actual 'self' was changed – and it became even more of a drama. Many patients were getting hold of them as wonder-cure drugs from the Internet, hoping for 'plastic surgery' for their brains!

Finally, after the dust inevitably began to settle, the position became clearer. This newer group of drugs, which will of course be superseded at some point, is of great value in depressive illness, especially when combined with a psychotherapeutic approach – looking at those very causes if they can be established. They actually bring about demonstrable changes in the hippocampus, the emotional seat of the brain, due to the action of a protein called BDNF (brain derived neurotrophic factor), so it is not just 'filling a hole', and is the reason they take weeks to take full effect. For the most part, people are helped to return to a healthy emotional state, rather than being changed into a new unfamiliar human being.

This drug, and its fellow SSRIs, represents many things to many people – but can be of huge benefit to patients, if used in a responsible manner.

psychiatric nurses

Psychiatric nurses are the unsung heroes of the mental health service. They will try to act in the patient's best interests, which is often not the same as what the patient wants them to do. This can make for some interesting discussions, usually involving a lot of shouting and abuse directed at the nurses who normally take it in their stride and as part of the job. Curiously enough, once the illness has subsided and come under control, a friendly relationship based on mutual respect often emerges.

psychiatrists, psychologists, psychotherapists

See **Therapists**, pages 298–303.

psychopath

An emotive term used by the tabloid newspapers to describe those who commit murder whilst mentally ill (in fact most of these rare crimes are committed by sufferers from schizophrenia, acting out of fear brought about by terrifying hallucinations or delusional beliefs). It is a little confusing – their behaviour in these circumstances might be described as psychopathic, from the Greek words *psych* (mind) and *pathos* (suffering) because they are at that time unwell in their minds; but a person with a treatable condition, such as schizophrenia, is not a 'psychopath'.

'Psychopath' is actually a medical and legal term used to describe individuals with what is clinically known as an anti-social personality disorder, and they act in a manner, though unacceptable, for which they are considered responsible. There is no doubt that these individuals cause a great deal of suffering to their fellow men. The diagnostic criteria for a psychopathy are a lack of empathy, shallow emotions, incapability to feel guilt or remorse, and an inability to learn from experience.

Psychopaths are also usually of above average intelligence and have considerable charm. They are seen as manipulative and dishonest individuals who will use bullying or violence to achieve their aims if lies and deceit fail.

There is a saying that there are no psychopaths in open society over the age of forty. This is due to the fact that they are either in prison (it is thought that a large proportion of inmates have undiagnosed personality disorders) or dead. They usually have a high occupancy rate in the mortuary fridges as they have a tendency to die young, either through drug overdoses, car crashes, suicide or altercations with fellow psychopaths. There are some that manage to achieve the emotional maturity needed to fit in with the general population. There is also some discussion that very successful and ruthless individuals may in fact be psychopathic. Most of us can think of someone who fits this description.

To be fair, it must be said that most psychopaths are made, not born. They usually have childhood histories of staggeringly horrifying abuse or neglect. Post mortem examinations of their brains (of which there have been plenty due to their high attrition rate) have shown that the areas that govern the emotions are underdeveloped. It is thought that the abuse they suffered as children did not allow these areas fully to develop and they are physically incapable of feeling any extreme emotions. When talking about their feelings, they will often describe themselves as feeling flat or bored most of the time. To combat this they will often engineer situations which result in violence, harm or chaos to others and excitement or amusement to themselves.

There are various treatment approaches available. These include therapeutic communities where they are expected to take responsibility for their actions and deal with being confronted and challenged by their peers. In some prisons and high security hospitals they take part in groups that force them to confront and face up to the damage and misery they have caused to others. The effectiveness of this treatment is still being debated.

There are some who say the condition is untreatable and those who commit offences should be dealt with by the criminal justice system as psychopaths who know exactly what they are doing. Others disagree and say that the mental health services provide the best chance of allowing them to live meaningful lives.

psychosis

A disorder of mind which disturbs the individual's ability to perceive the state as abnormal, i.e. generally lacking in insight. The category has an implication of severity, in that it contains some of the more unfamiliar symptoms to others, such as delusion or hallucination.

r

reality

Our interpretation of reality is entirely affected by our mood. When one is in a stable and healthy mood, it is difficult to imagine. When one isn't well, perception is distorted so that 'reality' appears distorted too. There is a theory that the human psyche is set to be abnormally optimistic by the 'computer' in our brains; from an evolutionary perspective it is quite attractive to a potential mate to be slightly high, apparently strong and confident. After all, if we regarded life as perhaps it really is, we would be depressed and believe, as the playwright Samuel Beckett says, 'We are born astride a grave.'

relapse

In general, this means to fall back to a former condition. It is a common occurrence in many chronic disorders and addictions that require behavioural adjustments to treat them effectively. A relapse might refer to resuming use of a drug, going back to the bottle or in general regressing after a partial recovery.

relate

Relate is the leading agency for the provision of advice and support for couple and family relationships.

website
www.relate.org.uk

Religion is often blamed for many of the terrible things going on in the world. The root of many wars, territorial disputes and attendant unhappiness frequently appears to have been religious conflict. Yet many religions successfully offer purpose and comfort to hundreds of millions of people. Many people, who write off religion as a load of boring codswallop, are often a trifle ignorant of what they are actually dismissing. Similar to the man who believed manic depression simply meant 'being very depressed', sometimes it's easy to think you know something, when in fact, you don't.

THE MAIN CHRISTIAN CHURCHES
church of england (protestant)

The Church of England is the officially established Christian Church of England which recognizes the monarch as its official head. Beliefs are that Christ was sent to earth to save humanity from its sins, and that he was the Messiah promised in the Old Testament. Worship and *The Book of Common Prayer* are permanent features, and central to worship is a celebration of the Lord's Supper or Mass.

roman catholic church

A 2000-year-old religion and the biggest religious institution in the western world, headed by the Pope, currently Pope Benedict XVI. Like Protestants, Catholics believe in the divinity of Christ, but also focus on other areas which make their teachings distinctive. These include devotion to the Virgin Mary, belief in transubstantiation, and that all life is sacred and begins from the moment of conception.
Website: www.catholic-ew.org.uk

Other main Christian denominations include Baptist, Methodist, Orthodox and Seventh-Day Adventist.

quakers

The Religious Society of Friends (commonly known as Quakers or Friends) is a spiritual movement founded in England in the seventeenth century by people who were dissatisfied with the existing denominations

RELIGIONS

of Christianity. Since its beginnings in England it has spread to other countries though its numbers are fairly small – around 600,000.
Website: www.quaker.org.uk

christian support organizations

Such a vast Christian community has both the enormous resources and desire to provide help and support in the field of mental health. Apart from the services and support networks found at local parish level – too numerous to list here – there are a number of Christian umbrella organizations dedicated to pastoral care for mental health.

Organizations concerned with faith, spirituality and mental health – information courtesy of the Mental Health Foundation website:

Acorn Christian Foundation
Whitehill Chase, High Street, Borden, Hampshire GU35 0AP
Telephone: 01420 478 121
Fax: 01420 478 122
Email: info@acornchristian.org
Website: www.acornchristian.org
The Acorn Christian Foundation offers a telephone resource for information. It represents an affiliation of six healing centres where support is available, and callers can be pointed towards approximately twenty other healing centres nationwide. Source: Acorn Christian Foundation website.

Association for Pastoral Care in Mental Health (APCMH)
c/o St. Marylebone Parish Church, Marylebone Road, London NW1 5LT
Telephone: 020 7383 0167
Email: apcmh@pastoral.org.uk
Website: www.pastoral.org.uk
The APCMH is a Christian based, ecumenical charity which recognizes the importance of spiritual values and support in mental health. This is the largest pastoral organization primarily concerned with the spiritual needs of people with mental health problems. They hope to encourage local initiatives in faith communities in order to support and empower mental health service users. Several befriending schemes and drop-in centres have been set up by APCMH members and the experience gained from them can be shared.

Association of Christian Counsellors (ACC)
29 Momus Boulevard, Coventry CV2 5NA
Telephone: 0845 124 9569
Fax: 0845 124 9571
Email: office@acc-uk.org
Website: www.acc-uk.org
The Association of Christian Counsellors is an interdenominational affiliation representing over one hundred Christian training and counselling organizations. The ACC can offer referrals to local counsellors on its register. Source: Association of Christian Counsellors website.

Connections Counselling Limited
8 Grafton Road, King's Lynn, Norfolk PE30 3HA
Telephone: 07050 694775
Fax: 07050 694776
Email: info@connections-c.com
Website: www.connections-c.co.u.k
Counselling centres help people around the world.

Life for the World Trust
Micklefield Christian Centre, Buckingham Drive, High Wycombe HP13 7YB
Telephone: 01494 462008
Fax: 01494 462008
Email: info@lftw.org
Website: www.lftw.org
A Christian charity committed to excellence in providing recovery from addiction.

buddhism

Buddhism is a 2000-year-old Eastern religion sometimes described as a philosophy, and is followed by 350 million Buddhists worldwide. Based on the teachings of Buddha, one of its central beliefs is the cycles of reincarnation that humans must go through to achieve Nirvana – a state free of suffering. At the heart of Buddha's teaching lie the Four Noble Truths and the Eightfold Path which lead the Buddhist towards the path of Enlightenment.

Buddhism is increasingly popular in the West and there are now estimated to be hundreds of Buddhist organizations, centres and groups in the United Kingdom.

buddhism and mental health

Buddhist Psychotherapy

53 Grosvenor Place, Jesmond, Newcastle upon Tyne NE2 2RD

Telephone: 01162 867 476 or 020 7209 3224

Email: amida@amida.demon.co.uk

Website: www.amidatrust.com/www.buddhistpsychotherapy.org.uk

Information from the Amida Trust on membership, training and retreat centres. Bookings and enquiries can be made to the Trust address outlined above.

Karuna Institute

Natsworthy Manor, Widecombe-in-the-Moor, Newton Abbot, Devon TQ13 7TR

Telephone: 01647 221 457

Email: office@karuna-institute.co.uk

Website: www.karuna-institute.co.uk

The Karuna Institute is a training centre in a Buddhist-oriented psychotherapy called Core Process.

The Buddhist Society

58 Eccleston Square, London SW1V 1PH

Telephone: 020 7834 5858

Fax: 020 7976 5238

Email: info@thebuddhistsociety.org.uk

Website: www.thebuddhistsociety.org.uk

Various classes for members and non-members. Meditation class on Saturday for the public. Public lectures.

hinduism

The oldest main religion at over 4000 years, Hinduism is a tradition that is based on a collection of Indian literature known as the Vedas, and has around 750 million followers. The term Hinduism in fact covers many religious rituals and traditions which would confound the novice attempting an exact definition. Some central concepts are belief in a universal soul called Brahman who can take many forms; the idea of reincarnation; and karma.

Website: www.hinducounciluk.org

sikhism

Sikhism was founded in the Punjab by Guru Nanak, and is one of the world's major religions with over twenty-three million followers. Over half a million Sikhs live in Britain making it the UK's third most popular religion. Sikhs are easily identifiable by their beards and turbans which are seen as important religious hallmarks. Core beliefs include that one god exists without form or gender, that a good life is achieved through honesty and caring for others, and that empty religious superstitions have no value.

Website: www.sikhs.org

islam

Islam is the world's second largest religion after Christianity at 1.5 billion followers worldwide. Believing in one all-encompassing god, and worshipping Muhammad as the final prophet of Islam, followers of the faith are known as Muslims. Britain has around 1.6 million Muslims, and the community has developed various bodies concerned with mental health.

The Muslim Council of Great Britain: Website: www.mcb.org.uk

Muslim Health Network

65a Grosvenor Road, London W7 1HR

Telephone: 020 8799 4475

Email: info@muslimhealthnetwork.org

Website: www.muslimhealthnetwork.org

Established to play a principal role in promoting, preserving and protecting health and health education amongst Muslim communities in the UK.

Muslim Women's Helpline

Room 7, 11 Main Drive, G.E.C. East Lane Estate, Wembley, London HA9 7NA

Telephone: 020 8904 8193

Website: www.mwhl.org.uk

The Muslim Women's Helpline is a telephone listening service for Muslim women. Source: Muslim Women's Helpline website.

An-Nisa Society
85 Wembley Hill Road, Wembley, Middlesex HA9 8BU
Telephone: 020 8902 0100
Email: an-nisa@btconnect.com
The An-Nisa Society works towards establishing a Muslim association of counsellors, acting as an accredited organization, training centre and counselling service.

Awaaz
464 Cheetham Hill Road, Cheetham Hill, Manchester M8 9JW
Telephone: 0845 644 1972
Email: altaff@aol.com
Website: www.awaaz.co.uk
Awaaz is primarily a resource for Asian people in the Manchester area. In addition, Awaaz is currently developing a network of Muslim counsellors in the north-west of England, and can provide information on accessing counsellors who practise a faith-centred model of therapy.

judaism
Judaism has around fourteen million followers worldwide, being one of the oldest religious traditions still practised today. It has a fairly well-developed network in the spiritual provision for mental health.

Jewish Association for the Mentally Ill (JAMI)
16a North End Road, London NW11 7PH
Telephone: 020 8458 2223
Fax: 020 8458 1117
Email: info@jamiuk.org
Website: www.mentalhealth-jamiuk.org.uk
Works to provide services and support to people with mental illness, people with learning disabilities and their carers. Committed to providing the care and support that embodies the culture and values of Jewish society.

Jewish Care
Stuart Young House, 221 Golders Green Road, London NW11 9DQ
Telephone: 020 8922 2000
Fax: 020 8922 1998
Email: jewishcaredirect@jcare.org

Website: www.jewishcare.org
Jewish Care is a voluntary organization operating in London and the South East. Jewish Care offers a variety of services including community psychiatric assessment by professional staff trained in mental health services. Source: Jewish Care website.

Jewish Care Scotland
Walton Community Care Centre, May Terrace, Giffnock, Glasgow G46 6LD
Telephone: 0141 620 1800
Fax: 0141 620 2409
Email: admin@jcarescot.org.uk
Website: www.jcarescot.org.uk
Range of social work services for vulnerable individuals and families from the Jewish community. Source: Jewish Care Scotland website.

MIYAD Jewish Crisis Helpline
Helpline: 0345 581999
Telephone: 020 8444 2044
Website: www.find.support.co.uk
The Jewish Crisis Helpline is a counselling service based in London and Manchester.

humanism
Humanism is a broad category of philosophies which seeks to emphasize the personal capacity of people to seek truth and morality in a way which transcends idols or religious texts.

British Humanist Association
Website: www.humanism.org.uk

paganism
Paganism has come to mean a broad set of spiritual or religious beliefs loosely defined by a reverence for nature, and also draws on the traditions of indigenous peoples of the world.
The Pagan Federation website: www.paganfed.org

bahá'í

The Bahá'í faith is an emerging global religion and was founded by Bahá'u'lláh in Iran in the nineteenth century.

The central idea of the faith is that of unity, and Bahá'ís seek to remove barriers of race, gender and belief. They believe that people should work together for the common benefit of humanity.

Website: www.bahai.org

rethink

Rethink is the largest severe mental illness charity in the UK. It used to be called the National Schizophrenia Fellowship. It provides a wide range of community services including employment projects, supported housing, day services, helplines, residential care and respite centres.

Rethink adheres to the recovery approach which means that people are encouraged to take control of their own lives and move away from a negative mental health system. It's about working out ways to help yourself, acquiring skills, knowledge and strength to reduce harmful experiences, taking responsibility and having hope. You can read more about this on their website. They provide a range of leaflets and a bibliography on recovery and self-management.

Rethink
28 Castle Street, Kingston Upon Thames, Surrey KT1 1SS
Telephone: 0845 456 0455
Email: info@rethink.org

National Advice Service
Helpline: 020 8974 6814 (open 10am – 3pm Monday to Friday)
Email: advice@rethink.org
Website: www.rethink.org
As well as the helpline, advice and information resources, Rethink can help with housing: Rethink have 117 housing services in the UK which range from intensive twenty-four-hour supported housing to crisis housing.

community services
Rethink's services are commissioned by local Primary Care Trusts and Social Services. Community services vary from area to area but may

include one-to-one or small group support, resource cafés, and opportunities to participate and train in community work such as practical conservation and environmental work, etc.

services for carers
They provide fifty-three carer services across England. These offer carers individual and group support, access to information, education and training, and assistance with Carer Assessments.

employment and training
There are thirty-seven Rethink employment services that provide or access real work. These include sheltered workplaces with access to training and intensive on-the-job support for those starting work in open employment. You can find more information and a list of all their employment services on the website.

rock bottom

Rock bottom is a term used in AA and other twelve step programmes to describe an addict or alcoholic at the end of their tether who has become financially, mentally and spiritually bankrupt. Many people find that once they acknowledge their 'rock bottom' situation and that they need help, it turns out to be the best thing that ever happened to them.

Interestingly, the Chinese do not have a single word for 'crisis'. The equivalent is made up of two characters – 'danger' and 'opportunity'.

S

SAD – seasonal affective disorder

This is not a joke, but a real kind of depression which sets in regularly at certain times of the year. Usually it starts in the autumn or winter, when daylight is reduced. A key feature is the desire to sleep more and eat carbohydrate foods.

Seasonal affective disorder (SAD) is a form of depression that affects approximately one in fifty or just over one million people in the UK between September and April.

SAD seems to develop from inadequate bright light during the winter months. It is thought to be caused by a biochemical imbalance in the hypothalamus, the part of the brain which controls mood, appetite, sleep, temperature and sex drive.

how can SAD be treated?

Light therapy has proved to be effective in the majority of cases and involves spending up to four hours per day exposed to light that is at least ten times the intensity of normal household lighting. You are advised to sit in front of a special light box, allowing the light to reach your eyes, and with consistent use, your low mood should lift.

sainsbury centre for mental health

Sainsbury Centre for Mental Health carries out research, development and training work to influence policy and practice in health and social care. Whilst not offering direct services, it may be worth looking at their website for up-to-date information.

website
www.scmh.org.uk

samaritans

Samaritans are available twenty-four hours a day to provide confidential emotional support for people who are feeling distressed, in despair, in crisis or suicidal.

Samaritans will not judge you or tell you what to do, but they will give you the time and space to talk, to think and find a way through. Samaritans listen with an open mind for as long as you need. They may ask you how you are feeling and invite you to talk about your feelings. They give you plenty of time and space to talk if you want to. Volunteers are trained in listening skills, recognizing your needs and responding appropriately.

Samaritans also offer support and advice for people who are worried about someone else, help spot someone at risk and what to do, and provide helpful advice if someone you know has died.

You can contact Samaritans by telephone, letter or email. You can also visit a branch for face-to-face support.

national telephone number
08457 90 90 90 – twenty-four hours a day from anywhere in the UK for the price of a local call. In the Republic of Ireland the number is 1850 60 90 90.

local branch numbers
You can find the number of your local branch in the telephone book or in their local branch index on the website. There are over 200.

visiting
You can visit your local branch. Their address is in the phone book or you can find your nearest branch address and telephone number on the local branch index on their website.

address
You can write a letter to any branch or write in complete confidence to: Chris, PO Box 9090, Stirling FK8 2SA

email

jo@samaritans.org

If you want your email address to be confidential and anonymous, you can create a free email address through www.btyahoo.com/bbdirect/basic-mail, www.hotmail.com or www.talk21.com. You can choose an address here which doesn't identify you. Protected by a password, no one else can access it. Samaritans aim to reply to your email within twenty-four hours. These replies are from real human volunteers and are not automated responses. However, it won't necessarily be the same person answering your emails each time.

festival branch

Festival Samaritans go to events throughout Britain and provide a twenty-four-hour service. Events are mainly outdoor music festivals like Reading and Glastonbury. You can find them by a large green SAMARITANS banner on display at the event.

website

The Samaritans website (www.samaritans.org.uk) provides information about their service and a local branch index. Their website also publishes useful fact sheets about depression, self-harm, suicide and other mental health problems.

confidentiality

All information given to a Samaritan will remain confidential unless:

- You have given informed consent to pass on information.
- The Samaritans have had to call an ambulance if it appears that you are unable to make rational decisions.
- The Samaritans have received a court order requiring them to divulge information.
- The Samaritans are given information about acts of terrorism or bomb warnings.
- A caller attacks or threatens volunteers.
- A caller deliberately prevents the service from being delivered to other callers.

Samaritans do not make recordings of calls. You can read more about confidentiality and the Samaritans' caller privacy statement on their website (www.samaritans.org.uk).

SANE is an organization which raises awareness about people with mental illness and their families. They provide information and emotional support to those experiencing mental health problems, their families and carers through SANELINE. They also undertake research into the causes of serious mental illness through the Prince of Wales International Centre for SANE Research. SANE initially focused on schizophrenia and now is concerned with all mental illness.

contact

1st floor, Cityside House, 40 Adler Street, London E1 1EE
Email: london@sane.org.uk
Telephone: 0845 767 8000 All calls are at local rate.

nationwide helpline: SANELINE

SANELINE is a national 'out of hours' telephone helpline offering practical information, crisis care and emotional support to anybody affected by mental health problems. Calls are totally confidential within the organization and are not traced. Very occasionally, under extreme circumstances where they feel life is in danger, they may breach confidentiality by calling the emergency services, but only if you have already given them your name and address.

SANELINE is accredited to the Mental Health Partnership Quality Standard.

Interpreters are provided through Language Line, a service offering interpretation in over 100 languages.

The calls are answered by volunteers who have had extensive training on a programme recognized by the Royal College of Psychiatrists. Volunteers will be non-directive and non-judgemental and will be able to listen and discuss options with you. There is no set time limit. SANELINE volunteers are trained to support people who are feeling suicidal. Highly experienced co-ordinators are on hand to help. SANELINE volunteers are able to:

- Offer support and a listening ear in times of crisis
- Give information to help you make decisions
- Put you in touch with services in your local area and give you up-to-the-minute details about current treatments, medication, side effects, etc.

- Help you with current mental health legislation and the mental health system.

Volunteers have access to a huge database of resources and information, which is updated daily.

You can be referred to a 'Caller Care' team, which means that particularly vulnerable people can be contacted during a period of crisis and feeling isolated, if they want to be. This service is staffed by trained mental health workers. It operates during office hours and also provides out of hours and weekend cover.

website

The website (www.sane.org.uk) has up-to-date information about mental health, treatments, legislation, etc. There are downloadable fact sheets on Alcohol and Drugs, Anxiety, Depression, Manic Depression, Medical Treatments, Obsessions, Phobias, Schizophrenia and Talking Treatments. There are also other books and publications available on request, many of which are free. For example, *Discover the Road Ahead* is a handbook which provides helpful information on detecting the early signs of schizophrenia, how to deal with the diagnosis, the progression of the condition, and the latest treatments and available support, and provides useful case studies. A mental health series of booklets are also available free on request.

saturn

The farthest known planet in the solar system was associated in the Middle Ages with darkness and misery, and had astrological significance in this character.

schizophrenia

The 'split' in schizophrenia refers to a splitting of the mind, not the personality. It is a label given to people who have a number of emotional and cognitive or thought-based symptoms.

DSM IV defines schizophrenia as a collection of symptoms that have been present for a month or longer against a background of symptoms present for at least six months. The symptoms are associated with social dysfunction. Two of the following symptoms are required for the diagnosis: delusions; hallucinations; disorganized or incoherent speech; disorganized behaviour; and 'negative' symptoms, which describe a lack of emotional and verbal responses.

The best-known symptoms are delusions and hallucinations that include hearing voices. Delusions are erroneous beliefs that cannot be shifted regardless of the evidence to the contrary. They are often part of a complex belief system, which may include a belief about being persecuted. Someone can be shown all the evidence to contradict their belief, but because the person with schizophrenia no longer knows whom they can trust or believe, he or she assumes the evidence is faked. The usual method of deciding what is significant and what is not significant have failed and somehow the person with schizophrenia has to account for everything that happens. In order to do so, 'delusions' are needed to fill the gaps. Moreover, everything that happens tends to become personally relevant. If there is one way of summing up the condition, it is as a 'disturbance of meaning'.

The second major symptom is hearing voices and hallucinations. Everyone has at least one voice inside his or her head. When asked 'How old are you?', if you think and listen for a moment, you will find the voice inside has already answered the question. At other times, the inner critic shouts, 'How can I be so stupid?' The difference between the average person and the person with schizophrenia is that the schizophrenic does not always recognize these voices as coming from inside their own head. The voices appear to come from the outside world and can sound like friends, family or acquaintances. The voices frequently say unpleasant and dangerous things. The person with schizophrenia responds to these voices as though they were from outside of themselves. They may answer them out loud, so appearing to talk to themselves, and they may do what the voices tell them to do. Rarely, these voices can be so aggressive and terrifying that they drive the person with schizophrenia to suicide or even murder.

Cognitive behavioural therapy can be extremely valuable in enabling people to learn to live more easily with their voices and to learn diversions such as music to help manage them more effectively. When asked, few people with schizophrenia want rid of their voices completely. With a brain prone to schizophrenia come accompanying talents and insights. For example, some people with schizophrenia have an almost uncanny way of sensing how other people are feeling. If the gift of manic depression is energy, the gift of schizophrenia is sensitivity.

sectioning

This term is often used in conversation about individuals who have been admitted to a mental health inpatient unit. The tone of voice used is probably similar to that used when describing someone who has just been caught smuggling heroin by the customs authorities.

The reality is that placing someone under a section of the 1983 Mental Health Act is usually used only in cases where someone is extremely unwell and is presenting as a danger to themselves and/or others. The powers granted to police and clinicians are wide ranging. In extreme cases it grants the power to enter people's homes and take them to an inpatient unit. Depending on the type of section, individuals are obliged to take the medication prescribed by the psychiatrist. Nursing staff also have a clear duty to administer it. This can lead to some interesting situations on the ward.

When a patient is under a section, it is not possible to leave the ward without the permission of the consultant and the nursing staff. Those placed under section are usually admitted to an open ward unless their illness is of such severity as to warrant admission to a psychiatric intensive care unit (PICU). These are small locked units with a high ratio of staff to clients where the most disturbed individuals are treated. Sufferers of manic depression usually only remain there for a relatively short period of time and are admitted to the open units as soon as possible.

Individuals admitted under section have wide-ranging rights in place to protect them from being unlawfully detained, such as: the right to free legal representation; the right of appeal to a Mental Health Tribunal; the right to an advocate from MIND or another MH charity to complain on the patient's behalf; and the right to have the section reviewed by the hospital managers. All hospitals have a complaints procedure that can be used to investigate any issues that a patient is unhappy with. In some respects being under section, ironically, can actually give a patient more rights than someone who is admitted informally.

Informal admission means a voluntary stay in an acute ward. This means that the patient can leave at any time. However, if the staff feel that this would be unsafe for both the individual and others, then it is possible to be placed under a section when in hospital. In some situations, a patient can be detained for up to six hours by a suitably qualified nurse, to give the doctor time to consider applying a section.

For more information *The Maze*, a book produced by the Maudsley Hospital, gives very clear guidance on every section covered by the 1983 Mental Health Act.

self-esteem

Effective self-esteem gives resilience in the face of difficulties. It requires a relatively accurate but generous assessment of one's qualities and talents. The assessment remains constant over time and is not dependent on immediate circumstances or supportive friends. Effective self-esteem holds someone in good stead when they are faced with a crisis. They are confident that they can handle it because they know their resources and how to manage them. The first breeze of adversity does not disperse effective self-esteem.

Improving self-esteem by telling someone how good they are has barely more effect than telling someone who is depressed to 'pull themselves together'. Low self-esteem comes with a set of beliefs attached to it. Those beliefs mean that someone with low self-esteem thinks, 'Yes, self-esteem is important and it is good. Everyone in the room needs good self-esteem, except for me. It doesn't apply to me because I am just so bad.' Someone with low self-esteem can deflect every compliment or simply not hear them. If they read a report that contains both positive and negative statements, they will only see the negative statements because the negative statements agree with their beliefs.

However, those who can see themselves in these statements can also understand that there are benefits to low self-esteem. For example, if you believe all the terrible things you say to yourself, it means you don't have to try and succeed. You know you are going to fail anyway, so why risk actual failure? Thus, low self-esteem can perversely protect an individual from risk.

However, it also shields them from success and fulfilment.

Good self-esteem is essential for good mental health. One easy way to improve self-esteem is to stop negative self-talk and putting oneself down, and to start asking better questions. Instead of saying, 'How stupid can I be?' or telling yourself off: 'That was stupid, I am stupid, I am never going to succeed,' try saying to yourself, 'What have I learnt from that experience?' or 'What do I know now that I didn't know before?' or 'What can I do to get a different result in the future?'

The aim of therapy is to help people reach that point of change, through reassessing their own self-worth and increased self-confidence, and through the healing power of a strong relationship with their therapist.

self-harm

what is self-harm?

Self-harm is a way of coping with distress that is, in itself, harmful. It's often called deliberate self-harm (DSH).

how do people self-harm?

People self-harm in many ways, including having unhealthy lifestyle habits such as drinking excessively, taking street drugs and overeating. However, 'self-harm' is taken to mean harming yourself in ways such as cutting, burning, scratching, taking overdoses (suicide attempts, otherwise known as parasuicide) and swallowing inedible objects.

who self-harms?

People can self-harm regularly or just once or twice in a lifetime. People who have had traumatic, abusive childhoods are vulnerable to self-harm.

why do people self-harm?

People say they self-harm for many reasons, for example:
- Keeping difficult memories at bay
- Trying to feel 'real and alive'
- Maintaining a sense of being 'separate' (e.g. from an abuser)
- Trying to feel less 'vulnerable'
- Releasing emotions

what can I do?

If you are hurting yourself you should consult your GP who should follow NICE (see website) guidelines when planning your care. Your care should involve either working on stopping self-harm altogether, or at least minimizing the damage you do to yourself when self-harming. Some health professionals may not be as sympathetic as others around self-harm issues so do seek alternative help or try another GP if this seems to be the case.

how can I help someone I know?
Be patient, talk to them. Acknowledge their pain, encourage them to seek help. DON'T ignore it.

if you self-harm
You are not alone – many people self-harm.

self-management

know your illness
Everyone's manic depression is different, yet there are patterns of illness. Everything is worse when one is tired. But different types of stress affect people differently. Self-awareness and an awareness of one's relationships are essential parts of the self-management of manic depression. Just as someone in a wheelchair cannot easily forget their disability, so the person with manic depression cannot easily forget what has happened to them. However, with careful planning, skill, courage and ingenuity very little is beyond the reach of the truly determined. Mountains can be scaled, and continents crossed! And the same rules apply across the board and to those with mental health problems. The diagnosis comes with certain constraints, but with ingenuity and determination, constraints need not be limitations.

know yourself
Self-knowledge does not come easily. People are socialized to follow other people's rules and plans. Self-knowledge is about knowing who you are beneath all the programming and social obligations. The nature–nurture debate focuses on how much of our character is due to upbringing and how much to our DNA. We are naturally an adaptable species. Self-knowledge is about knowing what is an adaptation and what is real. Self-knowledge doesn't mean you don't bend to the group, it means you

know when you do. That leads to knowing the difference when you flow to your own rhythms and march to the beat of your own drum.

Self-knowledge is about being honest, and accepting oneself for all the good and bad, social and antisocial characteristics that are an integral part of the nature of human beings.

sex

how mental health problems might affect your sex life
Mental health difficulties and relationship problems affect your sex life. How you feel about yourself reflects in how much you and your partner can enjoy sex. If you are feeling low and anxious, maybe tired, your self-image is likely to be low and this may contribute towards a loss of interest.

Some people experience anxiety over sexual identity and this can exacerbate or trigger mental health problems. People who have had abusive childhood experiences, and who are vulnerable to psychological distress, may experience difficulties around sex. Anxiety makes it difficult for people to 'let go' and 'enjoy' themselves – for example, some people find it difficult to reach orgasm (anorgasmia). Whilst it would be rewarding to have a fulfilling sex life, often sex is the last thing on your mind whilst you are experiencing mental health problems.

Some illnesses can actually increase the sex drive (libido). People who are experiencing a 'manic' episode, for example, may go through overwhelming feelings of sexual desire and may become quite promiscuous.

medication and sex 'drive'
Psychotropic medications, for example anti-depressants, may affect sex drive and performance. You may feel reduced libido. Men may also experience impotence (inability to get and sustain an erection), or delayed ejaculation.

how to get help if you're worried about your sex life
Discuss this with your GP/health care team. It might be worth considering drugs such as Viagra for men finding difficulty getting and sustaining an erection. You might discuss whether an alternative medication would be more appropriate for you. You can, of course, address any sexual issues with your therapist if you are receiving professional psychological input.

If you think you are experiencing sexual difficulties linked to past issues, discuss this with your therapist/GP.

top tips

- Try not to worry too much – worry only makes it worse!
- If men wake up with an erection in the morning it shows that they can still get an erection – but even if they don't, they probably still can!
- Concentrate on getting as healthy as you can with your initial psychological problem – for the time being that may well be far more important.
- Talk about the problem with your partner – you could think about ideas around satisfying your partner sexually whilst you are unwell. It may well be an opportunity to get closer in other ways, and improve your sex life when it resumes.
- Don't be ashamed – almost everyone experiences sexual difficulties at some time.

books

Sex Therapy – a Practical Guide by Keith Hawton (This is a professional's book but you may find it useful to find out what help you may be offered and what you may be able to do to help yourself.)

sex addiction

Sex addiction is seen as another type of compulsive behaviour which is causing harm to oneself and others, and deserves as much attention as gambling, drugs or food addictions. Sex Addicts Anonymous (International) (www.sa-recovery.org) provides a forum for change for those who feel their sexual behaviour is compulsive, destructive or perhaps dangerous.

shame

Mark Twain once wrote, 'Man is the only animal that blushes or needs to,' yet it is always possible to tell when an animal is ashamed of itself, normally on account of some misdemeanour involving peeing somewhere or stealing food. Likewise, it is fairly easy to tell when a human being is ashamed because of the way they lower their eyes, blush or bite their lip. However, understanding that somebody has a long-held sense of shame about something is another matter. Maybe the best way of defining shame is to look at the opposite – dignity. Perhaps somebody or some institution took away, belittled or attacked your dignity at some point in your life and left you with a wound of indignity. However, most of us feel shame about feeling shame and as a result it's rarely acknowledged to others. Like any other feeling that has been denied, shame resurfaces in a manifestation of mental ill health.

As the saying goes, 'secrets make you sick'.

Therefore, the answer lies in bringing things to the surface, out into the open, oxygenating them so that they lose their power.

simpsons, the

Originally created by Matt Groening as animated segments for the *Tracy Ullman Show* in 1987, *The Simpsons* has become the longest-running prime-time TV cartoon in history. Exceptional scriptwriting, the endearing voices and characters of Homer, Marge, Bart, Lisa and baby Maggie have all helped to win the show twenty-one Emmy awards and become a must-see programme for people of all ages.

Similar to their cartoon predecessors *The Flintstones*, the most important aspect of *The Simpsons* is the continuing unity of the family, despite innumerable disasters. However, unlike *The Flintstones*, *The Simpsons* are a loveable dysfunctional family who often 'react' against television stereotypes and find themselves in situations that are realistic to their audience.

The Simpsons is successful because it has a wide-ranging cast of characters who we can identify with. More importantly, they examine unfunny issues such as depression, alcoholism, gambling, loneliness and anxiety in an extremely funny and often moving way.

weird fact

James L. Brooks, the writer and director of *Broadcast News*, *Terms of Endearment* and *As Good As It Gets* co-wrote the first ever *Simpsons* series and, through his company Gracie Films, remains an executive producer to this day.

> 'Sleep that knits up the ravelled sleeve of care.'
>
> (*Macbeth*, Act 2 Scene 2)

Sleep is a necessary part of our lives; the quantity we take, the times we take it, the positions we choose may be different but we all need it. Sleep is not fully understood scientifically though there are certain things that are quite clear. Animals deprived of sleep lose weight and die. Sleep allows storage of energy and protein synthesis. REM (rapid eye movement) sleep is our prime dream time and deprived of it we make up for it the next night. It is thought that sleep allows 'sorting' of information, and creatures that have no REM sleep seem to have larger cortices (front part of the brain) than others, probably to store more unimportant unsifted information.

There are hormonal changes in sleep, and levels vary in prolactin, vasopressin (so we don't produce so much urine in the night), growth hormone and ACTH, as examples. The role of melatonin, produced by the pineal gland, which has a very clear role to play in many creatures, is less obvious in humans. When given for jet-lag it seems to benefit some but not others. Recently it has been discovered that peptides called orexins occur at abnormal levels in narcolepsy (sudden onset of sleep during the day) and studies of these may lead to treatments in the future.

One theory accounting for some forms of depression questions whether one of the symptoms, early morning waking, may occur due to unresolved psychological conflicts in dreams. There is even a treatment for depression involving sleep deprivation. In a trial of two groups taking antidepressants, the group deprived of sleep had greater initial improvement.

Lack of sleep brings on hypomania and hypomania brings on lack of sleep. Jet-lag often induces hypomania. Regular sleep patterns are very important for sufferers of MD.

Poor sleep is not only a symptom of depression, it is also a cause of depression. A mild depression can often be corrected by a few good nights' rest, even with the help of a sleeping tablet.

Rod Steiger was a Hollywood actor whose finest roles were his Oscar-winning performance in *The Heat of the Night* where he played a bigoted Southern police chief, *The Pawnbroker* and *On the Waterfront*. A devotee of method acting, Steiger became one of the most acclaimed actors of the 1960s and 1970s. He suffered from severe depression that lasted eight years in his later life. He successfully emerged from it and used his acting talents to help bring about a greater understanding of mental health.

> 'The most important thing is to be whatever you are without shame.'
>
> **Rod Steiger (1925–2002)**

stigma

Stigma has two parts: what we believe about ourselves and what other people believe about us. The most important part is what we believe about ourselves. If someone believes that people with mental illness have failed in some way, and then that person also has a mental illness, then it follows that he or she will see himself or herself in the same light and his or her self-esteem will suffer accordingly.

Mental illness is no more about failing or failure than a physical illness. It happens.

The second part of stigma relates to how other people and society view the condition. Just as with racism and intolerance of gays, prejudice against mental illness has been deeply ingrained in society; however, this has changed enormously in the last few years.

'Stigma', and thus rejection, is spread wide throughout the animal kingdom. It is the equivalent of intolerance. However, tolerance of others' imperfections is not just being 'nice'; it is a mark of social evolution. It represents a strength, not a weakness, and is the reason it survives in civilized cultures. That tolerance, or acceptance of others' limitations, has an implicit mirror image acceptance of one's own fallibility, that allows the individual (and thus society) to grow without struggling with the pretence of perfection. Unfortunately, we have not progressed far enough, as the débâcles of totalitarianism, fascism and imperialism have shown.

The National Institute for Mental Health in England is currently running a five-year initiative called 'Shift', which aims to tackle the stigma and discrimination surrounding mental health issues. More information can be found at www.shift.org.uk.

How you feel about your condition will be reflected in your attitude to yourself. If someone with a mental illness believes that it is a deeply shameful condition, and that mental illness should at all costs be concealed, the same person will appear as shady as a Great Train Robber. People will sense that they are hiding something and assume the worst, far worse than a manageable and fascinating condition, which comes complete with a wonderful sense of humour and quirky viewpoint!

As Mahatma Gandhi said, 'You must be the change you wish to see in the world.'

stress

what is stress?

Stress in a mental health context means excess load and the negative reaction you have to it. Strain would be a better word, but stress has come to be the familiar term. Stress can be a significant factor in all sorts of problems such as in triggering an old-fashioned 'nervous breakdown', which merely means an extreme reaction to stress. Stress can affect our immune system, making us more vulnerable to illness. The 'right' amount of 'stress' can be helpful in getting you motivated; too little can lead to depression and boredom and too much is really no good at all! External stress refers to the outside events that are stressing you and internal stress refers to patterns of thinking and reaction that are contributing to stress. Both act together to make up your levels of stress. For example, if you have loads of work to do for an exam and you're thinking, 'I'm bound to fail,' your stress levels will be greater than if you had loads of work to do and you were thinking more positively. Stress is cumulative; you might cope and cope and cope with massive stress and then be surprised to 'fall apart' when your pen breaks.

what could contribute to getting stressed

- Too much work
- Too much responsibility
- Unhelpful patterns of thinking
- Change
- Anything that you find 'too much' to manage
- Illness

how you can tell if you are experiencing an overload of stress

- Relationships are suffering
- Sleep difficulties
- Anxiety
- Taking time off work
- Not being able to 'see the wood for the trees'
- Irritability
- Not being able to eat/eating too much
- A feeling of not being able to cope
- Drinking too much alcohol or taking street drugs to excess

who gets stressed?

Anyone and everyone.

how to cope with stress

The first step is recognizing that you are experiencing too much stress. Take stock – add up what's going on in your life. Work on minimizing the number of tasks/responsibilities you have. Work on challenging and looking afresh at your thoughts and reactions. Look after yourself – diet, exercise, relaxation, meditation (if that's your bag), reducing caffeine, reducing alcohol and street drug intake. Take a systematic approach to reducing stress – set aside a specific time for thinking about how to cope, however hard it may seem to make time.

Consult your GP.

top tips

- DON'T try to reduce stress with short-term solutions, e.g. excess drink/drugs. They work in the short term but in the long term they make the problems worse. DON'T think 'I need it – it's the only way to relax.'

- DO talk to other people
- DON'T just keep going
- Learn to say 'No'
- Don't be surprised if something small sets you off – stress is cumulative – remember 'the straw that broke the camel's back'

books

Manage Your Mind by Gillian Butler and Tony Hope
How to Relax (audiotape/CD) – www.octc.co.uk

students and mental health

We hope that the contents of this Insider's Guide and the Manic Dialogues will be of some use, but students interested in finding out about mental health for personal reasons can find further information on the following website: www.studentdepression.org (part of the Charlie Waller Memorial Trust website: www.cwmt.org).

suicide

Up to fifteen to twenty per cent of unresponsive manic depressives kill themselves. When the condition is poorly controlled through incorrect medication, or combinations of them, and in harrowing life circumstances, suicide can happen, and it is vital to encourage sufferers to keep as much contact with carers as they can and, if possible, to join a group. It is vital that there is as much back-up as possible, so that when things start to go wrong there is help to prevent these crises.

statistics

Around 4500 people kill themselves in England and Wales each year (one in 100 deaths), while at least ten times that number of people attempt suicide.

In almost all cultures, the suicide rate rises with age, with the highest rates in the UK for those over seventy-five. In recent years, suicide has also increased in young men, and it is now the second leading cause of death in the fifteen to twenty-four age group, after accidents.

Certain factors are known to be associated with increased risk, including drug and alcohol misuse, unemployment, social isolation and family breakdown. People with a diagnosed mental health problem are at particular risk. Indeed, up to ninety per cent of suicide victims have been reported to have been suffering from a psychiatric disorder at the time of their death.

The highest risks of suicide are among alcoholics and those with a diagnosis of clinical depression (both fifteen per cent) or schizophrenia (ten per cent). Previous suicide attempts are also an indication of particular risk. Up to twenty per cent of survivors try again within a year, and as a group they are 100 times more likely to go on to complete suicide than those who have never tried before.

The number of children contemplating suicide has increased by fourteen per cent over the past year, a national charity has said. Childline has revealed that more than 1000 children who rang its helpline felt suicidal over problems such as abuse, bullying, stress and low self-esteem.

Be...foundation

Email: info@be-foundation.org

Website: www.be-foundation.org

Aims to offer a comprehensive source of help and information on youth suicide and deliberate self-harm.

CALM – Campaign Against Living Miserably

Gateway House, Piccadilly South, Manchester M60 7LP

Telephone: 0800 585858

Email: janepowell@thecalmzone.net

Website: www.thecalmzone.net

Launched in response to high suicide rates amongst young men, their aim is to try to reach young men before they become depressed.

LifeLink

Millburn Centre, 221 Millburn Street, Roystonhill, Glasgow G21 2HL

Telephone: 0808 8011315

Email: info@lifelink.org.uk

Website: www.lifelink.org.uk

LifeLink provides free support and advice to people in crisis and self-harming or at risk of suicide. They give the support you need, when you need it. They do not offer any easy solutions; however, they do listen and have helped many people find new ways to cope.

PAPYRUS – Prevention of Young Suicide
Rossendale GH, Union Road, Rawtenstall, Lancashire BB4 6NE
Telephone: 01706 214449
Fax: 01706 214449
Email: admin@papyrus-uk.org
Website: www.papyrus-uk.org
A voluntary organization committed to the prevention of young suicide and the promotion of good mental health and emotional well-being. Also home for HOPELineUK, advice and information to anyone who is concerned that a young person they know may be suicidal.
Telephone: 0870 170 4000.

Samaritans
10 The Grove, Slough, Berkshire SL1 1QP
Helplines: 08457 90 90 90 (UK) 1850 60 90 90 (ROI)
Email: jo@samaritans.org
Website: www.samaritans.org.uk
Charity that provides confidential emotional support to any person who is suicidal or despairing and that increases public awareness of issues around suicide and depression (see **Samaritans**, pages 279–80).

Suicide and Mental Health Association International
PO Box 702, Sioux Falls, South Dakota, USA
Telephone: 1-57101-0702
Website: suicideandmentalhealthassociationinternational.org
Dedicated to suicide and mental health related issues.

t

Psychiatrists, psychologists and psychotherapists: 'What's the difference?' is a question people in these professions get asked all the time. The reality is that much of what they do overlaps. Over recent years, for example, all these professions will have had training in psychotherapy/'talking treatments'. Psychiatrists are doctors and can thus prescribe medications. There are, however, moves to give psychologists certain prescribing rights. It is confusing too, because a psychiatrist can be a psychotherapist, a psychotherapist can be a psychologist, and so on. They are all 'shrinks'!

PSYCHIATRISTS

Psychiatrists (popularly known as 'trick cyclists'!) are doctors who have taken a further three years of general psychiatric training, i.e. have trained further in order to specialize in mental health and illnesses. As part of this, those more recently trained will have received instruction in psychotherapy. Some psychiatrists specialize in psychotherapy, as opposed to having skills in what is often called 'organic' psychiatry, which is related more to 'physical' psychiatric illnesses which are treated with medications, though of course there is no line between these. Psychiatrists can diagnose, prescribe medication or organize other treatments. They can arrange for you to be admitted to hospital either voluntarily or 'under section' (see **Sectioning**, pages 284–5). Psychiatrists usually hold ultimate responsibility for your care despite the input of other professionals or team members.

when should I see a psychiatrist?

You should see a psychiatrist if you and your GP agree this is an appropriate option. If you wish to see a psychiatrist privately your GP can also arrange it.

how to get to see a psychiatrist

Your GP can refer you to a psychiatrist who you would normally see in your local community mental health team rooms or psychiatric hospital. If you are not happy with the treatment you receive from your psychiatrist you are entitled to ask for a second opinion.

what can you expect?

Normally, you would expect your psychiatrist to make an initial diagnosis (this may take time as some illnesses cannot be diagnosed immediately). Your psychiatrist will also make a 'risk assessment' (e.g. suicide/self-harm) for yourself or others if you are very unwell. He/she and you would then normally plan together an appropriate approach to helping you cope better with your symptoms. This could include: 'talking treatments'/psychotherapy, medication, hospitalization, ECT (not normally a first line of treatment), social work input if your circumstances are causing you problems, or referral to a community psychiatric nurse, and so on. He/she will usually take the primary responsibility for your care and will, if appropriate, arrange follow-up appointments for you. Your psychiatrist should be up to date with government and other directives on standards in patient care such as the NICE guidelines.

websites

Royal College of Psychiatrists (www.rcpsych.ac.uk)
MIND (www.mind.org.uk)
NICE (www.nice.org.uk)

PSYCHOLOGISTS

A psychologist will normally have completed a degree, followed by at least a further three years of training. Psychology means the study of the mind and behaviour, so it is not only related to illness and is a science-based profession, including research.

The type of psychologist you are likely to see if you are experiencing mental health difficulties is likely to be what is called a clinical or a counselling psychologist (see BPS website overleaf). If your mental health difficulties have contributed to your involvement in criminal activity you may be referred to a forensic psychologist.

Your GP/health care professional can refer you to a psychologist either on the NHS or privately. You can also seek private treatment with a psychologist yourself.

THERAPISTS

top tips

- Be aware that, at present, the NHS waiting list for psychology is often very long.
- Use personal/professional recommendations and/or consult professional bodies when seeking psychological help.

websites

British Psychological Society (www.bps.org.uk)
Oxford Cognitive Therapy Centre (www.octc.co.uk)

PSYCHOTHERAPISTS

A psychotherapist is someone who has trained in the delivery of 'talking treatments' for emotional/psychological/mental health difficulties. A psychotherapist can be anyone who has trained in any form of 'talking'-based therapies, and is a more general term. Thus it can include people who already have a professional qualification in mental health, including psychiatrists, psychologists, psychiatric nurses, occupational therapists, counsellors and social workers.

There are many different types of psychotherapy:

- *Cognitive Behavioural Therapy* – A focused, collaborative, often short-term, problem-centred treatment based on finding and instituting more helpful ways of thinking and behaving. You might consider CBT if you think you have an identifiable problem that you would like to work on in a focused, practical way.
- *Psychodynamic Therapy* – The major emphasis in psychodynamic therapy is on helping the client to work towards understanding themselves and their difficulties. Psychodynamic therapy will not necessarily be as long and intense as 'full-on' psychoanalysis. You might consider psychodynamic therapy if you feel that you need to explore and talk about issues to 'make sense' of things and/or you feel you have particularly difficult issues around relationships. One of the values of one-to-one psychotherapy is that it allows 'stuff to come up'; enabling the individual to shed some of the 'baggage' we all have. Put another way, it can help one to come to terms with issues that have been negatively influencing one's life, and then move on, in a more balanced manner. That's the theory! And it does work! It works for many psychological issues, especially if one is lucky enough to find a good professional who can remain detached, though caring, and be patient and understand-

ing. This carer may come to represent a parent figure while the individual 're-runs' life, learning to reappraise life experiences in a supportive atmosphere. The individual comes to value themselves more and, yes, 'love' themselves more. It can be a real opening for individuals who had unsupportive parenting. If necessary it is worth spending money on, if it cannot be done within the NHS. It may be the best money spent, especially if it puts the demons of the past in the right place, turning them into life experiences that one can grow from.

- *Cognitive Analytic Therapy* – Roughly speaking, a mixture of psychodynamic and cognitive therapies. CAT is a problem-focused individual therapy based on working on repeating patterns in relationships, the difficulties these lead to and the often unhelpful ways we have found to overcome them. A course of CAT might last around sixteen to twenty-four sessions. You may consider CAT if you feel that your problems might benefit from a part-psychodynamic/part-cognitive/behavioural approach.

- *Psychodrama* – A therapy, often group based, in which problems are worked on through guided dramatic action. Clients may work through issues by acting out significant relationships and events in their lives. A course of psychodrama might last between one and two years. You might consider this a helpful option if you enjoy working in a group with other people, if you are perhaps finding relationships problematic, and feel that it would be useful to resolve issues through working with action.

- *Art/Creative Therapy* – Creative therapies encourage self-expression through creativity. Clients might be asked to draw their family, to discuss what their sketch represents and then to draw how they would LIKE the family to be. You might consider this therapy if you like working creatively, if you often tend to think in terms of images, and/or find it difficult to put your feelings into words.

- *Family/Systemic Therapy* – Therapy based on ideas around the importance of your family/system and how you and it might maintain difficulties. In family/systemic therapy, members of that group may be asked to attend with the client. The therapist works with the family/individual to look at patterns in relationships and to help to understand their difficulties. In systemic therapy there may often be more than one therapist. Family therapy is also used in supporting families who are living with people with serious mental illness.

THERAPISTS

- *Group Therapy* – Almost any form of psychotherapy can be offered in group form. People find it helpful to work in groups for many reasons, such as discovering that they are not 'the only one' with difficulties in life. The waiting list for group psychotherapy in the NHS is often shorter than for individual therapy.
- *Brief Therapy* – Any form of therapy carried out over a brief period – historically, therapies tended to last for months or years, whereas now more focused treatments are often felt to be effective. You may prefer this method if you favour a time-limited approach to your therapy and particularly if you feel you have a relatively identifiable problem.

how to access psychotherapy

You can access psychotherapy either through your GP/health care team (private or NHS referrals) or directly. When looking for a psychotherapist, value personal recommendations and consult professional websites. A professional psychotherapist should be able to tell you after the first meeting whether they think their model of psychotherapy is appropriate for you and, if it isn't, suggest other forms of therapy.

top tips

- Do your homework – unfortunately anyone can set themselves up as a psychotherapist, so do as much research as you can, or be advised by someone in whom you have confidence.
- If you are using private health insurance to access psychotherapy you will often need a psychiatrist's referral.

books

Therapists should be grounded in three conditions for therapy as described by Carl Rogers – unconditional positive regard, congruence and empathy. These are described in:

On Becoming a Person by Carl R. Rogers

The Road Less Travelled by M. Scott Peck

websites

British Psychological Society (www.bps.org.uk)

British Association of Behavioural and Cognitive Psychotherapists (www.babcp.org.uk)

United Kingdom Council of Psychotherapists (www.ukcp.org.uk)
Oxford Cognitive Therapy Centre (www.octc.co.uk)
Association for Family Therapy (www.aft.org.uk)
Association of Cognitive Analytic Therapists (www.acat.me.uk)
Institute of Family Therapy (www.instituteoffamilytherapy.org.uk)
Psychodrama (www.psychodrama.org.uk)
British Association of Art Therapists (www.baat.org)
MIND (www.mind.org.uk)

PSYCHOANALYSIS/PSYCHOANALYSTS

Psychoanalysis is, perhaps, the classic layman's image of what psychotherapy might be like. It really is often lying on the 'couch', talking about anything and everything that enters your head (free-associating) and describing dreams, with almost total silence from your analyst. Your analyst will, occasionally, make relevant, hopefully helpful, insightful comments. You are likely to meet with your psychoanalyst regularly over a number of years, although some analysts practise brief therapy.

what is a psychoanalyst/psychoanalysis?

A psychoanalyst is someone who practises psychoanalysis, which is a kind of psychological treatment based on understanding the unconscious mind. A psychoanalyst's work draws largely on the writings of Sigmund Freud and others who have developed his ideas, such as Melanie Klein. Psychoanalysis can be thought of as a way of understanding yourself and your relationships, as well as understanding and coping with psychological distress. A psychoanalyst will have undergone a long, rigorous period of training including going through analysis themselves. Although there is, at present, no firm evidence base for the efficacy of psychoanalysis, many people report finding it very helpful and well worth the long hours of treatment.

how to find a psychoanalyst

Consult your GP, look at personal/professional recommendations and consult professionally based websites.

websites

The Tavistock and Portman Institute (www.tavi-port.org)
The Institute of Psychoanalysis (www.psychoanalysis.org.uk)

THERAPISTS

toast

Toast can be eaten at any time of the day or night and can best be described as comfort food. Strongly favoured by the majority of the British population, toast is a perfectly acceptable and economic accompaniment to a cup of tea or coffee. It can be the snack that keeps you going during the day or the most nourishing fare to offer a passing friend.

trivia

In 1978 a song celebrating the wondrous qualities of cheese on toast was recorded and turned into a novelty hit record by Paul Young and the Streetband.

triggers

Just as pressing the trigger fires a gun, so a trigger can set off an episode of depression or mania. Triggers are events that cause difficult stresses that put people at risk of further illness. With recurrent episodes, a pattern often emerges, whether it is seasonal, or whether it relates to specific events such as changing jobs. For a teacher it may be the school exams, or a time when work and home life pressures combine to cause extra stress. The best way to identify triggers is to look back over past episodes, both highs and lows, and find the common thread that runs through them. It is often helpful to write them down and to ask a friend to look through them with you, as they may see patterns from the outside that you cannot see from the inside.

By identifying the events that lead up to illness, it is possible to understand what areas of life someone finds hardest to handle. By knowing what his or her triggers are, it is possible then to take specific action to avoid a full-blown episode, by asking for extra help at particular times, using a different approach, changing expectations, and so on. Knowledge is power and self-knowledge is the first step towards self-mastery.

twelve step programmes

The 'Twelve Step Programme' was created and developed in 1935 by the two founders of Alcoholics Anonymous, New York stockbroker Bill Wilson and Ohio surgeon Bob Smith. Since then, the Twelve Step Programme has been the basis of AA's recovery plan, and has been used and adapted by numerous other self-help groups ranging from Narcotics Anonymous to Gamblers Anonymous.

The Twelve Step Programme carries a strong spiritual message and attracts both loyalty and criticism – perhaps partly because of its strong Christian language, and the encouragement to surrender to a higher 'Power' on the journey to recovery. Following the Twelve Steps involves working towards various milestones in the presence of the support group. These include, amongst others, admission of the problem, seeking help, self-appraisal, sharing your story with the group in confidence, achieving a spiritual awakening and supporting others who want to recover.

For some people suffering from addiction problems, the required practice of the Twelve Steps may not be enough to solve the root cause of the problem, and they may need to find a good therapist to work with. The Twelve Step process requires commitment and determination and can stretch what a person is capable of. In the words of one member, the best thing about it is that, 'It's like a spiritual and mental carwash – while the worst thing is that at times, it can feel a little bit like going back to school.'

other support groups who follow the twelve step structure

Cocaine Anonymous
Website: www.ca.org

Gamblers Anonymous (UK)
PO Box 5382, London W1A 6SA
Telephone: 08700 50 88 80 or 020 7384 3040
Email: webmaster@gamblersanonymous.org.uk
Website: www.gamblersanonymous.org.uk
Gamblers Anonymous is a fellowship of men and women who have joined together to do something about their own gambling problems and to help other compulsive gamblers do the same.

Gamblers Anonymous Scotland
Head Office, Central Halls, 304 Maryhill Road, Glasgow G20 7YE
Telephone: 0870 050 8881
Email: info@gascotland.org
Website: www.gascotland.org

Marijuana Anonymous
Website: www.marijuana-anonymous.org

Nicotine Anonymous
Website: www.nicotine-anonymous.org

non-twelve step organizations
Drugs in School Helpline
Telephone: 0345 366666

Drugscope
Website: www.drugscope.org.uk

National Drugs Helpline
Telephone: 0800 77 66 00
Email: frank@talktofrank.com
Website: www.talktofrank.com
A user-friendly and frank resource on drug use and abuse. It is a free confidential drugs information and advice service twenty-four hours a day.

GamCare
2 & 3 Baden Place, Crosby Row, London SE1 1YW
Telephone: 0845 6000133
Fax: 020 7378 5237
Email: info@gamcare.org.uk
Website: www.gamcare.org.uk
Voluntary organization committed to promoting responsible attitudes to gambling and to working for the provision of proper care for those who have been harmed by gambling dependency.

sex addiction websites
Sex Addicts Anonymous (International) (www.sexaa.org)

Sexalcholics Anonymous (International) (www.sa.org)
Sexual Compulsives Anonymous (USA based) (www.sca-recovery.org)
Sex and Love Addicts Anonymous (USA based) (www.slaafws.org)

twenty-first century

Is manic depression a disease of the twentieth/twenty-first centuries? Even though the number of people who have a tendency to manic depression remains the same, people's levels of stress are higher and it is likely that more people are precipitated into crisis, whether they're depressive or on the high side.

V

van gogh, vincent

Born in 1853 in Holland he became an artist after limited success as a minister of the church and a teacher. He spent time in London at the age of twenty-two and then moved to Paris. He was spurned in love and self-mutilated by burning his hand years before the reputed cutting off of an ear in anger while with Gauguin, and delivering it to a local prostitute. He painted furiously 2000 works, finding that the intensity of the light in Arles suited his temperament as did his vigorous, brightly coloured and heavy paintwork. He was an excessive drinker of absinthe, which contains the hallucinogenic toxin thugone, and this may have been fuel for his tempestuous episodes lasting many years, before his suicide in 1890. He had a sister with schizophrenia (and four other siblings) and probably had manic depressive psychosis, though other diagnoses included epilepsy, porphyria and neurosyphilis.

voluntary work

There are hundreds of forms of voluntary work but one of the easiest is to start by helping to clean up around the house. It can easily extend to helping a next-door neighbour in their garden or shopping for an elderly aunt or taking a friend's dog for a walk. It's often better to get away from home and go to work in an organization that requires volunteers. This can be helping to serve behind the scenes in a high street charity shop such as Mind or Oxfam all the way up to joining VSO (Voluntary Service Overseas). Voluntary work is a good way to get back to work and mix with other people without placing yourself under too much pressure. You do not need to be a superstar or have a trillion qualifications, but merely be willing to roll up your sleeves and help. A sure way of improving your self-esteem and confidence.

For more information: www.timebank.org.uk

W

world health organization

In 1990 the WHO listed unipolar depression as the number one cause of disability worldwide. Despite manic depression being much less common (particularly in the more severe forms), it is listed as the sixth. This is because of the fallout from episodes of severe illness that can be so life-shattering, and not only affect the individual but friends, family, work colleagues, etc.

y

Yoga combines asanas (physical poses) and deep breathing to create a 'moving meditation', reducing stress-related anxiety and depression. The practitioner focuses fully on the combination of movement and breath, thereby eliminating stressful thoughts, and creating a sense of peace. When a yogi was complimented on the results of the laboratory measurements he had achieved during meditation he reversed the compliment, congratulating the team for designing such clever instruments able to prove that which he knew all along!

Yoga might be regarded as a stress-relief method working 'from the bottom up', as one is using 'physical' movements and control to induce 'mental' change. Here is another example of how the division between body and mind is passé – they should be regarded as the same; one whole organism (put another way, Cartesian duality is no longer regarded as correct!). Research into the vagus nerve (the tenth cranial nerve) has shown it is eighty per cent sensory and twenty per cent motor, and this nerve that supplies the heart, stomach and diaphragm feeds back to the brain; in this way relaxed, calm and controlled breathing helps reduce psychological tension.

Z

z cars

Z Cars was an immensely popular police drama that ran on the BBC between 1962 and 1978. Focusing on the gritty issues of inner city crime and social deprivation, *Z Cars* solidified the career of Stratford Johns who played the formidable Inspector Barlow, and set up Frank Windsor's career playing his deputy. It was deliberately issue-driven, with ground-breaking storylines highlighting problems of poverty, racism, mental illness and addiction. Viewing figures topped fourteen million in the first series and made the actors household names. Alongside the tough themes of law and order, the drama also portrayed glimpses of the personal lives of the policemen, and how their work could compromise their relationships. *Z Cars* paved the way for all of the current British police dramas on TV today.

Z Cars also featured the acting talents of Leonard Rossiter, Brian Blessed, James Ellis and Colin Welland. The programmes were directed by numerous up-and-coming directors including Ken Loach and Ridley Scott.

zyprexa

The tradename of olanzapine – one of the newer atypical anti-psychotics which are now being used in some centres as first-line treatment for manic depressive illness.

acknowledgements

The authors would particularly like to thank Dr Liz Miller and Karen Cowan for their invaluable support and contributions to the Insider's Guide section and also Chris Filmer-Sankey and Sarah Cellan-Jones.

Grateful thanks are also due to the following for their help with the whole book: Janet Walsh, Steve O'Connor, Simon Frodsham, Sally and Rod Harvey, Gareth Richards, Jamie Moon, Chris Eastwood, Helen Helm, Ellen Oakes, Anthony 'George' Osborn, Alex Fontaine, Prabjote Osahn, Mark Harnden, Jane Oakley, Max Carlish, Maurice Phillips, Ian Shemilt and Andrea Christie. Thanks also to Simon Pearsall for his fantastic illustrations, and the wonderful staff of the Blue Bay Hotel.

Grateful appreciation is due to the anonymous contributors of the Life Stories section, to Katie Southall for her poem and to Dom Antony Sutch for his prayer.

Many thanks to the many doctors and scientists who have given up time to meet and give us pearls of wisdom, including Professors Guy Goodwin, Jan Scott, Stephen Williams, John Stein, Sophie Frangou, Tim Crowe, Paul Harrison, Mary Phillips, Nick Craddock, Robin Murray, Michael Crawford, Lewis Wolpet; Kay Jamison on a visit to London; Dr Mark Salter for the tour of his unit at the Homerton; Dr Robert Lefever at The Promis centre for addiction; and Rose Barton for the visit to the Ashcroft residential centre in Norfolk.

Eternal gratitude to Fiona Brown for copy-editing beyond the call of duty, and to Sarah Rollason and Kate Adams for so expertly guiding the book in and out of the delivery room.

Special thanks to the staff at the MDF, to Ross Wilson and Lindsey Douglas at IWC, to Antony Topping from Greene and Heaton, to the indomitable Jane Villiers at Sayle Screen for her belief and support, and to Dr Orlane Holmes-Clouet for her encouragement and comment.

Last, but certainly not least, thank you to Stephen Fry.

recommended reading

books recommended in text

AA *Living Sober*. AA General Services Office, PO Box 1, Stonebow House, Stonebow, York YO1 7NJ

Butler, Gillian and Hope, Tony *Manage Your Mind*. Oxford Paperbacks 1995

Cleese, John and Skynner, Robin *Families and How to Survive Them*. Mandarin 1984

Consumers Association, The *What to Do When Someone Dies*. 1967

Eron, Judy *What Goes Up: Surviving the Manic Episode of a Loved One*. Barricade Books 2005

Fisher, Carrie *The Best Awful*. Pocket Books 2004

Graham, Katherine *Personal History*. Vintage 1998

Greenberger, Dennis and Padesky, Christine *Mind Over Mood*. Guilford Press 1995

Greenfield, Susan *The Private Life of the Brain*. Penguin Books 2002

Haddon, Mark *The Curious Incident of the Dog in the Night-Time*. Vintage 2004

Hawton, Keith *Sex Therapy – a Practical Guide*. Oxford University Press 1985

Jamison, Kay Redfield *Exuberance: The Passion for Life*. Vintage 2005

Jamison, Kay Redfield *Touched With Fire: Manic Depressive Illness and the Artistic Temperament*. Free Press Paperbacks 1994

Jeffers, Susan *Feel the Fear and Do It Anyway*. Rider & Co 1997

Kennerley, Helen *Overcoming Anxiety*. Constable & Robinson 1997

Kramer, Peter D. *Listening to Prozac*. Fourth Estate 1993

Kubler Ross, Elisabeth *On Death and Dying*. Routledge 1973

Laing, R. D. and Esterson, A. *Sanity, Madness and the Family*. Penguin 1964

Larsen, Earnie *Stage II Recovery: Life Beyond Addiction* HarperCollins 1985

Larsen, Earnie and Hegarty, Carol *Believing in Myself: Daily Meditations for Healing and Building Self-Esteem*. Simon & Schuster 1991

Lewis, C. S. *A Grief Observed*. Faber & Faber 1976

Mate, Gabor *Scattered Minds*. Vintage Canada 2000

Oxford Cognitive Therapy Centre *How to Relax* (audiotape/CD) – www.octc.co.uk

Rinpoche, Sogyal *The Tibetan Book of Living and Dying*. Harper San Francisco, 1992

Rogers, Carl R. *On Becoming a Person*. Constable & Robinson 2004

Sacks, Oliver *An Anthropologist on Mars – Seven Paradoxical Tales*. Picador 1996

Scott Peck, M. *The Road Less Travelled*. Arrow 1990

Thomas, Jeremy *Taking Leave*. Timewell Press 2006

other recommended books

Bipolar Disorder

Goodwin, Guy and Sachs, Gary *Bipolar Disorder*. Health Press 2004

Hunt, Neil *Bipolar Disorder: Your Questions Answered*. Elsevier 2005

Jamison, Kay Redfield *An Unquiet Mind*. Picador 1996

Jamison, Kay Redfield and Goodwin, Frederick K. *Manic Depressive Illness*. Oxford University Press 1990

Schwarz, Dorothy *Behind a Glass Wall*. Chipmunkapublishing 2005

Scott, Jan *Overcoming Mood Swings*. Constable & Robinson Ltd. 2001

Sutherland, Stuart *Breakdown* (second edition). Oxford University Press 1998

Whybrow, Peter C. *A Mood Apart*. Picador 1999

Depressive Illness

Milligan, Spike and Clare, Anthony *Depression and How to Survive It*. Arrow 1994

Solomon, Andrew *The Noonday Demon*. Vintage 2002

Styron, William *Darkness Visible*. Vintage Classics 2001

Wolpert, Lewis *Malignant Sadness*. Faber & Faber 1999

General Reading

Andreasen, Nancy C. *The Creating Brain*. Dana Foundation 2005

Damasio, Antonio R. *Descartes' Error*. Quill 2000

Jamison, Kay Redfield *Night Falls Fast*. Vintage Books 2000

Laurance, Jeremy *Pure Madness, How Fear Drives the Mental Health System*. Routledge 2003

Mithen, Steven *The Prehistory of the Mind*. Phoenix 1998

Ridley, Matt *Nature Via Nurture*. Harper Perennial 2004

Storr, Anthony *The Dynamics of Creation*. Pelican Books 1976

Thompson, Tony and Mathias, Peter (eds.) *Lyttle's – Mental Health and Disorder*. Balliere Tindall 2000

Autobiography/Criticism

Behrman, Andy *Electroboy*. Penguin Books 2003

Caramagno, Thomas C. *The Flight of the Mind: Virginia Woolf's Art and Manic-Depressive Illness*. University of California Press 1992

Fry, Stephen *Moab is my Washpot*. Arrow Books 2004 (reissued)

Pegler, Jason *A Can of Madness*. Chipmunkapublishing 2002

Storr, Anthony *Churchill's Black Dog*. HarperCollins 1989

really useful websites

www.iop.kcl.ac.uk/iopweb/contact/getting-help-for-someone-with-mental-illness.com

www.mentalhealthcare.org.uk

www.ahealthyme.com

www.bbc.co.uk/health/conditions/mental_health

www.netdoctor.co.uk/menshealth/facts/addiction.htm

www.connects.org.uk